Wichita Kinship & Culture

Dr Jay Miller, ed.

CONTENTS

Famed for their haystack-shaped grass houses and their body tattoos, especially on eyelids, Wichita, who accordingly call themselves *kirikir'i•s* "raccoon eyes", are Caddoan speakers of the central Plains. Documentation of and for them ranges from early French and Spanish explorers and soldiers to painter George Catlin, who called them Pawnee Picts for their tattoos, to scholars like George Dorsey, with the Carnegie comparative Caddoan project, Karl and Iva Schmitt until his tragic death, and especially William Newcomb in Texas. Spier's classic kin study is included because it was vital to the Schmitts' conclusions. Karl's & Iva's obituaries end our volume.

Editorial changes relied on clarity so Schmitt's teachers, sources, consultants ("~~informants~~") now have a # before their capital letter, particularly in the case of #A. The Latin abbreviations *ibid* (= *ibidem*) and *idem* 'in/at same place' is now *same*. All footnotes are now numbered continuously, though in some original texts each page starts at #1. The original variety of dash lengths now includes a tilde ~ between kin terms and categories, and spaces have been added before and after these dashes to free up the formatting.

Robert Bell, Edward Jelks, and William Newcomb *Wichita Archaeology and Ethnohistory*: *A Pilot Study*. DC: National Science Foundation Grant GS-964 1967.

George A Dorsey *The Mythology of the Wichita*, DC: Carnegie Institution, 1904; University of Oklahoma Press, 1995: 16-17, 25-29.

William Newcomb, jr The Wichitas: Nations of the North. *The Indians of Texas ~ From Prehistoric to Modern Times*. Austin: University of Texas Press 1984: 247-277.

Wichita. Handbook of North American Indians. Washington, DC: Smithsonian. *Plains* #13 Part 1: 548-566 2001.

Douglas Parks Kitsai. Handbook of North American Indians. Washington, DC: Smithsonian. *Plains* #13 Part 1: 567-571 2001.

David Rood Sketch of Wichita, A Caddoan Language. Handbook of North American Indians. Washington, DC: Smithsonian. *Languages* #17: 580-608 1996

Karl and Iva Osanai Schmitt *Wichita Kinship ~ Past and Present*. Norman, Oklahoma: University Book Exchange. 1950

F Todd Smith *The Caddos, The Wichitas, and the United States, 1846-1901*. College Station: Texas A&M University Press. 1996

Leslie Spier, The Distribution of Kinship Systems in North America. University of Washington Publications in Anthropology 1 (2): 69-88, Maps 1-9. August, 1925.

WICHITA FIRST CREATION

Man-never-known-on-Earth creates land and water.[1] Darkness everywhere. He makes man, Having-Power-to-Carry-Light, and woman, Bright-Shining-Woman. They receive things through dreams. Woman is given Mother-Corn, to be food for people. Having-Power-to-Carry-Light is drawn by man in grass-lodge toward east. There is light in lodge. Man of grass-lodge says more people will exist. While men are talking voice tells them to come and shoot deer. They are only to shoot last deer, which is half black and half white. Man of grass-lodge makes arrows. White deer, black deer, and black and white deer come out of water and man shoots last one. He follows deer and becomes Star-that-is-always-moving. Shooting black and whale deer signifies there shall be days and nights. Having-Power-to-Carry-Light sees man across water who says he shall be called Man-Reflecting (Sun) who will give light. Having-Power-to-Carry-Light sees sun coming up. He returns home and has light to travel in. When darkness comes he sees three stars which are three deer, and fourth star which is man who wounded deer. Villages spring up. Having-Power-to-Carry-Light and woman go from village to village teaching people how to make and use things. Man tells them about bow and arrows and gives men ball with string to it and teaches them how to play game. Teaches them shinny game. He tells them how to travel fast on arrows and ball. Man travels like spirit, is at place at once. Woman gives women Mother-Corn to plant to eat. They are to offer food to Man-never-known-on-Earth and rub over children before eating. The woman teaches them double-ball game and tells them use of ball in traveling. Says she will become something else, and that by her they will know whether they are pregnant. She teaches them to foretell things about to happen, and to make offerings to heavenly bodies and earth powers. Woman disappears and becomes Moon. Man tells men that in bringing game from hunt they are to offer to heavenly bodies and earth powers. Says if children bathe before daylight they will get powers. Man tells them he will sometimes be seen in early morning as star and his name will be "Bringer-of-the-Daylight."

Longer Epic

In the times of the beginning there was no sun, no stars, nor anything else as it is now. Time passed on. Man-never-known-on-Earth (*Kinnekasus*) was the only man that existed, and he it was who created all things. When the earth was created it was composed of land and water, but they were not yet separated. The land was floating on the water, and darkness was everywhere. After the earth was formed, Man-never-known-on-Earth made a man whose name was Having-Power-to-Carry-Light (*Kiarsidia*). He also made a woman for the man, and her name was Bright-Shining-Woman (*Kashatskihakatidise*). After the man and the woman were made they dreamed that things were made for them, and when they woke they had the things of which they had dreamed. Thus they received everything they needed. The woman was given an ear of corn, whose use she did not know, but this was revealed to her in her heart; that it was to be her food; that it was Mother-Corn; that it was to be the food of the people who should exist in the future, to be used generation after generation; that from Mother-Corn the people should be nursed. Still they were in darkness, not knowing what was better than darkness.

Once upon a time it came into the mind of Having-Power-to-Carry-Light that he should go

---

[1] Told by Towakoni Jim (Towakoni) to George A Dorsey, *The Mythology of the Wichita*, DC: Carnegie Institution, 1904; University of Oklahoma Press, 1995: 16-17, 25-29.

toward the east. He went further and further, not knowing where or why, but still wanting to find out what he was after. He kept on until he came to a grass-lodge. He found somebody existing on the earth besides himself. As he entered the grass-lodge there was light. He saw the man of the grass-lodge. This man of the grass-lodge said to him: "Well, I have brought you here. I put it in your mind to come this way and visit me. Therefore, you are here, and I am told to tell you of some things that are to come to pass. You have always thought you were the only person living, but I am here too. I have been created the same as you. The man that creates things is about to improve our condition. Villages shall spring up and more people will exist, and you will have power to teach the people how to do things before unknown to them." While they were talking they heard a voice from the east, saying: "Hurry, you men in the grass-lodge! Come out with your arrows and shoot the deer that are now starting [26] out to your shore!" The man of the grass-lodge replied to the voice:

"All right, I will be ready to meet the deer, but I have not yet made my arrows, nor have I got my bow. I must cut and make these first." The man of the grass-lodge went and cut the bow and arrows. Again the voice came, saying; "Hurry, the deer are about to land on the shore that you are on. You are not to shoot the white deer or the black deer but shoot the last one, that is half black and half white." The man replied: "All right. I will have my bows and arrows ready for him." The man peeled the bark off from his arrows and dried them.

The voice came again, telling him to make haste and finish the arrows. The man of the grass-lodge again answered, telling how much he had done on the arrows, and that he was feathering them. After a time the voice came again, saying: "Hurry!" The man of the grass-lodge said; "I have my arrows ready, but I have yet to put on the string." After he had put on the string the voice came again, and said: "The deer are about to land." The two men went out and saw the deer coming out of the water toward them. When they got to the bank the white and black deer jumped out, and as it was jumping out the man of the grass-lodge shot it. After shooting it he heard a voice from above, saying he had done well. This meant that everything would move, that the sun would rise, the stars would move, and the darkness and the light would move on. After shooting the deer he followed all of the deer. Now the voice was heard from above, saying: "You have done the right thing." The white deer went ahead, then the black one, then the one that was wounded. The man of the grass-lodge followed them. This man now became Star-that-is-always-moving (*Kinni'hequidikidahis*). Having-Power-to-Carry-Light stayed there after the other man had left to follow the deer. By shooting the deer that was half black and half white it was signified that there should be days and nights. Having-Power-to-Carry-Light, as he stood there, looked toward the east, where he heard the voice telling what to do, and there he saw a man standing across the water on the other shore, who said that thereafter he should be called Reflecting-Man (*Sakidawaitsa*), the sun. The man on the other shore thought that as he should be known as the sun, he would give light, that he would be seen at all times by the people and give them light, and by his powers he would aid them in having-great powers. After looking, Having-Power-to-Carry-Light looked back at the man who had been speaking to him and he was gone; but he saw the sun coming up. He then turned back to his home. As he went along he began to find out the object of his visit to the grass-lodge. This he liked very much. He had light to travel in and could [27] see a long way. He found that light was better than darkness. On his way back home he found he could travel faster than he could travel in darkness. In a very short time he reached his home. When he got home the sun went down and darkness followed, and he saw up in the sky three stairs coming up, followed by a single star. Having-Power-to-Carry-Light made up his mind that the three stars were the three deer and that the other star coming behind was the man that had wounded the deer.

The three stars represented .the three deer as they had come out of the water, while the fourth star, which came later, represented the man who had wounded the deer.

This was a new start for the man and the woman. They enjoyed this kind of life better than living in darkness. Time went on, and Having-Power-to-Carry-Light saw that the promises which were made by Man-never-known-on-Earth to Star-that-is-Always-Moving were being fulfilled. He saw villages springing up. There were more people existing, and this was as had been promised.

After these things had happened the man and the woman went from one village to another, showing the people how to use the things they had, how to make them, and what to use them for. The people in the village had things that they knew nothing about, and they did not hitherto know how to make or use them. They simply knew that they were existing as human beings. They knew neither where they had come from nor how to live. The woman and the man were greatly helped by the day. Having-Power-to-Carry-Light then began his work among the men, teaching them what bows and arrows were; that the bow was a weapon of great strength; that the arrow was a thing to shoot and kill game with. He gave the men a ball, smaller than the shinny ball. He told them that this ball was to be used to amuse themselves with; that the men were to play together and the boys were to play together. Whenever a child was born, if it was a boy, this kind of ball was to be given to it, that he might observe it .and learn how to move around. The ball had a string to it. The further the ball rolled — that is, the older the child should get, the faster it would move around. He went on and taught the men how to play the game, for the people were ignorant and did not know what the things were for. Finally the men were shown how the ball should be used. He showed them the clubs for the shinny game. He told them they should be divided equally in the game, one party on one side and the other party on the other side. Many men were interested, for the game was new to them. Many of the men were fast on their feet. The game was to be won by the side that should get the ball to the goal first. Having-Power-to-Carry-Light [28] also told them how to travel with the arrows and ball. This marks the time when they learned to travel fast from one place to another. The men went out hunting animals after they had been taught that animals existed for their use, and they traveled with their arrows and ball. They would shoot an arrow in the direction they wanted to go, then would go with the arrow as it went up. This is the way they traveled. They would hit the ball and as it flew the person would be on .the bail. When the ball would hit the ground they would hit it again, and so they would go from place to place. Having-Power-to-Carry-Light traveled like a spirit. When he heard of a place he would be right there, but the people who were made after him were a little slower in traveling. This sort of traveling was fast enough for these people. From this place he went to other places, and he taught the people how to use things. He would make the things for them at first, then would teach them how the things were made.

When the woman began her work among the women she gave them Mother-Corn, and told them that this was -theirs, and this was their mother; that from this time they should be nursed; that with the use of Mother-Corn they could live and it would strengthen the young ones; that Mother-Corn was to be used as long as the world should last. There were no certain times for the women to plant the corn, because the time passed pretty fast. When the women planted their corn it would grow right up and .they would gather their corn at once. The Moon told the women that whenever Mother-Corn was eaten by them, whether ground or dry, they must offer some food to Man-never-known-on-Earth. Then they were to eat of it, and as a prayer for blessing before eating of the food they were to take four kernels of corn and rub them over the child. These were the Moon's instructions to the woman. Things progressed very rapidly. The young ones grew quickly.

The woman told the women that Mother-Corn should be used for many different purposes. She gave them the things that they should use to enjoy themselves — namely, the double-ball game. She showed them how to play the game and told them that the ball was for their use in traveling. Now she told them the time was drawing near when she would have to leave them, for she had gone from one place to another, showing the women what to do, how to travel, how to raise Mother-Corn, how they must eat it and offer it, in all the ways that Mother-Corn was to be used. She told the women that after she had become something else she would ask the people, especially the women, to look upon her once in a while. She said that by her face women should be able to tell their condition; by their monthly flow, whether [29] they were pregnant or not. She was to show herself a certain number of times, and by keeping count they might know what time the child would be born. She said that when she made her appearance the parents of the young child should turn its face toward her, implying a prayer, and asking her that the child might grow as fast as she did. By keeping track of the days and the months and the seasons they could foretell what things were about to happen. After the woman had given all .these instructions to the women, telling them how to make their offerings to her and to the stars and other heavenly bodies, and all the important supernatural beings of the earth, she told the women that she had all their powers and they were to know their conditions at all times, through her. She then told the women she would be seen after the sun had gone down, then she disappeared. Late that evening after the sun had gone down, they saw her-in the sky, and she had become the Moon.

Now, the man told the men that they, in bringing their game from the hunt, must offer to the moon, to the stars, and other heavenly bodies and to the important supernatural beings on the earth. After he had told them how to use all the other things he said he would have to leave them and become something else. He had told them all the things they were to have, to use and to do, that there was a place for him to go and that he was about to go to that place. He told them that when the should go to his place he would show himself early in the morning, before daylight, and if, at that time, people should take their children to the nearest flowing water and put them in the water and bathe them (but they must drink before bathing them) he might help them to grow up and enjoy life. He told them that that place was the one at which they would get powers that he would give them. He then told them that he would sometimes be seen in the early morning as a star, and sometimes as a human being, and that his name was to be known as the First-Star-seen-after-Darkness-passes-by (*Hoseyasidaa*).

In the religious organization of the Wichita, the same liberality which is so characteristic of the tribe in general was strikingly manifested. While we find certain religious ceremonies in control of quasi-secret societies, they do not prove to be esoteric to the same extent as are those of the Pawnee. As a consequence, not only the salient features of their religious belief, but the mass of tribal lore constituting their mythology is open to all who can afford the slight compensation asked by the narrator of traditions.

While intensely conservative in many ways, as already pointed out, the religious ceremonies of the Wichita began many years ago to decline. This was largely due to the fact that the Wichita were a race of warriors, and their societies were largely concerned with acts of war. We do not find the extended and beautiful rituals, so characteristic of the Skidi and other bands of Pawnee, nor do we find, to any degree, extended ceremonies based upon the dramatization of myths, so characteristic of the tribes further to the west and south. Membership in all religious organizations seems to have been based almost entirely upon the wish of the individual. No organization is known to have existed the basis of membership in which was hereditary.

Standing at the head of the ceremonial societies was the *deer dance*, or the ceremony of the medicine-men. According to my ~~informant~~, the last ceremony was performed in 1871. From my .scant knowledge of the ceremony, it seems not to have been unlike that of the Skidi. No one could participate in the ceremony except medicine-men, each of whom had his own song or songs, in which was set forth the story of the origin of his magic power. In addition there were certain rituals sung, in connection with the opening and closing rites of the ceremony. The dance was held generally three, occasionally four, times a year; the first occasion when the grass had just appeared, the second when the corn was ripe, the third, when the corn was harvested. The ceremony was never held in the winter. One of the special features of the ceremony was the administering to the novitiate of a small red bean, which produced a violent spasm, -and finally unconsciousness, this condition being indicated by the inability of the novitiate to suffer pain when the jaw of a gar-pike was drawn over his naked body. During the ceremony offerings were made to the different gods, and at the end of the ceremony and following the feast was a ceremonial foot race, in which all members of the tribe, both male and female, were permitted to compete. This was followed on the part of those engaged in the [17] ceremony by violent vomiting. The foot race was supposed to give the participants great endurance while on the war-path. The chief efficacy of the ceremony was the removal from the camp of all evil influences and the promoting of good health, long life, and general prosperity.

Next in importance was the ceremony of the *calumet pipe* sticks, during which feathered pipe-stems were carried to some chief or other prominent individual of the tribe or to some neighboring tribe. This ceremony abounded in ritual and had its origin in one of the early myths, and its performance was supposed to confer lasting benefit upon the tribe. It is claimed by the Wichita, and there is evidence that their claim is valid, that they originated this ceremony, and that it was obtained from them by the Skidi, who, in turn, passed it on to the other tribes of the Pawnee.

Next in importance, and having their origin in times comparatively modern in the legendary chronicles of the Wichita, were the *rain bundle* ceremonies, the first having to do with the maturation of the corn; the second with the propagation of the buffalo. The chanting of the rituals was the chief feature in both of these ceremonies, the time of the singing being marked by the drawing of a stick over a notched dub, one end of which rested on a buffalo rawhide resonator. Both had their origin in the animal gods.

Next in importance were two ceremonies similar in nature, and known as "*Surround-Fire,*" and "*Small-Robes.*" These ceremonies also were of ritualistic nature, the first having its origin in the stars, and the second from the animals. The performance of both ceremonies was supposed to be efficacious in obtaining certain power or magic from various animals.

Next in rank were two societies, the first known as the *Many-Dogs*, and the second as the *Horn.* The time of the origin of these societies, like that of the rain and buffalo, was comparatively recent. They may be characterized as singing societies, in which ritualistic songs were sung, and they were preparatory to the setting out of a war-party.

Forming the last group were certain ceremonies or dances, all of which had more or less to do with the return of the successful *war*-parties. These were the *Scalp*, the "*Etwat's,*" the *Rubbing-Bone*, the *Turkey*, the *Squng*, the *Singers*, and the *Flat*, the last four being danced exclusively by the women.

In addition to the ceremonies just enumerated, the Wichita played the well-known forms of games common to the other Plains tribes, but always in a ceremonial manner. Among the most noted and sacred of these games were the shinny, the double-ball, and the ring-and-javelin games.

Wichita

WILLIAM W NEWCOMB, JR

Since 1835, when they first signed a treaty with the United States, a number of once autonomous but culturally similar tribes and subtribes have been known collectively as the Wichita ('wichito). Before their consolidation the principal groups were the *Taovaya*, Tawakoni, *Iscani*, Wichita proper, *Waco*, and *Kitsai*. The I*scani* disappeared in the last decades of the eighteenth century, and apparently other groups in earlier years also became extinct or were absorbed by others. The Waco emerged as a separate village group in the second decade of the nineteenth century. The name Wichita is drawn from one of the smaller and historically less prominent tribes.

Most of the progenitors of the modem tribe spoke Wichita, a Northern Caddoan language, which had several dialects.[2]* The *Kitsai*, who became amalgamated with the Wichita during the reservation period, spoke a distinct Northern Caddoan language, more closely related to Pawnee than to Wichita (Parks 1979: 203; "Kitsai," this vol.).

History Until 1845

Contact, 1541-1601

The first contact ancestral Wichita groups had with Europeans was in summer 1541 when Francisco Vasquez de Coronado and his army discovered the scattered settlements that they called Quivira along the Little Arkansas River, the farthest near the Smoky Hill River in Kansas (Winship 1896: 590: Hammond and Rey 1940: 304; Bolton 1949: 427-428; Wedel 1942: 12, 1959: 585-587; M.M. Wedel 1982: 121). These people were variously portrayed as comprising six or seven settlements, or as inhabiting 25 villages, some reported to be as large as 200 houses. The people were extensively tattooed, lived in grass houses, hunted bison, and cultivated maize, beans, and squash. The archeological remains of the people of Coronado's Quivira are [b] known as the Little River focus of the Great Bend phase (Wedel 1968: 371).

In 1601 Juan de Onate, governor of New Mexico, led another expedition to Quivira where he met an encampment of 5,000-6,000 tattooed and nearly naked Indians, probably about 25 miles northeast of present Ponca City, Oklahoma (Hammond and Rey 1953; Bolton 1916: 199-267; Newcomb and Campbell 1982). The Spaniards termed these Indians Escanjaque, after the word they uttered in greeting, but their name for themselves was Aguacane. They were composed of eight "pueblos" whose home territory likely lay along the North Canadian River in western Oklahoma (fig. 1). They may have spoken a Wichita dialect (Newcomb and Campbell 1982: 37) and were primarily bison hunters. Of the 600 movable dwellings in their camp, one kind was circular, dome-shaped, and covered with bison skins or grass; the other was similar to the hide-covered conical tepees the Spaniards had seen used by Apaches.

---

[2] *The phonemes of Wichita are: (voiceless stops) k^w, t, k, ʔ; (voiceless affricate) c; (voiceless spirants) s, h; (resonants) w, /ř/ (r, n), y; (short vowels) i, e ([ɛ], [æ]), a; (long vowels) i•, e•, a•; (overlong vowels) i:, e:, a:; (high pitch) v; (low pitch) v unmarked; (unpredictable secondary stress accompanying low pitch) v. The phoneme /ř/ is pronounced as an alveolar flap or tap or as the nasal [n], depending on the environment; in this orthography these major allophones are written distinctly as r and n. This phonemic analysis and the transcription of Wichita words follow David S Rood (Vol. 17: 580-586).

The Aguacane volunteered to join Oñate in a campaign against a nearby people of a "Great Settlement," whom they blamed for the murder of two Spaniards. Not only were the two peoples old enemies, but they "killed and ate each other" (Hammond and Rey 1953: 843). Oñate rejected the offer.

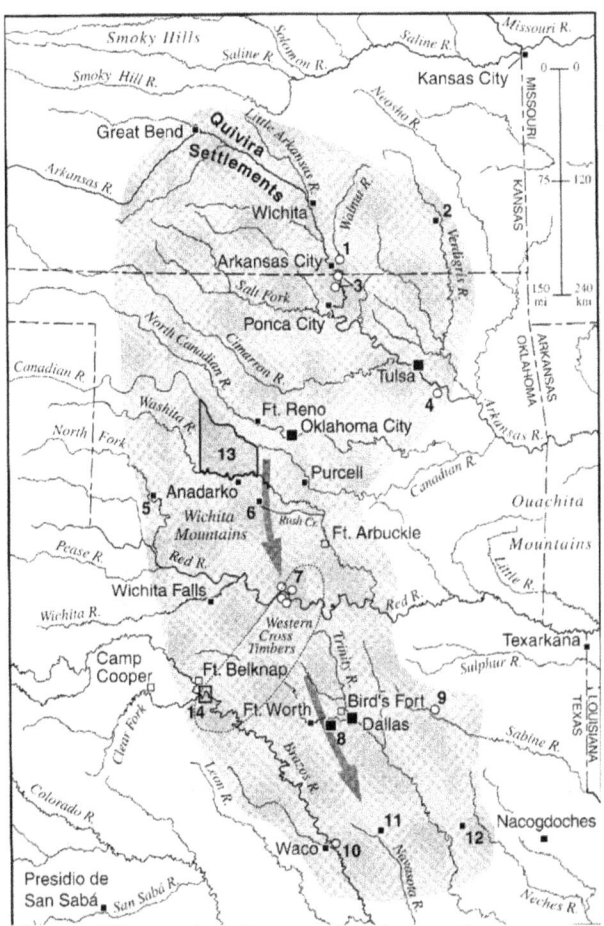

Figure 1. Wichita territory in the late 16th to early 18th centuries, showing villages and southward migration in the 18th century. 1, Great Settlement, which stretched along both banks of the Walnut River for 30 miles; 2, Taovaya villages and town of Neodesha; 3, Taovaya villages; 4, Tawahoni village; 5, Wichita village and town of Lugert; 6, Wichita village and town of Rush Springs; 7, "Spanish Fort" villages; 8, Waco and Kitsai villages and town of Arlington; 9, Tawakoni and Iscani twin villages: 10, Tawakoni and Waco villages; 11, Tawakoni village and town of Tehuacana; 12, Kitsai village and town of Palestine; 13, Wichita Reservation, 1872-1901; 14, Brazos Reservation, 1854-1859.

The Great Settlement was about 21 miles beyond the Aguacane encampment, probably on the Walnut River, just above its junction with the Arkansas near present Arkansas City in southern Kansas (Wedel 1942: 18-20, 1959: 223; Newcomb and Campbell 1982: 30). The archeological remains have been designated as the Lower Walnut focus of the Great Bend phase. The natives' name for themselves was not recorded, but they were later called Jumanes (or Jumanos), a name employed indiscriminately by New Mexican Spaniards for any Indians who painted or tattooed their bodies (Scholes and Mera 1940: 274; Newcomb 1961: 225-226).

The Great Settlement extended along both sides of the river for three or four days' travel, perhaps a distance of 30 miles. Estimates of the number of houses ranged from more than 1,200 to close to 2,000, and more houses could be seen in the distance. One member of the expedition guessed that the population of the settlement was 20,000. The Spaniards also were told that this settlement was small compared to others located to the north, and the Aguacane indicated that there were other dispersed settlements farther down the Arkansas. The houses were the distinctive [549] grass-covered lodges that the Wichita continued to construct until the late nineteenth century. They were built 30-40 paces apart, clustered in groups of 30-40. These clusters were separated from one another by 200-300 paces, and gardens of corn, beans, and squash occupied these intervals and extended beyond them but not out of sight of the houses (Hammond and Rey 1953: 754, 844-845, 847).

When the natives of the settlement discovered the Spaniards approaching, accompanied by Aguacanes, a number of their warriors challenged them to battle by throwing dirt in the air, said to be a "universal sign of war" in that land (Hammond and Rey 1953: 753). But Oñate was able to meet them peacefully, apparently by employing the sign for peace — arms stretched toward the sun, then touched to the [b] chest (Hammond and Rey 1953: 855). Presents were exchanged; the Indians gave the Spaniards the small beads they wore around their necks, ears of corn, and "some round loaves of corn bread as big as shields and two or three inches thick" (Hammond and Rey 1953: 753, 857). [b]

The Aguacane had informed Oñate that these enemy people held a Spaniard captive. Ostensibly to gain his freedom, six or eight natives were seized and placed in chains, including the principal chief, whom Oñate referred to as *catarax* (Hammond and Rey 1953: 754). Miguel, an Aguacane, later related that this settlement had two chiefs, a "main one and a lesser one" (Hammond and Rey 1953: 874). Various members of the expedition described the people of the settlement, presumably men, as dark, well-built, and mostly naked, although "some wore buckskin hanging to the knee" (Hammond and Rey 1953: 57). They painted their bodies and painted "stripes extended from eye to ear" (Hammond and Rey 1953: 42), apparently referring to tattooing.

Migration and Change, 1719-1803

French explorers probing westward from the Mississippi valley were aware of groups ancestral to the Wichita by 1673. Their maps indicate Paniassa villages scattered along the Arkansas River valley in Oklahoma and Kansas (Tucker 1942; Delanglez 1943). In 1719 a French trader, Jean-Baptiste Benard de La Harpe, established a post near modern Texarkana just above the great bend of the Red River. In August, accompanied by two Kitsai guides and about eight other men. La Harpe traveled by horseback to the Tawakoni settlement on the south bank of the Arkansas River below Tulsa, Oklahoma, near the town of Leonard (M.M. Wedel 1981a: 28, 1982: 124).

La Harpe and his party were ceremoniously met some distance from the settlement by the principal Tawakoni chief and six chiefs of other "nations," all mounted on beautiful horses. Following mutual assurances of friendship, the French were presented with cornmeal bread mixed with squash and smoked meat. La Harpe was provided with a fine horse, and the group proceeded to the settlement. There the Indians had La Harpe dismount, and two eminent men, with heads bowed, carried him to the chief's dwelling where he was sealed on a buffalo robe spread over a platform. The leading men encircled him, and one after another put a hand in his as a token of goodwill. La Harpe presented the young Tawakoni chief with muskets, powder, balls, and cloth, and the chief gave La Harpe an eagle-feather headdress adorned with many colored feathers, and two "calumet feathers" (probably pipestems), one for peace and one for war (Margry 1876-1886, 6: 288-290).

About 7,000 persons had come to see the strangers, and during the next several days the elaborate calumet ceremony was conducted for the French by the Taovaya and Iscani chiefs, both of whom were old men. The calumet was danced, speeches made, and presents exchanged. On [550] the second day of the ceremony La Harpe was carried to an arbor, his face was painted, and was presented with 30 buffalo robes, rock salt, tobacco pressed into loaves, some mineral pigments, and an eight-year-old Apache captive. The chief said that 17 other captives had been eaten a week before, apparently in a ritual feast. La Harpe learned that the settlement would be abandoned in November for the winter hunt, from which the Tawakoni would not return until March (Margry 1876-1886, 6: 291-292).

At almost the same time that La Harpe reached the Tawakoni settlement on the Arkansas, Claude-Charles Dutisné, heading westward from the mouth of the Missouri River, reached a Taovaya village, probably located on the Verdigris River near modern Neodesha in southeastern Kansas (M.M. Wedel 1982: 124). This village had 130 grass houses and 200-250 warriors; another village of the same size was located several miles upstream. The population of each village was about 1,000-1,250; between them they had only about 300 horses, but they reluctantly traded to Dutisné two horses and a mule with a Spanish brand. The Frenchman learned that the Taovaya were at war with the Apache, ate Apache captives, and used leather armor to protect their horses. In warfare they skillfully employed the bow and arrow as well as a long lance tipped with the blade of a European sword. He was told there were other Wichita villages to the west and northwest.

In 1748-1749, deserters from French Louisiana making their way from the Arkansas Post on the Lower Arkansas River to New Mexico passed through two Wichita villages about one and one-half miles apart on the west side of the Arkansas. These are identified as the Deer Creek (34KA3) and Bryson-Paddock (34KA5) archeological sites, in northern Oklahoma (M.M. Wedel 1981a: 4, 1982: 127; Thomas 1940: 82-89; Wedel 1959: 533-534). Their population was variously estimated at 1,500-2,500, and one of the villages was fortified with a stockade and ditch. Identified as Panipiques and Jumanos, one or perhaps both villages were probably mostly Taovayas (M.M. Wedel 1982: 127). For a time this was an ideal location since in the late 1740s the Comanche and some or all of the Wichita-speaking groups agreed to a mutually advantageous peace, which made the Taovaya prosperous middlemen in the lucrative trade between the Comanche and the French. French traders could ascend the Arkansas as far as these villages by boat, and the villages were easily accessible to nomadic Comanche (Febre et al. 1749).

By 1757 these villages had moved far to the south out of the Arkansas drainage to the Red River just west of the Western Cross Timbers, about 50 miles east of Wichita Falls, Texas. A fortified Taovaya village was built on the north side of the river (the Longest site 34JF1), and an Iscani village was located a short distance downstream. By 1765 a village of the Wichita proper was north of the Taovaya village, and the Iscani village was south of the river (apparently the Upper Tucker site 41MU17) (Bell, Jelks, and Newcomb 1974: 269-271). [b]

According to a captured Spanish soldier, Antonio Trevino (who lived in the village in 1764), and from what is known about the site archeologically, the fortification consisted of an oval-shaped palisade about 88 by 136 yards, situated in the middle of a dispersed village on the north bank of the river. It was constructed of split logs set vertically in the ground; outside the palisade was an earthen rampart about four feet high, and beyond it a ditch about four feet deep and more than 12 feet wide. Inside were four underground chambers large enough to shelter all noncombatants (Bell, Jelks, and Newcomb 1974: 84-85, fig. 26).

About the same time the Taovaya were establishing their fortress on the Red River, to the east the Tawakoni and a band of the Iscani were also migrating south. Before 1742 they were on the Canadian River, but soon afterward migrated to the Red River, and in the 1740s moved farther south into Texas (M.M. Wedel 1981a: 32). They apparently first settled in a twin village located on the upper Sabine River, probably at what is known as the Pearson site (41RA5), about 50 miles east of Dallas (Johnson and Jelks 1958; Duffield and Jelks 1961). The migration put many miles between them and their Osage enemies, and it gave them easier access to the French at Nalchitoches (John 1975: 305-306).

The southward migration of the Wichita tribes in the mid-eighteenth century brought them into closer contact with the Spaniards of Texas, and into a relationship that was uneasy, sometimes hostile, and never wholly resolved. When the longstanding anti-Apache policy of the Spaniards was reversed in 1757, a mission and presidio were built for the Lipan Apache on the San Saba River in west-central Texas. This was a clear signal to the Wichita that the Spaniards had allied themselves with the Apache, ancient enemies of the Wichita. Consequently, in spring 1758 a combined Indian force sacked and burned the mission, killing two of the missionaries and eight others. Composition of the attacking force is only partly known, but it did include Comanches, Hasinais, Bidais, Tonkawas, Kitsais, almost certainly Yojuanes, probably Taovayas, and others. In the following year Col. Diego Ortiz Parrilla, commander of the San Saba presidio, with an army of over 600 men, rode northward from the presidio to surprise and decimate a Yojuane camp, then continued northward to attack the fortified Taovaya village on the Red River. Armed with French firearms, supported by other Wichita allies, and apparently assisted by the Comanche, the Indians inflicted a stinging defeat to Parrilla, even capturing his two cannons (Parrilla 1759; Bell, Jelks, and Newcomb 1974: 260-265).

Soon afterward, in response to Tawakoni overtures of peace relayed through Caddo intermediaries. Fray Joseph de Calahorra, a veteran Spanish missionary at Nacogdoches, with a small retinue of soldiers and settlers joined along the way by about 100 Caddoes, visited the twin Tawakoni and Iscani villages. They were met, as was customary, about 10 miles out and were escorted in. Only a "street" separated [551] the Tawakoni and Iscani villages, which totaled 47 large dwellings. The villages had 250 warriors. Located in a meadow with the houses, streets, and gardens, there was abundant pasturage for the "fine breeding horses" they raised. Several miles from the villages was fertile farm land where they communally raised and shared equally in the abundant harvest of maize, beans, and squash. The villagers were also constructing a fort with an underground shelter to defend themselves (Johnson and Jelks 1958: 412).

The Tawakoni-Iscani settlement on the Sabine probably was abandoned before 1770, perhaps because of dissension over their relationship with the Spaniards or attacks by the Osage. They and apparently other migrant Wichita groups reestablished themselves in small and relatively impermanent scattered settlements and villages on the middle reaches of the Trinity and Brazos rivers and the headwaters of the Navasota.

After the transfer of Louisiana from France to Spain in 1769, Athanase De Mezieres became the Spanish commandant at Natchitoches. In autumn 1771 he concluded a treaty of peace with the Taovaya, Tawakoni, Iscani, and Kitsai, and during the following decade he made three tours to their villages. In his 1779 tour he visited for the first time the Spanish Fort villages on the Red River. There were 37 grass lodges on the north bank, apparently of the Wichita proper, and 123 in the Taovaya village on the south bank. Each lodge had 10-12 beds, and De Mezieres estimated there were more than 800 men and youths in the two villages. Although it was April, each lodge had 27-34 bushels of dried corn as well as beans and squash. They also raised large quantities of watermelons and tobacco. They dressed in skin shirts, leggings, and moccasins, and their shields, tepee covers, and horse equipment were also of skins. De Mezieres was particularly impressed by the women's industry. He noted that women as well as men participated in their system of government. Men could become "petty chiefs" not through inheritance but through their own abilities (Bolton 1914, 2: 201-204).

Consolidation and Subjugation, Nineteenth Century

By the opening of the nineteenth century the peoples who were to compose the Wichita tribe were scattered in small villages from southwestern Oklahoma to east Texas. They faced a declining population, poor trading relationships in Spanish Texas and with Americans who were filtering westward, and continued enmity of other tribes.

The Spanish Fort villages suffered from a smallpox epidemic in 1801, leaving about 400 men, half the number of a quarter-century earlier (Sibley 1832: 723). There was at that time a Tawakoni village on the north bank of the Red River and on its south side villages of the Taovaya and Wichita proper. The principal chief of the three villages was *Awakahea* (or *Awahakei*) of the

Tawakoni village, who died in 1811. No agreement could be reached on his successor, and each group went its own way (Garrett [b] 1946: 403; Bell, Jelks, and Newcomb 1974: 289-301). When the villages dispersed, part or all of the Tawakoni, subsequently known as the Huico (Waco), the name of one of their bands (John 1982-1983: 416,434), moved south to the Brazos in the vicinity of other Tawakoni settlements, establishing their village at the location of Waco, Texas (the Barren Branch site, 41ML95).

The Waco and their Tawakoni allies came into conflict with Anglo-Americans soon after Stephen F. Austin and other empresarios began to attract colonists to their Spanish land grants in southeast Texas in the 1820s. In 1824, when a Waco war party in pursuit of Tonkawas was blamed for killing a White man, the settlers retaliated by surprising the war party and slaying 12 of them (Wilbarger 1889: 204-205). In June 1824, commissioners were dispatched to the Brazos River villages to seek peace. Most of the Waco were away on a buffalo hunt and an expedition against the Osage. The Waco village contained 60 houses, and the inhabitants had about 400 acres of corn, beans, squash, and melons under cultivation. It was estimated that they could raise no more than 100 warriors. There was also a Tawakoni village, three miles below the Waco village on the east side of the Brazos, which had only seven houses; this was probably the Gas Plant site (4IML1) (Bell, Jelks, and Newcomb 1974: 45-49). At both villages defensive dugouts had been created by digging shallow pits and throwing the excavated dirt up around them (De Shields 1912: 67; Berlandier 1969: 44).

When the Mexican government ordered Austin to destroy the Waco village, he invited the East Texas Cherokee to participate in a joint campaign against them. Although the Mexican government rescinded its order, in 1829 the Cherokee assaulted the Waco village, exacting a heavy toll. The following year the Cherokee attacked a Tawakoni village at Tehuacana on the headwaters of the Navasota, but this village apparently was not abandoned until after an unsuccessful Texas Ranger assault on it in 1835; the Waco village was vacated about the same time.

About the same time that the Waco, Tawakoni, and Kitsai were being driven from central Texas, the United States government made contact with Wichita peoples north of the Red River. The dragoon expedition led by Col. Henry Dodge in 1834 visited a Wichita village in Devil's Canyon near modern Lugert, Oklahoma (Wheelock 1834; Catlin 1841, 2: 70-75). It paved the way for the Camp Holmes treaty of 1835 in which the Indians agreed to peace and perpetual friendship with one another and with the United States. It was the first treaty of the Wichita with the United States, it eased the Osage threat, and it established the usage of the term Wichita as their collective name (Harper 1953; Kappler 1904-1941, 2: 435-439).

The Waco, Tawakoni, and Kitsai retreated well beyond the rapidly expanding Texas frontier to establish villages in the upper valleys of the Trinity and Brazos and the lower Wichita rivers. But it was not far enough to escape the increasingly aggressive Texans, who in 1841 assaulted [552] Kitsai and Waco villages on the West Fork of the Trinity near present Arlington and caused their abandonment.

In September 1843 the Republic of Texas signed a peace treaty at Bird's Fort on the Trinity River with a number of Indian groups including the Waco and Tawakoni, which established a boundary between the settlements and Indian country (Winfrey and Day 1959-1966, 1: 242-245). However, raids against settlers' horses continued, primarily by Waco and Tawakoni (Winfrey and Day 1959-1966, 2: 50-53).

Culture, 1850-1875

Subsistence

Until the reservation era the Wichita pursued a varied subsistence pattern, sharply divided by sex: men hunted, women gardened. When game was scarce, greater reliance could be placed on the women's gardens, and when floods, droughts, or other conditions harmed or destroyed the gardens, game could be more intensively sought by the hunters.

Throughout much of their history the Wichita followed a semisedentary seasonal cycle. They remained in their settlements throughout the spring and summer while the women worked the gardens. Following the harvest they abandoned their settlements to become tepee-dwelling hunters.

The gardens were typically located along the terraces of rivers and smaller streams, where the women cultivated maize, beans, squash, gourds, and tobacco. Muskmelons and watermelons probably were acquired from French traders during the first half of the eighteenth century. By the [b] mid-eighteenth century the gardens were enclosed with brush or rail fences to keep out horses and other livestock. Men hunted bison primarily, but also deer, elk, bear, antelope, and other game. A variety of wild fruits (some of which, like plum trees, were apparently cared for), berries, nuts, and other plant products were utilized. Fish were not eaten (Bolton 1914, 2: 202; G.A. Dorsey 1904a: 4; Curtis 1907-1930, 19: 37).

The women dried surplus garden produce and stored it in hide bags, both in their lodges and in underground cache pits. Their method of preserving squash was first mentioned in the eighteenth century by De Mezieres (Bolton 1914, 2: 202), who observed that squash were cut into long narrow strips, flattened by pounding, woven into mats (braided according to G.A. Dorsey 1904a), and then dried (fig. 2). They were easily stored and were an important item in the trade with the Comanche and other nonhorticultural Indians. Surplus meat was smoked or sun-dried. Green corn was roasted or boiled in pottery vessels with other vegetables and meat; dried corn was ground into meal as needed in wooden mortars (fig. 3) and also on stone slabs. Cornmeal was often made into large round loaves and baked in the ashes (Curtis 1907-1930, 19: 37).

Settlement Pattern

Wichita communities in the sixteenth and seventeenth centuries are well characterized as scattered or dispersed settlements. Matrilineally related relatives lived close to one another in a cluster of grass lodges in the midst of cultivated fields, next to other similar clusters, which were near others, often extending for considerable distances in favored locales. [553] Hostilities during the early historic period must have been sporadic; they did not force the Wichita into more compact and secure settlement patterns. The spread of the horse complex, the introduction of firearms, depopulation, and the other factors related to European invasion forced them to abandon their dispersed settlements during the eighteenth century for compact villages, often built near similar villages. Some villages soon came to be fortified.

Structures

The beehive-shaped grass lodges of the Wichita (fig. 4) were substantial dwellings that varied from 15 to 30-40 feet in diameter and were constructed of cedar posts and crossbeams surrounded by upright poles sunk into the earth and lashed together at the top (Douglas 1932b). Willow rods were lashed to the upright poles and covered with grass thatching (Curtis 1907-1930,

19: 38). The lodges and arbors described by members of Oñate's expedition (Hammond and Rey 1953) did not differ materially from those described 300 years later. Originally each lodge had two small willow and grass doors, low and narrow, one on the east, the other on the west, and vestigal doors on the north and south sides, which had earlier been used ceremonially (G.A. Dorsey 1904a: 4-5). Six to as many as 12 beds, constructed of light poles and raised well above the floor, were arranged around the interior walls. Beds were covered with bison hides, and painted hide curtains were hung around the beds [b] to afford privacy. A slight excavation was made in the center of the lodge for a fire. The fireplace was considered sacred as many offerings and medicinal preparations were made there. A small smoke vent was provided near the top of the roof. A three to four-foot peak, formed from bundles of tightly wrapped grass, capped the apex of the lodge, and from its base four poles extended for about three feet, one pointing in each of the cardinal directions. They symbolized the deities of the directions, and the peak symbolized the Wichita creator god. As late as 1900, 90 percent of the Wichita lived in grass lodges (Kiowa Agency 1931).

Adjacent to the lodges were several kinds of arbors, the largest being oval in floorplan and like the lodges in construction except that they were open-sided and had a raised floor, providing a shady retreat for work and relaxation. Raised platforms, 10 to 20 feet square, reached by notched tree-trunk ladders, were employed for drying corn, meat, and squash. At one time, small sleeping platforms were constructed for the confinement of young women. When hunting, the Wichita used hide tepees, which apparently were like those of the Plains Apache; they also constructed some form of sweatlodge (Bolton 1916: 260; G.A. Dorsey 1904a: 4-5).

Clothing and Adornment

During the first centuries of European contact Wichita peoples dressed for the climate. In warm weather men wore little more than a breechcloth and moccasins, and [554] women a short skirt (fig. 3). In cold weather a robe was added. Hide moccasins appear to have been aboriginal, and after the adoption of horses, leggings were added. By 1834, Wichita attire had been considerably altered. Catlin (1841, 2: 74) remarked that the women wore dresses reaching from chin to ankles, fringed and ornamented with rows of elk teeth.

The most striking feature of Wichita personal appearance was extensive tattooing, said to have been revealed in [b] a vision by the buffalo. Men were tattooed on both eyelids, with a short horizontal line extending from the outside corner of each eye. Short tattooed lines also extended downward from the corners of the mouth. On the back of their hands were clawlike designs, placed there after a boy had killed his first bird. Small crosses, symbolizing war honors, were tattooed on the arms and chest and represented the stars of Flintstone Lying Down Above, the mythic guardian of warriors. They also pierced their ears, [555] usually in four places, and suspended numerous ornaments from them.

Women's tattoos were less individualistic but even more intricate than those of men. A tattooed line ran down the bridge of the nose to the upper lip, encircled the mouth, but just before the lines met below the lower lip the ends turned downward to the chin. Between these two lines were two other parallel lines, and all four terminated at the chin and intersected with a line along the chin line. This chin-line tattoo ran from ear to ear, above which were tattooed a row of solid triangles. Other triangles were tattooed on the neck and upper breast and a series of parallel zigzag lines coursed up and down the arms. The breasts, including the nipples, were tattooed with several short lines, and around them were tattooed three concentric circles, said to prevent pendulous breasts in old age. The tattooing of women was a form of social identification that distinguished them from female captives and from the women of other tribes (G.A. Dorsey 1904a: 2-3).

Social Organization

A woman, her husband, unmarried children, and married daughters with their husbands with children composed the basic social and economic unit. A family might occupy one lodge, or perhaps several close together if the family was large, and the oldest woman of such households was its head and supervisor. Other related families built their dwellings nearby. The women of the household cooperatively tilled the gardens, gathered firewood, tanned hides, sewed clothing, prepared food, and built houses. During menses, husband and wife did not sleep in the same lodge, and normal female duties were suspended.

The men helped in the physically more demanding tasks of house-building. During the hunting season, the household groups were broken up, but they maintained cohesive-ness by pitching their tepees close to one another. Before European pressures forced alterations in Wichita life, it is probable that the matrilineal emphasis was greater than it was in later years (Schmitt and Schmitt 1952: 59).

Kinship

The Wichita used the terms 'brother' and 'sister', and behavior appropriate for siblings, to include all cousins. A child lived in the same household with the children of his maternal aunt (his mother's sister), and, in fact, because men sometimes married sisters, she also might be married to the child's father.

A person termed his mother's sisters 'mother', qualifying the term with 'little' or 'big' depending upon whether they were younger or older than one's biological mother. Similarly, a father's brothers were 'little' or 'big' fathers. Inasmuch as the Wichita practiced the levirate, a custom in which a man marries his brother's widow, the brothers of a child's father were potential fathers. A father's sister was [b] also termed and treated as a 'big' or 'little' mother, but a mother's brother, who lived elsewhere if married, was termed uncle. In the grandparental generation all relatives were referred to as grandfather or grandmother, with the qualifying 'big' or 'little' depending upon the relative age of the connecting grandparent. Reciprocally, all grandchildren of a person's siblings were termed grandchildren (Schmitt and Schmitt 1952: 11).

Life Cycle

At the birth of a child a mother moved to a tepee pitched near her lodge. Husbands were barred from entering the tepee until four days after the birth lest they cause mother and child to become ill. Expectant women were attended by experienced, elderly midwives. Shortly after birth an older woman took the infant to a river, where she held it aloft and offered prayers to the moon and the creator god. The child was then immersed in the river and prayers were addressed to the powers of the water. A woman chosen for her good health would construct a cradle using materials ritually prepared by the father (fig. 5). If the child grew to be healthy, the cradle might be purchased and used by other families (G.A. Dorsey 1904a: I 1-12; Curtis 1907-1930, 19: 41).

Children were often named prior to birth as a consequence of dreams of the mother or other relatives. Later, they might be given another name based on some personal mannerism or significant act. People who were experiencing poor fortune or continued illness often changed their names in later life by means of a name-giving ceremony or through purchase (G.A. Dorsey 1904a: 8; Curtis 1907-1930, 19: 40).

Fathers played an important role in the instruction of their sons in hunting, the use of weapons, and the other male skills. Mothers and the other women of the household trained girls in female activities. Girls approaching marriageable age (said to be 16 years) were kept away from men and boys. Families of marriageable boys usually arranged, through go-betweens, marriage with the family of the chosen girl, ideally a girl of the same village. But if a girl's parents favored a particular boy for a son-in-law the procedure might be reversed; this may have been more common prior to reservation days. Marriages were formalized by giving presents to and a feast for the bride's relatives (G.A. Dorsey 1904a: 9-11).

A newly married couple lived in the household of the bride's parents, and the new son-in-law was expected to perform a number of duties for the family, the most important being to supply them with meat. His standing with the family depended upon how well he fulfilled this and other obligations. If the bride's parents were not satisfied with his behavior, he was sent home, thus constituting divorce. The relationships between in-laws, particularly those of the opposite sex, were always reserved and formal. Thus, a man's mother-in-law might talk to him through his wife rather than directly to him, and a man would never tease or [556] joke with a mother-in-law no matter how successful or prestigious he might become.

When a person was on the verge of death, relatives began to gather around, and all relatives were expected to be present when the body was buried. Nonrelatives took charge of the last rites, because the souls of the dead were believed to attempt to persuade relatives to join them. [b] Relatives cut their hair in mourning, close relatives cutting off more than distant ones. Burial generally occurred two to four days after death, in a shallow grave over which was erected a shedlike structure. Prayers were addressed to the earth. The corpse's head was oriented to the east, and graves were normally located on hills near the villages. A man's war gear was buried with him except for his shield, which was given to a friend who knew its medicine. The family of the deceased often impoverished itself through giveaways. Relatives mourned for four days and surviving spouses for several months (G.A. Dorsey 1904a: 12-16; Curtis 1907-1930, 19: 42; Schmitt and Schmitt 1952: 11-14; Schmitt 1952).

Political Organization

The dispersed settlements of the early historic period were clearly autonomous but also in contact with other related settlements. Chiefs wielded considerable authority within their communities and were accorded respect and obedience by their followers. Chiefs acquired their position through their bravery, generosity, kindness, and the reciprocal love and respect of their people. They were elected by the head warriors who controlled village affairs through their ability to demote a chief if his performance was unsatisfactory. However, retiring chiefs frequently nominated an outstanding young man to fill their position (G.A. Dorsey 1904a: 6; Curtis 1907-1930, 19: 43). The primary responsibility of chiefs may have been conducting the calumet ceremony, which established and maintained relationships with other groups.

A "lesser" or second chief was called 'the one who locates', referring to his duty of being constantly on the lookout for better village sites. He was also responsible for the removal of the village and for laying out new village sites. How long aboriginal settlements were maintained in one location is unknown, but by the eighteenth century and the onset of frequent removals, selection of new village sites had become a vitally important task. Next in the hierarchy were the medicine men, who conducted important ceremonies. One of their number filled the important office of crier. Helpers or assistants might become highly ranked medicine men after years of apprenticeship. Social status for the remaining population was determined by wealth and prowess in war (G.A. Dorsey 1904a: 6-7).

During the eighteenth century, with continuing population decline, migration, warfare, and the other changed conditions imposed by the European onslaught, the traditional political structure was not able to hold the various tribal components together, much less to lead them to consolidate their depleted and scattered villages into effective entities. The Iscani, for example, split into at least two bands, and the Tawakoni in Texas splintered over relations with the Spaniards. During the nineteenth century, the authority of some particularly able village chiefs, as in the [557] case of *Awakahea*, expanded in that they were recognized as the leaders of several villages (John 1982-1983). But there were few such leaders, and their successors were unable to hold various factions together.

Warfare

Wichita captives among the Pueblos in 1541 and the animosity of the *Aguacane* for the Wichita of the Great Settlement in 1601 indicate that conflict was present before European intervention. Whatever its nature, after the advent of Europeans and the development of bitter competition between tribes for firearms, horses, and European goods, intertribal strife apparently increased dramatically. The traditional enemies of the Wichita were the Plains Apache, Osage, and Tonkawa. Captives of both sexes and all ages were tortured and eaten, apparently in response to religious beliefs (Margry 1876-1886, 6: 291-292). By the mid-eighteenth century captives had become an important article of commerce, and cannibalism disappeared prior to the nineteenth century.

Militarily, the Wichita reached their peak in the mid-eighteenth century. Nonetheless, they were not aggressive in that their migrations were prompted in large part by a desire to distance themselves from enemies, and the fortifications they built were for defensive purposes. Warfare consisted of small raiding parties, composed of a handful of volunteers, whose aim was to steal horses, take scalps, and capture women. Men painted depictions of their war deeds on tepees and robes. Victorious war parties were received in their villages with rejoicing, sparking scalp and victory dances. The death of any warrior required ritual expiation on the part of the leader, after which the entire village mourned for four days. War tales could be narrated only during the winter, when men gathered at night to relate their war deeds (G.A. Dorsey 1904a: 7, 15).

Mythology

In 1719 La Harpe reported that the Wichita venerated "a great spirit" under diverse forms and offered to him the first fruits from their gardens (Margry 1876-1886, 6: 296). This was 'Man Never Known on Earth', the creator who was closely associated with the sun, Man Reflecting

Light (G.A. Dorsey 1904a: 26; Newcomb 1961: 270-272).

According to one origin myth (G.A. Dorsey 1904a: 25-29), before any celestial beings were created, Man Never Known on Earth was alone and in darkness. After the land was created floating on water, he made the first humans and placed them on the earth. They were the moon, Bright Shining Woman, and the morning star, Having Power to Carry Light, who was regarded as the founder of Wichita culture. Bright Shining Woman was the protector of women and source of procreative power for humans, animals, and plants. [b]

Everything they needed to live was given to them through dreams. Moon received the four Corn Mothers (different types of corn) to nourish the people. Morning Star journeyed to the east where he found a grass lodge inhabited by Star That is Always Moving who taught him how to makes bows and arrows and to hunt. When Star That Is Always Moving wounded a black and white deer, he initiated the cycle of day and night. Sun told Morning Star to return to Moon, after which the people multiplied. Morning Star taught the men to make offerings after successful hunts, then he and Moon ascended to the sky where the people offered them prayers.

A separate origin myth tells of a great flood during which most people and animals were drowned. As Wind journeyed forth and dried the land he discovered a woman lying on the ground who, after giving birth to a female child, sunk into the earth. The child was raised by Wind in the underwater home of the beaver. There she married and gave birth to a boy. Morning Star, who led the people out of the beaver lodges, gave them corn, and taught them to hunt (Curtis 1907-1930, 19: 53-56).

Woman Forever in the Water was the primary water power and granted health and well-being as well as protecting the virtue of women whose husbands were absent. The earth was the great keeper of medicines and the mother of everything. Prayers were also offered to many other stars, meteors, and the various winds. Four distinct epochs were recognized as constituting the world cycle, the last of which was believed to lead to the destruction of the present world and the beginning of a new world cycle (G.A. Dorsey 1904a:18-21; Curtis 1907-1930, 19: 44-48).

Religion and Ceremonies

Every sort of object might contain or could be imbued with more than natural qualities. Animals often assumed special power and appeared to men in dreams or visions to become their spirit helpers, but there was no structured vision quest. All spiritual knowledge was believed to come from dreams and visions. To disregard instructions given by spirits brought ill fortune to the offender, as spirits knew at all times the thoughts of the individual (Curtis 1907-1930, 19: 47). Deities and spirit-helpers were spoken of as "dreams" and divided into 'above dreams' and 'dreams down here', the later classified as 'dreams living in water' and 'dreams closest to man' (G.A. Dorsey 1904a: 20).

The Wichita believed in a continuing existence after death in a spirit world, where they held the same social standing as in life; those who had taken their own lives were unable to enter (G.A. Dorsey 1904a: 14). According to La Harpe, the dead departed in a great canoe under the guidance of a black man with horns who took warriors and other reputable people to a prairie where there were buffalo in abundance, and others to a dry, barren place where life was difficult (Margry 1876-1886, 6: 296). [558]

Semisecret religious societies were responsible for maintaining and strengthening relationships with the important deities who controlled tribal welfare. Membership in these societies was apparently open to anybody who wished to join, and in the early years of the twentieth century 14 dance societies, three of which were composed of women and some of which were probably secular, were remembered (Curtis 1907-1930, 19: 43-14).

The most important of these was the Deer Dance, a ceremony of the medicine men, which was held three or four times a year during the warm months. Last performed in 1871 (G.A. Dorsey 1904a: 16), it was thought to remove evil influences, promote abundant crops, good health, long life, and general prosperity. The rite, which originated in a vision of the 'red bean man', took place in a ritually constructed lodge. Attended by both male and female shamans, the dance involved smoke offerings; the opening of medicine bundles; trance states possibly induced by the ingestion of mescal beans (*Sophora secundiflora*), during which the participants received power from animal visions; and conjuring acts. The ceremony was led by a chief shaman dressed as a deer. Offerings to various gods also were made, and following a feast the ceremony was concluded with a foot race open to all tribal members (including women), which presumably gave participants great endurance on the warpath (Curtis 1907-1930, 19: 64-71).

Another important ceremony was that of the calumet in which feathered pipestems were presented to a prominent person or chief of a neighboring tribe. First described by La Harpe in 1739, its performance was thought to confer lasting benefit to the tribe (Margry 1876-1886, 6: 290-292).

Other ceremonies, originating in visionary experience, involved the use of sacred bundles, the bear medicine bundle being one of the most important. Rain bundle ceremonies were held annually for both the maturation of corn and the calling of the buffalo. These ceremonies were held in ritually purified lodges and involved singing and the opening of the bundles. The Surround the Fire ceremony was directed to the spirit of the dogwood tree for the increase and health of children (Curtis 1907-1930, 19: 72-85). The Many Dogs and Horn societies performed ceremonials for success in war. Victorious war parties participated in numerous scalp dances, four of which were led exclusively by women (G.A. Dorsey 1904a: 17).

A Wichita secret society of sorcerers was reported, whose members could cause "silent death" to their enemies, Membership in the society required sacrificing the life of a relative or a close friend. This was accomplished by procuring a lock of hair or some possession of the victim and placing it either in the knurl hole of a tree for "slow death" or in the mouth of a toad, which was then killed, for "fast death." Poisoning was also practiced. Those found guilty of witchcraft would be killed and their bodies left on the open plain without ceremony (Curtis 1907-1930, 19: 57-558 59). [b]

History Since 1846

Reservation Period, 1846-1901

When Texas achieved statehood late in 1845 it retained claim to public lands; Indians living in the state became the responsibility of the federal government, in effect denying them any claims to land within the state. In 1846 and again in 1850 the federal government negotiated treaties with all the local Indians it could assemble, by which the Indians acknowledged that they were under the protection of the United States (Winfrey and Day 1959-1966, 3: 43-61, 130-136). In 1853 the Texas legislature authorized the federal government to establish Indian reserves on vacant Texas land. The Waco, Tawakoni, and remnants of other tribes — Caddo, Delaware, Shawnee, and Tonkawa — were soon gathered on a reserve on the upper Brazos River. But nearby Texas settlers became so hostile and menacing that by June 1859 it was evident that the reserves would have to be abandoned. In August 1,050 Indians of the Brazos Reservation, including approximately 375 Wacos and Tawakonis, escorted by federal troops, made the trek to the Leased District in Indian Territory, purchased by the government from the Choctaw and Chickasaw (Winfrey and Day

1959-1966, 3: 193-209; Bell, Jelks, and Newcomb 1974: 295-298; Elam 1971: 314-317).

The Wichita north of the Red River had in October 1858 abandoned their village on Rush Creek, following its destruction by Maj. Earl Van Dorn with four companies of cavalry, coincident to a battle with the Comanche. They fled to Fort Arbuckle, where Indian agent Elias Rector, anticipating abandonment of the Brazos Reservation, designated a reservation for them all. But the Wichita, now considered a single tribal entity, were hardly well settled before they were uprooted by the Civil War. The bulk of the tribe fled to Kansas in the winter of 1862-1863 and remained there until 1867. The site of one of their refugee camps is now the city of Wichita, Kansas (Bell, Jelks, and Newcomb 1974: 299-302).

Although the Wichita were returned to their old homes along the Washita River after the Civil War, they were unable to secure government recognition of their right to its possession. In autumn 1872, a reservation embracing 743,610 acres between the Canadian and Washita rivers and west of 98° longitude, was agreed to by the Wichita, but Congress never ratified the agreement. The Waco and Tawakoni (late of Texas), the Wichita from north of the Red River, and the Kitsai established themselves in what the agents termed separate "neighborhoods" (Randlett 1901; Schmitt 1950: 155). Each group had a chief and one of them was acknowledged as head chief of the tribe. By the end of the reservation period the position of local chief had disappeared. These tribal (or subtribal) fragments were too weak to rebuff or reject overtly whatever policies or actions the government might wish to impose. [559]

In 1878 the Kiowa-Comanche and Wichita agencies had been combined, and after the reservations were broken up official reports seldom dealt specifically with its various tribes. Agents often were able to exact compliance with governmental policy by withholding annuities and trust funds. This enabled them to discourage attendance at the summer and fall dances, which frequently lasted as long as 10 days. In 1882 the Wichita were settled at Rush Springs south of the Washita River (Elam 1971: 372).

Although the Wichita were reported to have about 100 acres under cultivation as early as 1869, it was a consequence of women's labors (ARCIA 1869: 382). Typically the women enclosed garden patches of three to four acres with split rail fences, in which they grew corn, squash, watermelons, and a variety of garden vegetables. Efforts to induce the Wichita to become American-style farmers were furthered by plowing fields for them and planting in rows for easy cultivation of corn (and later cotton).

As late as 1875 it was reported that many of their farms were still worked with hoes by the women. Occasional floods, frequent droughts, and grasshoppers often destroyed or severely reduced crop yields, discouraging farming by whatever means by either sex. Wichita men felt it was degrading to labor in the fields, and most of them did not become willing farmers until the twentieth century. They were interested in raising horses, not cattle or crops. They regarded themselves as hunters, and with their agent's approval, continued to pursue bison in off-reservation hunts until the animal's virtual extinction. [b]

A boarding school was opened near the Wichita Agency in 1871, which emphasized agricultural arts for boys and domestic training for girls.

Attempts to convert the Wichita to Christianity were less overt than those associated with farming. A Baptist mission was established in 1878, and its success was credited to Tula-Mico (Tulsey-Micco ~ John MacIntosh), a Seminole Baptist missionary. By 1880 a meeting house had been constructed with donated funds for its 70 members. Services attracted 100-300 persons (ARCIA 1880: 75).

When the Ghost Dance swept the plains, the Wichita embraced the movement enthusiastically (fig. 7). Throughout the summer of 1891 they danced (Mooney 1896: 902-903), but when the millennium failed to arrive, the Ghost Dance attracted fewer and fewer followers. Despite opposition by the authorities, reservation Indians, apparently including the Wichita, continued to dance until at least 1917.

The religious use of peyote was also adopted by the Wichita as early as 1889, as it was highly compatible with the Surround the Fire ceremony *(hacthiyas* 'fire tied around'). La Barre (1938: 120) noted that many medicine bundles contained peyote before a Kiowa named Old Man Horse introduced the Peyote religion to the Wichita, about 1902. In 1924, the Wichita sent representatives to the annual meeting of the Native American Church indicating their continued interest in the sacramental use of peyote (Stewart 1987: 226).

The Wichita resisted the determined efforts of the Cherokee Commission, under the provisions of the Dawes [560] Severally Act of 1887, to break up their reservation. They were discouraged from seeking and for a time denied legal counsel, and then they were offered about 50 cents an acre for their "surplus" land. But on June 4, 1891, 152 Wichitas out of an adult male population of 227 were persuaded to sign an agreement with the commissioners. Litigation over what the Wichita had agreed to, and the Choctaw and Chickasaw claims to reservation lands, postponed dismemberment of the reservation until December 1900. A Supreme Court decision then led to allotment in severally, compensation [b] of $1.25 an acre for surplus land, and the opening of the reservation in 1901 (B.B. Chapman 1933, 1944; Wright 1951; 260; Newcomb 1976).

The Twentieth Century

Allotment of the reservation meant not only a drastic reduction in land holdings but also destruction of the last vestiges of the old neighborhoods since families had to scatter out to establish homes on their allotments, often at [561] considerable distance from their old residences (Randlett 1901). Even when families moved to potentially more productive lands, most could not plant a crop in 1901, and those who were able to do so suffered from a serious drought that summer. With no annuity or other funds due, and near starvation, the beginnings of post-reservation life were bleak for the Wichita.

By the second decade of the century the number of Christian denominations active among the agency's Indians, in addition to the Baptists, included the Methodist Church, Reformed Church of America, Reformed Presbyterian Church, and Mennonites. By this time the Peyote religion had spread to the Kiowa, Comanche, and Wichita agency, and it was reported that peyote was used by approximately 50 percent of the Indians there (Stinchecum 1917).

The Wichita adopted a constitutional tribal organization following the congressional enactment of the Oklahoma Indian Welfare Act in 1936. Its governing body was composed of a chairman, vice-chairman, treasurer, secretary, and three other members, elected for four-year terms of office. Among economic ventures, the tribe in 1974 built a 30,000-square-foot office building in Anadarko (fig. 9), which it leased to the Bureau of Indian Affairs. The Wichita joined with the Caddo and Delaware tribes as WCD Enterprises, Inc., to undertake light industrial and other ventures, and a number of buildings were completed in an industrial park. When the federal Riverside Indian Boarding School in Anadarko was closed in the 1950s, its 2,500 acres [b] reverted to the three tribes, and 10 acres of this land were set aside for the Wichita. Through revenue sharing and donations a community building, dance pavilion, and picnic and camping areas were built. The tribe also benefited from various government programs, apart from those of the Bureau of Indian Affairs, particularly during the Great Society years of the 1960s, obtaining funds to improve the nutrition of low-income families and for an improved water system. The tribe began a number of programs aimed at preserving the tribal heritage and identity, including projects to record tribal songs; however, by 1998 none were fluent in Wichita.

In the early 1970s, the Wichita Indian tribe pursued compensation from the United States for the taking of Wichita aboriginal lands within the present states of Kansas, Oklahoma, and Texas. The Wichita were authorized to file their claim before the Indian Claims Commission even though the deadline for submitting such claims had already expired. The case was transferred to the Court of Claims, which in 1981 determined that the Wichita were not entitled to compensation and dismissed the petition "on the basis that the tribe had abandoned the lands ... being claimed by the time the United States acquired sovereignty over Kansas and Oklahoma in 1803 and Texas in 1845" (Bureau of Indian Affairs 1985b: 1). In 1983, the United States Court of Appeals reversed the dismissal and asked for the United States Claims Court to determine the boundaries of Wichita aboriginal lands. Such a finding was never issued by the court because in [562] 1985 the Wichita Tribe settled all claims by accepting $14,000,000, with both the United States and the tribe agreeing not to seek further review or appeal of the case.

Population

The documents of the 1540 Coronado expedition at first glance appear to be internally contradictory concerning the settlement patterns in Quivira and at odds with the population figures of the Oñate expedition 60 years later. Coronado reported that he visited or heard of 25 villages in Quivira (Winship 1896: 582), but Jaramillo, who accompanied him, wrote that there were "six or seven settlements, at quite a distance from one another, among which we traveled for four or five days" (Winship 1896: 590). Coronado may have noted some sort of geographical or political divisions of the settlements; and following this line of reasoning it is possible the expedition passed through six or seven "settlements" each composed of three to five "villages." The villages had "as many as 200 houses" (Winship 1896: 577). Using 8 to 10 occupants per lodge, the figure employed by Oñate 60 years later, the villages had 1,600-2,000 inhabitants, and Coronado's Quivira a total population of 40,000-50,000. It should be noted that the settlements were unequal in size.

Population data, gained from members of the 1601 Oñate expedition who were interrogated the following year in Mexico City, reported that the Great Settlement contained variously 1,200, 1,700, and "close" to 2,000 lodges (Hammond and Rey 1953: 846). But in their three-day scout alongside the settlement they failed to reach its far end. One soldier estimated the settlement's population at 20,000, and at 8-10 persons per lodge this estimate is reasonable. There was general agreement that there were other settlements up and down the river, and two soldiers learned that other settlements were larger than the one they visited.

By 1719, when Europeans next visited the Wichita, there had been a dramatic decline in the native population. The dispersed village La Harpe visited on the Arkansas apparently had a population of 6,000 (Margry 1876-1886, 6: 289). The village Dutisné reached, presumably of Taovaya, and the other village nearby had between them 2,080-2,600 persons. Even if the contact-period population has been overestimated and the 1719 population underestimated, it is apparent that there had been a major and catastrophic population loss.

During the remainder of the eighteenth century Wichita population continued to decline, and disease is mentioned frequently in the documents of the period. In the 1770-1780 decade, for example, primarily following the estimates of De Mezieres, all the Wichita peoples, including the Kitsai, had a population of 3,000-4,000, Early in the nineteenth century, after being "again ravaged by smallpox" (Mooney 1910: 948), the consolidated tribe had a population of about 2,600. Their nadir population was reached in 1896 when they numbered 365 (G.A. Dorsey 1904a: 2). [b]

Population figures for the first decades of the twentieth century are confusing, as the Wichita were often counted with other groups. For example, in 1900 the "Wichita and affiliated tribes," excluding the Caddo, numbered 428 (ARCIA 1900, 1: 648), while according to Mooney (1910: 949) during the same period "the whole Wichita body [was estimated at] ... only about 310, besides about 30 of the confederated Kichai remnant." Fourteen years later, the combined Wichita and Caddo population amounted to 1,094 (ARCIA 1914: 81), probably almost equally divided between the two tribes (cf. Fletcher 1907a: 181). Adding to the confusion is the enumeration of 597 Wichita in 1930 (ARCIA 1930: 44) as compared to "300 Wichita and Kichai" reported the same year by the census; however, this source noted that "since there were 645 Indians in Caddo County not reported by tribe, it is quite likely the numbers of both the Wichita and the Caddo are considerably understated by the census enumeration" (U.S. Bureau of the Census 1937: 41, 59).

The undercount must have continued into the following decades, with perhaps 460 Wichita residing on the reservation in 1945 (U.S. Congress, House Committee on Interior and Insular Affairs 1953: 715). By 1960, over 700 Wichitas were living in the northern portion of Caddo County (U.S. Department of Health, Education, and Welfare 1960: 15). The number dropped to 470 in 1972 (U.S. Department of Commerce 1974: 478-479). In 1984 the total enrollment for the Wichita tribe was 1,170, with about half that number residing on the reservation (The Confederation of American Indians 1986: 243). In 1989, the number of reservation residents was reported at 869 (Bureau of Indian Affairs 1989: 5). Tribal enrollment grew to 1,912 members in 1998 (Jonelle Fields, communication to editors 1998).

Synonymy[3]

The name Wichita, now the designation of formerly separate tribes or bands, was originally the name of one village group. The earliest citation is on the 1718 Delisle map, where it appears as Ouachitas (Tucker 1942: pl. XV). Other French versions are Ousita, 1719 (La Harpe in Margry 1876-1886, 6: 293); Ouedsitas, 1772 (de Mezieres in Bolton 1914, 1: 289); and Ouitcitas, 1807 (Robin in Hodge 1907-1910, 2: 949). Spanish variants include Ovagitas, 1723 (Barcia 1723: 288); Ovedsitas, 1771-1772 (Bolton 1905: 91); Guachitas, 1786 (Cabello in Bell, Jelks, and Newcomb 1974: 379); Guichitas (Trevino et al. 1765; Cabello 1784, both in Bell, Jelks, and Newcomb 1974: 388, 379); Huichita, 1809 (Salcedo in Bell, Jelks, and Newcomb 1974: 387); and Huichites, 1828 (Mier y Terán in Ewers 1969: 149, n. 231). Later American variants reflect the modern spelling; for example, Whitchetaws and Witcheta, [464] 1807 (Sibley 1922: 94); Wichetas, 1847 (Neighbors 1847: 4); Wichetaws (Schoolcraft 1851-1857, 6: 689); and Witchita (Marcy 1853: 69).

Borrowings of the name by other tribes, probably dating to the postreservation period, include Caddo wic'itah (Chafe 1979), Kansa mitsitta (Dorsey 1883c, retranscribed), Osage Witsita (Dorsey 1883), Quapaw wisitta (Dorsey 1883b, retranscribed), Shawnee wi-čita (Voegelin 1938-1940, 5: 414), and Creek wicita (Haas 1942).

In the twentieth century the Wichita name for themselves was kirikir²'i•-s 'raccoon eye(s)' (Lesser and Weltfish 1932: 10; David S. Rood, personal communication 1987), said to be a reference to tattoos around the eyes (Scott 1912-1934). Formerly, this self-designation was also the name of one band, later generalized to the other groups (Lesser and Weltfish 1932: 11; Lesser 1979: 260). Historical citations of the name are Quicasquiris, 1719 (La Harpe in Margry 1876-1886, 6: 289), more correctly Quirasquiris, 1720 (Beaurain in Margry 1876-1886, 6: 289); in the nineteenth century it was recorded as Kiddĕkĕdissĕ (ten Kate 1884: 10) and Kĭ'tikĭiti'sh (Mooney

---

[3] This synonymy was written by Douglas R Parks based in part on a draft by Newcomb and Ives Goddard.

1896:1095). The designation is reflected in Pawnee *kiriku•ruks* and its Arikara cognate *čiriku•nUx,* literally 'bear eye(s)' (Parks 1965-1990, 1970-1990). The Pawnee name was borrowed into Omaha as ki•¢i-ku-¢uc (Dorsey 1880a).

A similar, related name occurs in Dhegiha and Chiwere Siouan as Omaha-Ponca *ppaði wasábe* (Dorsey 1878 in Hodge 1907-1910, 2: 949, retranscribed; misidentified as Caddo in Fletcher and La Flesche 1911: 102) and Iowa-Otoe-Missouria *pʰanⁿi waθewe,* literally 'black bear Pawnee' (Dorsey 1879 in Hodge 1907-1910, 2: 950, retranscribed). This name appears in Illinois as *Pani8assa* and Paniassa (Gravier 1700), which appear in late seventeenth- and early eighteenth-century French sources as Paniassa, 1673-1674 (Marquette in Tucker 1942: pl. V), Pancassa, 1680 (La Salle in Margry 1876-1886, 2: 168), Paneassa, 1688 (Franquelin in Tucker 1942: pl. VIA), Paniouassa and Panioussa, 1720 (Beaurain in Margry 1876-1886, 6: 289, 290). Later variants and mistranscriptions are in Hodge (1907-1910, 2: 949).

A related eighteenth-century French designation was *Panis noirs,* 1742 (Fabry de la Bruyere in Margry 1876-1886, 6: 4746) and 1751 (La Jonquiere in M.M. Wedel 1981a: 46), translated as Black Pani (Charlevoix 1761, 2: 246). Lewis and Clark (Moulton 1983-, 3: 445) reported that the Wichita were "formerly known by the name of the *White* Panias," an anomalous designation.

In the seventeenth and eighteenth centuries the Wichita groups were often designated by the generic name Pani, used interchangeably for the Pawnee, Arikara, and Wichita, usually cited as Panis (Gaignard in Bolton 1914, 2: 82, 85; Sibley 1832: 723; M.M. Wedel 1981a: 18-25), Panics, 1807 (Sibley 1922: 69), and Pana (Garraghan 1927: 312; M.M. Wedel 1973), which in the nineteenth century came to be applied exclusively to the South Band Pawnee. However, 564 designations for Wichita groups generally used a modifier [b] to specify them. The phrase "Little Pawnees," for example, was reportedly used to differentiate the Wichita from the Pawnee of Nebraska (Carter 1934-1962, 19: 59).

In the eighteenth and nineteenth centuries another common name used by the French for the Wichita was *Panis Piques* 'tattooed Pawnees'. It is cited as Panipiques, Panipiquets, and Panipiqueles, 1749 (Febre et al. in Bell, Jelks, and Newcomb 1974: 333), Paunee Pique, 1805 (Lewis and Clark 1832: 721), Panias picque (Jefferson 1804), Pawnee Piquas (James 1823, 2: 104), and Panies-Piques, 1839-1840 (Tixier 1940: 151). Similarly, Spaniards sometimes designated the Wichita, and perhaps specifically the Waco, as Flechazos, 1785, 'pricked ones' (Vial and Chavez in John 1994: 51). The name is cited in American sources as Pawnee Picts (Hildreth 1836: 160), Pania Pickey, 1804 (Lewis and Clark in Moulton 1983-, 3: 445) or simply Picks, 1837 (Dougherty 1838: 16), as well as Skin Pricks, 1804 (Lewis and Clark in Thwaites 1904-1907, 1: 190), and Prickled Panis or Freckled Panis (Buchanan 1824: 155), and Speckled Pani (Imlay 1793: 231).

The preceding designation referring to tattooing is reflected in several tribal names for the Wichita generally. The Cheyenne name is *Evxsohetan* 'tattooed people' (Fetter 1913-1915: 583), cited also as *Hew'soitäneo* (sg. *Hew'sóitän*) (Mooney 1907: 426). Two names reflect tattooing of the breast: Comanche Pitchinavo 'tattooed chests' (ten Kate 1885: 136) and Otoe *báðe grexé* 'spotted breast' (Parks 1988). Others refer to facial tattooing; Kiowa *'t'o-kut* 'face mark' (Laurel Watkins, personal communication 1979), cited also as *Do'gu'at* (Mooney 1896: 1095); and Kiowa-Apache *gonǰče?ịsna* 'they have painted face' (Bittle 1952-1953).

Other tribal designations that are descriptive of Wichita culture are Comanche Sonikanik 'grass houses' (ten Kate 1885: 136) and Kiowa *e-p'ɔ'-dɔ* 'pumpkin braid' (Laurel Watkins, personal communication 1979; La Barre 1935). The Arapaho name *Hinasau,* also recorded as *Hinasso*

(Gatschet in Hodge 1907-1910, 2: 949), is of unknown origin.

In the eighteenth century, the Spanish of New Mexico often designated the Wichita as Jumanos and Jumanes. However, the name, which is generally interpreted to mean 'striped', has been applied to various entirely distinct groups that practiced tattooing or facial painting (see Hodge 1907-1910, 1: 636; Bolton 1911, 2: 66-84; J.D. Forbes 1959; M.M. Wedel 1981a: 33-35).

The sign language gesture for Wichita symbolized tattooing. One sign used the extended forefinger of the right hand to make a circle or ring several times around the eyes or over the right cheek, or even over the breast, all representing the parts of the body that were formerly tattooed (Mallery 1881: 476; W.P. Clark 1885: 403; Scott 1912-1934; G.A. Dorsey 1904a: 2-3). An alternate gesture was to extend the fingers and thumb of the right hand, semiclosed, and repeatedly bring the hand toward the face, nearly touching it, imitating the motion of tattooing (Mallery 1881: 476). [565]

• *taovaya* The origin of this band name is unknown but is possibly from their name in an extinct dialect of Wichita. The spelling is Bolton's (1914; Hodge 1907-1910, 2: 705) normalization of the Spanish variants. The only French recordings are Toayas and Toajas, 1719 (La Harpe in Margry 1876-1886, 6: 289, 290). The earliest Spanish recording is Tabas, 1542 (Jaramillo in B. Smith 1857, 1: 160), if this is the same. Eighteenth and early nineteenth century Spanish recordings include Tauaiases and Tavaiases, 1770 (De Mezieres in Bolton 1914, 1: 211,215); Taoiiiaches, 1779 (De Mezieres in Bolton 1914, 2: 241); Taouaiazes, 1771 (De Mezieres in Bolton 1914, 1: 256); Tavayas, 1772 (de Ripperda in Bolton 1914, 1: 270); Tavoyache, 1774 (Gaignard in Bolton 1914, 2: 85); Tahuayas, 1795 (Troike 1964: 387); Taobayaces, 1778 (Croix in Bolton 1914, 2: 228); Tabuayases, 1804 (Salcedo in Nasatir 1952, 2: 749); Taouayaches, 1807 (Robin in Hodge 1907-1910, 2: 707); Tahuaiasses, 1830 (Berlandier 1969: 143-145); and Tamayacas, 1828 (Mier y Teran in Ewers 1969: 149, n. 231). For other variants in early Spanish documents, see Bolton (1914) and references in Hodge (1907-1910, 2: 706-707).

Examples of American spellings include Towaahack, 1805 (Sibley 1832: 723); Towiache and Towe-ash, 1807 (Sibley 1922: 40, 94); Toweaches (Schermerhorn 1814: 26); Towaches (Morgan 1871: 55); Towiash (Latham 1856: 104); Toyash (Hildreth 1836: 160); and Towoashe (Domenech 1860, 1: 444). For other variant forms see Hodge (1907-1910, 2: 705). The form Tawehash, which is Mooney's (1896: 1095) transcription of the name he obtained as the Caddo and Kitsai form, is often cited as a standardized spelling of this band's name (Hodge 1907-1910, 2: 705; Swanton 1952: 303).

• *tawakoni* The Wichita form of this name is *tawa•khariw* (David S. Rood, personal communication 1987), recorded also as *tawa•khariwa* (Parks 1988; Gatschet in Hodge 1907-1910, 2: 704), the origin of which is obscure. It was borrowed as Caddo *tawakunih* (Chafe 1979), Kitsai *tawăkăru* (Mooney 1893), Tonkawa *Tawakal* (Gatschet in Hodge 1907-1910, 2: 704), and Quapaw *ttahukkani* (Dorsey 1883b, retranscribed).

In European and American sources the name occurs in numerous recognizable variants, including Teucarea, 1542 (Jaramillo in B. Smith 1857, 1: 160); Touacara, 1719 (La Harpe in Margry 1876-1886, 6: 289); Tavakavas, 1742 (Fabry de la Bruyere in Margry 1876-1886, 6: 492); Tuacanas, 1772, 1777 (De Mezieres in Bolton 1914, 1: 289, 2: 145);Taovacanas, 1779 (Galvez in Bolton 1914, 2: 243); Taguacanes. 1778 (Bonilla in Bolton 1914, 2: 165); Tahuacanas and Tahuacanes, 1804 (Salcedo in Nasatir 1952, 2: 749); Tawakenoes, 1805 (Sibley 1832: 723); Toweca (Gallatin 1836: 117); Towiachs, Towakenos, Tawacani and Towacarro (Latham 1856: 102-104); and Yo-woc-o-nee (Marcy in Schoolcraft 1851-1857, 5: 712). For other examples, including misprints, see Hodge (1907-1910, 2: 704). A French corruption was Trois Cannes, 1712 [b] (Penigaut in McWilliams 1953: 156), as if literally 'three canes', which occurs as Three Canes, 1805 (Sibley 1832: 723), and misprinted as Three Cones (Schermerhorn 1814: 25) and Three Cranes (Alcedo in G.A. Thompson 1812-1815, 4: 515).

Quiscat, an eighteenth-century village named after a chief, occurs in several forms, including Quiscat, 1779 (De Mezieres in Bolton 1914, 2: 277); and Quiscate and Quisquate, 1787 (Vial in Hodge 1907-1910, 2: 346). Another eighteenth-century village named after a chief occurs as Flechazo (Bolton 1914, 2: 277; Chabot 1932: 8) and Flechasos (Cabello 1786).

• *iscani* This name occurs in the eighteenth century and has been thought to be an earlier designation for the Waco (Bolton in Hodge 1907-1910, 2: 1002). Variants include Isconies and Ysconies, 1684 (Mendoza in Hodge 1907-1910, 2: 1002); Ascani, 1719 (La Harpe in Margry 1876-1886, 6: 289-290); Hiscanes, 1749 (Parrilla in Bolton 1914, 1: 21 l); Yscanis, 1770 (De Mezieres in Bolton 1914, 1: 211); Iscanis, 1772 (De Mezieres in Bolton 1914, 1: 284); Yscan, 1770 (Chirinos in Bolton 1914, 1: 222); Niscaniche, 1774 (Gaignard in Bolton 1914, 2: 85); Yascale, 1759 (Parrilla in Bell, Jelks, and Newcomb 1974: 333); and Yxcanis (Chabot 1932: 8).

• *waco* The Wichita form of this name is *wi•ko•*, which is of unknown etymology (David S. Rood, personal communication 1998). Examples of borrowings are Caddo *we'ku* and *wi'ko* (Gatschet in Hodge 1907-1910, 2: 888), Kitsai weko (Mooney 1893), Tonkawa *weyko?* (Hoijer 1949: 36), and Quapaw Wi'-ku (Dorsey 1883b). Spellings in European and American sources reflect the Wichita form. Early French variants include Quaineo, 1718 (Delisle in Tucker 1942: pl. XV); and Huanchane, Huane, and Honechas, 1719 (La Harpe in Margry 1876-1886, 6: 277, 289). Spanish forms are Huecos, 1830 (Berlandier 1969: 125-126; Austin 1829) and Wacos (Sanchez 1926: 265). American forms include Wachos (Gallatin 1836: 117); Wacoah and Wico (Hildreth 1836: 166, 177); Whacoe, 1807 (Sibley 1922: 94; Burnet in Schoolcraft 1851-1857, 1: 239); and Wecos (Domenech 1860, 2: 25).

• *tokane* The Wichita form of this name, tó•kanne'?e (David S. Rood, personal communication 1987; Lesser 1979: 260; Parks 1988), survived into the late twentieth century as a band name. The earliest citation of it is Thacanhé, 1700 (Iberville in Margry 1876-1886, 4: 374). In the late nineteenth century it was recorded from Dhegiha Siouan speakers as Osage *Tu'-ka-nyi* (Dorsey 1883), Kansa *ttókkale* (Dorsey 1883c, retranscribed), and Omaha *Tu-ka-0a* (Dorsey 1880a), all of which were mistakenly glossed as Tawakoni (Hodge 1907-1910, 2: 704). It also appears in the late nineteenth-century form *Tooc-a-nie* Kiowas, the name of a group said to be part Wichita and part Kiowa (Richards in ARCIA 1875: 289).

This band name is also the source of one Comanche designation for the Wichita, *tuhka?naai?* (Robinson and Armagost 1990: 123) or *tu•hkanai* (Jean Chamey, personal [566] communication 1987), cited also as *Tokunai* (Curtis 1907-1930, 19: 229), a borrowing that was generalized to all the Wichita bands. It has subsequently been folk etymologized. Thus one citation, *Do'kana*, is translated as 'tattooed people' (Mooney 1896: 1095), while other sources cite and translate the form as *To-can-a* 'dark lodges' (Scott 1890) and *Toughkanne* 'dark, gloomy houses' (ten Kate 1885: 136) or Toechkanne 'dusky lodges' (ten Kate 1884: 373), the last three meanings said to be a reference to the grass lodge.

• *akwits* The name of this Wichita group has been recorded several times but does not appear in the historical literature. The first citation is Akwech (Hodge 1907-1910, 1: 34, based on information provided by James O. Dorsey), where it is given as a Wichita subtribe. The Wichita form, recorded in the early twentieth century, is $ak^{w'}i\bullet c$ (Lesser 1979: 260).

• *quivira* The name Quivira, Quibira, or Aguivira that Coronado's expedition, 1541 (in Hodge 1907-1910, 2: 147) gave to Wichita settlements in the sixteenth century cannot be identified with any modern Wichita name. Although it was said to derive from the Wichita self-designation *kirikir$^?$i•s* (Hodge 1907-1910, 2: 346), that association is unlikely. Historical variants of the name include Quiuira, 1554 (Gomara 1587: 470), Quivirenses, 1788 (Alcedo 1812-1815, 4: 305), and Quivera (Schoolcraft 1851-1857, 4: 28). See Hodge (1907-1910, 2: 347) for other forms.

• *mento* For a 50-year period in the late seventeenth and early eighteenth centuries, the name Mento appears in French sources as a designation for the most southerly of three Wichita groups, although sometimes the term may have been used for the Wichita in general. The origin of the name is obscure; the Illinois word assumed in the explanation of M.M. Wedel (1981a: 21-25, 1973a: 161-162) does not exist (Ives Goddard, personal communication 1998). The earliest recording of it appears to be Matora, 1673-1674 (Marquette map in Tucker 1942: pl. V). Other variants are Meintens, 1697 (Louvigny in Tucker 1942: pl. XIV); Mentous, 1700 (Tonti in M.M. Wedel 1981a: 21; Delisle in Tucker 1942: pl. XIII); Mentos (La Harpe in M.M. Wedel 1973a: 161; Fabry de La Bruyere in Margryl876-1886, 6: 474); and Mantou, 1702 (Iberville in M.M. Wedel 1981a: 33), cited as Manton in Margry (1876-1886, 4: 599). For later citations see Hodge (1907-1910, 1: 844). [b]

The only recorded tribal citation is a late nineteenth century Kansa form *mᶐttowe* (Dorsey in Hodge 1907-1910, 1: 844, retranscribed).

Sources

A number of studies have focused on various aspects of Wichita history. Harper (1953, 1953a, 1953b) emphasizes trade and diplomacy between 1719-1835. Her broader and more ambitious study of Spanish and French interaction with Southwest Indians between 1540 and 1795 places the Wichita within this larger context (John 1975). Elam (1971, 1979) presents historical accounts of the Wichita to 1868 and 1895, respectively. The brief articles by Bolton (1910: 701-706, 1910a: 1002) and Mooney (1910: 947-950) on various Wichita subgroups are now rather outdated. The probing studies of Wichita ethnohistory by M.M. Wedel (1971, 1981a, 1982), particularly of the Coronado expedition and the journeys of La Harpe and Dutisné, are essential to comprehending the location, cultural nature, and the forces that affected the Wichita from the sixteenth through the eighteenth centuries. La Harpe (in Margry 1876-1886, 6: 239-306) and De Mezieres (in Bolton 1914) provide firsthand accounts from the eighteenth century. For later centuries and an extensive bibliography see Bell, Jelks, and Newcomb (1974). Winfrey and Day (1959-1966) reproduce documents relating to the Wichita in Texas. Blaine (1982) discusses the historical relationship between the Wichita and the Pawnee. M.L. Tate (1986) covers the Wichita in his annotated bibliography of the Indians of Texas. Tiller (1996: 536-537) gives a social and economic profile of the Wichita Tribe in the mid-1990s.

George A. Dorsey (1904a) presents a succinct description of Wichita culture and a large body of mythology. Curtis (1907-1930, 19: 35-104) also describes Wichita culture, emphasizing religion and mythology. Newcomb (1961: 247-277, 1967) provides summaries. Wichita kinship is described in Schmitt and Schmitt (1952) and Lesser (1979). Extensive field notes recorded by Karl and Iva Schmitt in the 1940s are deposited in the Western History Collections of the

University of Oklahoma; they were not utilized in the preparation of this chapter. Linguistic investigations have been made by Lesser and Weltfish (1932), Taylor (1963, 1963a), Rood (1976), Chafe (1979), and Parks (1979).

Rock Springs Church. Baptist, north of Anadarko, which serves not only the Wichita, but also the Caddo, Pawnee, Seminole, Creek, Choctaw, Delaware, Comanche, and Kiowa tribes. Its founder was John McIntosh, a Creek Indian born in Indian Territory, who arrived among the Wichita in the 1870s. The first church was constructed in 1880; the present church was built in 1910. The open-sided building is used for outdoor services and overflows at funerals and revivals. Photograph by Ardina McAdams, 1998.

WICHITA KINSHIP
past and present

BY KARL SCHMITT
Associate Professor of Anthropology
University of Oklahoma

and

IVA OSANAI SCHMITT
Research Associate
University of Oklahoma Museum

UNIVERSITY BOOK EXCHANGE
NORMAN, OKLAHOMA
[1950]

PREFACE

The following paper on Wichita Kinship is based on data gained by weekly visits to Anadarko, Oklahoma and vicinity during the school years of 1947-48, 1949-50, and in the course of residence among the Wichita during June, July, and August of 1949 and June and July of 1950. Since methods of field work and analysis of data can affect results, some statement concerning these procedures is considered in order and is given below.

As published data on the Wichita are meager, actual field work as a necessity. Data were desired for the older way of Wichita life and because that way of life has essentially disappeared, it was necessary that old ~~informants~~ who had participated in or who had information concerning it from older relatives be interviewed. We were most fortunate to be able to work with one woman, Mrs. Cora West, who had actually taken part in the older culture patterns, who had in effect left the tribe during the 1880's, and who had not returned to participation in Indian affairs until after 1940. Although this woman is half white, she was culturally a full Wichita during her early years, and her information is, as it were, uncontaminated by later changes in Wichita life. Admittedly, without her aid this work would be considerably briefer and much less instructive as she gave a wealth of information which had high internal consistency. Some material was also gained from a somewhat younger man who had participated in Wichita culture before disintegration of the consolidated villages. Other individuals gave data based partially on parents' teachings and partially on participation in patterns persisting into the transition period. Because this was to be a study in change, information was also obtained from middle-aged and younger individuals. As a result of formal interviews, fourteen full genealogies from individuals of both sexes and ranging in age from 85 plus to 15 years were secured. After a genealogy had been obtained, each relative was given a number and then kinship terminology of both vocative and non-vocative nature was recorded for each relative by use of that individual's name. Reciprocal terminology was also solicited. It should be mentioned that genealogies are extremely difficult to collect among the Wichita since there is an aversion to "calling names" of deceased individuals. A great deal of additional terminological material was obtained by informal conversation with a wide number of ~~informants~~ as opportunities offered themselves. Modern terminological data were also gained by actual observation of, or listening in on, present day situations.

Older behavioral data were largely acquired by formal interviews of intensive nature. However, leading questions were avoided and used only as a last resort. Instead, open-ended questions such as "How did Wichitas get married?" or "What did Wichitas do when a child was born?" were posed. These most often resulted in ideal descriptions of such events and contained much information concerning ideal kinship behavior. Then, as descriptions of specific marriages or births were obtained, some checks on ideal patterns were possible. Most of our older kinship behavior material was not gotten as a result of a direct effort, but as a by-product of making a general survey of Wichita life. Other behavioral data were obtained from casual conversations, and in the modern situation, kinship behavior was continually observed and noted.

Analysis of data was along lines of patterning. The basic assumption made was that cultural behavior is patterned and that such patterns are discoverable. It was not assumed that all patterns were of the same rigidity or looseness, that all patterns are known to the carriers of the culture, or that all patterns necessarily harmonize in the total cultural picture. Ascertaining the overt patterns of Wichita kinship was relatively easy. Terminological patterns were remarkably consistent and where discrepancies in information occurred, older ~~informants~~ would even volunteer that one was the old way and the other the new. Behavioral data also fell into easily determinable patterns. Wichitas were cognizant of a most important one — that all relatives belong in either a respect or joking category and that with some one can joke only mildly while with others one can joke very roughly, or that with mothers-in-law the respect is of a near-avoidance nature while with parents' siblings there is no avoidance, but circumspect behavior. On further examination of the data some minor patterns were discernible of which the Wichitas were not aware or which they could not define in English words. The possibility of dealing only in ideal patterns, or verbal patterns to which varying degrees of lip-service are paid, was realized and an attempt has been made to point up observed behavioral patterns and some individual variations. Our interpretation of the older data is that patterns in the past were more rigid, or [iv] that ideal verbal patterns and behavioral patterns were more in agreement than at present. Our assessment of the data on the older culture would be that they are of high reliability. The major proof that this is so, is the fact that information from many informants on different occasions hews closely to the same discernible patterns.

In the modern Wichita situation, similar techniques were used, but observation was now possible. Actually the present situation is complex since the group has been, and is, undergoing rapid acculturation to American life. In the living generations wide variation of behavior and terminology occurs. Our work in the modem situation is less complete than that on the older culture since two years work was spent on features of the latter and one year on the former.

Dorsey's work on Wichita mythology[4] was found to be of immense help. The tales included many examples of kinship behavior and some of these have been quoted to illustrate patterned behavior. This is done since we consider the small cultural details which are unessential to advancement of the story to be phrased in good Wichita ideal patterns. It should be pointed out that, while the tales contain many examples of respect behavior, no examples of extreme joking behavior were noted, and this indicates that Wichita mythology as reported, does not completely reflect everyday Wichita life.

We have also used as examples of older type kinship behavior a number of incidents from modern times which came to our attention. The possible fallacy of mixing recent data and old patterns is recognized, but when this is done, we, and our ~~informants~~, feel quite certain that the behavior is really illustrative of old Wichita ways that have persisted to the present day.

Interpretive sections of the paper involve arranging our data in what appears to us the most meaningful order, and in viewing them against hypotheses and conclusions put forth by kinship experts. To facilitate possible reorientations of our data we have endeavored to keep factual material separate from interpretations.

We wish to express our appreciation to the Department of Anthropology, The Institute of Human Studies, and the Faculty Research Committee – all of the University of Oklahoma, for their monetary aid toward field work, and to the Alumni Development Association and the Faculty Research Committee for financing the publication of this monograph.

Many, many Wichitas were cooperative in our field work and among them were the following:

~~informants~~ for schedules and behavior:

Minnie Caley	Christine Miller	Wallace Miller	Sarah Smith
John Haddon	Florence Miller	Mary Rose	Rollin Stephenson

---

[4] Dorsey, 1904.

Schmitts

Frieda Luther	Gladys Miller	Myra Rose	Cora West
Vernon Miller	Homer Segar		

~~informants~~ for behavior:

George Bates	Rose Hunt	Bertha Provost	George Standing
Nellie Brown	Walter Lamar	Eben Rose	Helen Stevens
Moses Caley	George Lamb	Dan Ross	Oscar Stevens
Emma Curleychief	Stacy Luther	Frank Ross	Nuss Stephenson
Flora Gabbard	Belle Miller	Elmer Ray Smith	Max Thomas
Carrie Haddon	Frank Miller	Richard Smith	Bertha Wallace
Norman Hendrix	Houston Miller	Bertha Standing	Albert Wits
Dan Hunt	Arthur Ponley	Clarence Standing	Catherine Wolfe

Other Wichitas gave additional data which, while often meager in words, were of greatest value in understanding Wichita behavior. We also appreciate the great privilege of being present at functions of the Wichita Mission, the Rock Springs Church, and the Camp Creek organization; the permission to reside for two summers at Camp Creek; and the hospitality offered us at so many Wichita homes. The officials of the Western Consolidated Agency graciously permitted us access to records, and personnel of the Riverside Indian School near Anadarko furnished us quarters for one summer and pleasant friendship.

We are deeply indebted to Paul L. Garvin for transcription of terms and for his help in preparation of the manuscript. We also thank William Hunt, a former student of the University, for use of a Caddo schedule he collected, and Robert E. Bell and Alexander Spoehr for reading the manuscript. Finally, we wish to express our debt to Fred Eggan for our training in kinship and social organization and for his suggestions concerning the manuscript. [v]

TABLE OF CONTENTS

RESPECT AND JOKING:
PROBLEMS OF CLASSIFICATION AND
THEORETICAL CONSIDERATION 79

TABLES AND FIGURES

INTRODUCTION

In 1924, Leslie Spier published a list[5] of Wichita kinship terms collected from John Haddon, a native speaker of the Wichita language. During recent field work of the present authors, additional information was gained and a more extended treatment of Wichita kinship is now possible. The purposes of this paper may be summed up as follows: (1) to present further terminological data, (2) to present material on kinship behavior and attitudes, (3) to discuss changes which have occurred in the kinship system, (4) to consider some theoretical implications of the data.

The present day Wichita tribe comprises a group of between 450 and 500 individuals, most of whom live in the region just north of Anadarko, Oklahoma. They are the descendants of three sub-tribes — the *Wichita* proper, the *Waco*, and the *Tawakoni* — and an affiliated tribe, the *Kichai*. These four groups were loosely joined into a confederacy during the 18th and 19th centuries.

Recorded history of these associated groups is extensive but sporadic and indicates that the early historic period was of a most complex nature, involving numerous migrations and shifting alliances. In 1541, Coronado visited the province of Quivira and described the people there as living in grass-covered houses, sometimes concentrated into villages, and practicing agriculture. Most historians have equated the inhabitants of Quivira with the Wichitas,[6] and recent archaeological work has furnished additional evidence that this identification is correct and that Coronado's Quivira extended from central Kansas south to the Arkansas River.[7] From this time on, there seems to have been a general drift southward of the Wichita-speaking groups; however, the details of the movements are difficult to interpret because of the sporadic nature of early historical references and because of the use of many different names for Wichita groups. Present-day Wichita individuals separate the Waco, Tawakoni, and Wichita proper but report they were all "bands" of the Wichita and that the native term for the Wichita proper is *kiřikiř?i'•s* or "raccoon-eyed people," a reference to the former practice of tattooing or painting around the eyes. This is obviously a close cognate of the Pawnee word for the Wichita, *kiriku•'ruks*.[8] Modern individuals have a folk etymology for the term <u>Wichita</u> but its actual origin is not yet clear. The term first appears in 1719 as *Ousita*.[9] One of the writers' ~~informants~~ reported the name *Ta•'uwa•'ias* for the Wichita proper, saying this was a Kichai word for that group; variants of this name are used for Wichita groups in many 16th century Spanish sources.[10] The early French referred to the Wichita as Pani Piques[11] or Tattooed Pawnee, and the Americans sometimes called them Pawnee Picts.[12] But, the French and the early Americans at times appear to have confused the Pawnee Picts or true Wichitas with the Pawnee proper. The Waco and Tawakoni, who seem to have always ranged south of the Wichita proper, are referred to in Spanish and French reports by obvious cognate forms, such as *Hueco* and *Tuacanes*. The term *Waco*, with its cognate forms, appears relatively

---

[5] Spier, 1924.

[6] Winship, 1896, p. 591.

[7] Wedel, 1942, pp. 21-2.

[8] For a discussion of tribal and band names, see Lesser and Weltfish, 1932, pp. 10-13.

[9] Haas, 1942, pp. l64-5.

[10] Bolton, 19l4, p. 23.

[11] Same, p. 250.

[12] Catlin, 1926, Vol. 2, p. 83.

late and Bolton reasons that it replaces an earlier form, *Iscani*,[13] which was applied to a group closely affiliated with the Tawakoni.

The Kichai were formerly a separate tribe which was associated with, or lived near, the Kadohadacho in the late 17th century.[14] During the following centuries, the Kichai came to be closely associated with the Wichita-speaking groups and at the [viii] present have essentially disappeared into the Wichita group. The term Kichai has close similarities to many used by the Spanish and French during the 18th Century.[15]

The best interpretation of the evidence at the present is that at the time of Coronado the Wichita-proper were north of the Arkansas River and that closely related groups, perhaps even Waco and Tawakoni at this time,[16] were in the contiguous area of central Oklahoma. The subsequent southward drift may have been partially stimulated by a desire to be nearer the sources of French and Spanish trade and horses. By 1760, the Wichita-speaking groups were located primarily along the Red River and south into Texas though some groups probably ranged into Oklahoma. Later, the movements were toward the north and into the Indian Territory.

In 1834, a United States dragoon expedition, accompanied by {George} Catlin, visited the Wichita proper at their large village near Devils Canyon in the Wichita Mountains of present Kiowa County, Oklahoma. Some Waco, Tawakoni, and Kichai at this time were still in Texas. Shortly afterward, the Wichita village was moved to the confines of present-day Fort Sill at the east end of the Wichita Mountains in Comanche County, Oklahoma. In 1852, Marcy[17] visited the main Wichita village, which then was located near present Rush Springs in Grady County, Oklahoma, and also a village of the Waco situated only a mile distant. The Tawakoni and other Wacos were still in Texas.

The Wichitas signed treaties with the United States Government in 1835 and 1846. These finally culminated in the Wichitas' accepting in 1859 a reservation comprising portions of the present day Caddo, Grady, and Canadian Counties of Oklahoma. At this time, those of the Waco, Tawakoni, and Kichai who had remained in Texas were brought to the new Wichita reservation. At the same time, many Caddo "bands," remnants of the former large Kadohadacho and Hainai confederacies, and Black Beaver's band of Delawares were also placed on the Wichita reservation. All these groups were lumped together by the government as the "Wichita and Affiliated Bands," though all tried, and to a large extent have succeeded, to maintain their tribal identities. Shortly thereafter, at the outbreak of the Civil War, most of these groups moved north to Kansas. The Wichitas, as it were, returned to their old homeland and settled in several villages near present-day Wichita, Kansas. In 1867-8 the various Wichita-speaking groups came back to their reservation and settled near what is now Anadarko, Oklahoma. At this time, though they were situated near each other, the Waco, Tawakoni, Wichita-proper, and Kichai inhabited separate villages.[18]

Linguistically the Wichita-proper, Waco, and Tawakoni were closely related. Older ~~informants~~ state that they spoke the same language with only very minor differences, which were

---

[13] Bolton in Hodge (ed) 1907, p. 1002.

[14] Swanton, 1942, p. 89.

[15] For example *Quitseys* in Bolton, 1914, Vol. I, p. 285.

[16] The testimony of a Tawakoni chief in 1885 indicates a later origin of the name Tawakoni, but this seems invalidated by the early Spanish and French sources. See Gatchet, 1891, for the testimony.

[17] Marcy and Foreman (ed.), 1937, pp. 123-129.

[18] Schmitt, 1950b.

on the order of having different words for "horse". Furthermore, while Wichita and Pawnee languages are not mutually intelligible, Wichitas recognize them to be related; it is said that "we have many words that are almost alike." Wichita and Pawnee — along with Caddo, Kichai, and Arikara — comprise the Caddoan group of the Hokan-Siouan language family.[19] Living Wichitas do not recognize a relationship between their language and Kichai and Caddo and are not acquainted with Arikara although they have heard that it is like Pawnee and Wichita.

Culturally, the Wichita and associated groups belong to the so-called Village Tribes of the Low Plains area. They shared the wide-spread subsistence pattern of summer agriculture of corn, beans, pumpkins, and melons and the fall or winter hunt for buffalo meat and hides. During the summer the groups lived in villages of grass houses, the women tending rather extensive gardens and the men hunting for game relatively near the village. After the harvest, surplus garden produce was dried and stored in cache pits and the people left the villages for the fall buffalo hunts, during which they lived in tipis and by means of which an effort was made to secure a surplus of meat for drying. Some food was obtained by gathering the wild vegetable products, and another important source was the trade of garden produce for dried meat which such tribes as the Comanche and Kiowa had obtained during their summer buffalo hunts. Thus, basically there was a strong cultural similarity to the Mandan, Hidatsa, and Arikara along the Missouri River; the [ix] Pawnee, Omaha, and Ponca of the Central Plains; and the Oto, Osage, and other tribes along the eastern margin of the Plains.

In cultural details, the Wichita groups seen most closely allied to the Pawnee and somewhat less so to the Caddo groups. Points of relationship to these groups are the mythological emphasis on stars and details of ceremonies involving performances by "doctors" banded together into societies. Concerning the Wichita proper, Waco, Tawakoni and Kichai, older ~~informants~~ state there were only minor differences in culture; and this seems to have been particularly so by 1850. It should be pointed out, however, that meager information on the Kichai kinship system indicates that it is significantly different from that herein presented for the Wichita. After establishment of the reservation, most Kichai learned the Wichita language; and descendants of all four groups are now Wichita and carriers of modern Wichita culture. The older data presented in this paper refer to the Wichita-Waco-Tawakoni group of the 1850-1875 period.

The culture of the present day Wichitas is obviously much altered, and is still changing, from that of their ancestors. In understanding their kinship behavior, two time levels appear as immediately important; first, the 1850-75 period, which is the oldest date for which Wichita cultures can be reliably reconstructed; and second, the present date. Data have been gathered from older individuals, one of whom was born in the early 1860's, from middle-aged individuals, and from persons of high school age. No two individuals reported absolutely identical kinship schedules, but the variations, when viewed with respect to age and relative amount of acculturation of the person, indicate the manner and direction of change which has occurred. This change correlates with the shift from a relatively autonomous political unit to an encysted group dependent on white American culture for continued existence in its present form. [1]

OLDER KINSHIP TERMINOLOGY

A list of the kinship terms as they were used by the Wichita group of 1850-75 is given in Table I. Terms[20] are listed in two columns; the first gives vocative forms and the second, non-

---

[19] Lesser and Weltfish, 1932.

[20] Orthography is that developed by contributors to the *International Journal of Linguistics* for

vocative. A third column presents free translations, offered by ~~informants~~, and a fourth column lists the relatives in the English system called by these terns. Terms published by Spier[21] are given in parentheses. The important vocative forms appear to be "bare" stems; for most non-vocative forms various prefixes to the stem, corresponding to possessive pronouns, are used. First person singular forms are listed, it not being considered necessary to give the complete paradigms of terms. Some of the stems were never used without prefixes and others, such as those for "husband," "wife," "brother," and "sister", have vocative forms which were only rarely used and which some ~~informants~~ have never heard.

Table I

Consanguineal Relatives

Vocative	Non-vocative	Translation	Relatives to which applied
áka•ʔ (ukʷ)	ʔřatiʔáka•tasʔih	grandparent, my grandparent	grandparent, spouses of grandparents, great-great-grandparents
áka•ʔsiwa•cʔ	řatiʔaka•siwa•cʔih	big grandparent, my big grandparent	older sibling of grandparent great-great-grandparent
áka•ʔsikicʔ	řatiʔaka•siwkicʔih	little grandparent, my little grandparent	younger sibling of grandparent
řʼi•haskʷuřiks		old man	great-grandfather, grandfather, occasionally father after ego is adult and has children of own
ka•hi•ra•ʔi•cʔ		old woman	great-grandmother, grandmother after ego is adult and has children of own
ta•'ta (dada)	řatita•tasʔih	father, my father	father, step-father
tá•tasiwa•cʔ (datasiwatsa)	řatita•tasiwa•cʔih	big father, my big father	father's older brother, great-grandfather, male children of paternal grandparent's siblings older than father
tá•tasikicʔ (dátasikitsa)	řatita•tasikicʔih	little father, my little father	father's younger brother, male children of paternal grandparent's siblings younger than father

---

recording American Indian Languages. The major ~~informant~~ for Dr. Garvin's phonemics was Mr. John Haddon, but he has used speech of several other ~~informants~~ for comparative purposes. The phonemic transcription of these terms was checked in several interviews with native ~~informants~~ by Garvin. Their morphemic composition has, however, not yet been properly determined, and possible word boundaries within terms have not been checked. The transcriptions are still somewhat tentative in nature from that standpoint, and for the same reason, the literal translations are not sufficiently accurate.

[21] Spier, 1924.

Vocative	Non-Vocative	Translation	Relatives to which applied
řatɛ•ʔasiʔi adult spk	řati•ʔasiʔi i (natiase'i)	my father	father, God
	řakiri•á•ckski (nakiri yortsski)	one who helped raise me	step-parent
ɛ•ciɛ• (atsia)	řatiʔɛ•ciɛ•ʔih child spk	mother, my mother	mother, step-mother, mother's sister in sororal polygyny
ɛ•ciɛ•siwa•cʔ	řati•ɛ•ciɛ•siwa•cʔih (natiatsiatsiwatsi)	big mother, my big mother	father's older sister, mother's older sister, female child of grandparent's sibling older than connecting parent, great-grandmother
ɛ•ciɛ•sikicʔ	řati•ʔɛ•ciɛ•sikicʔih (natiatsiatsikitsa)	little mother, my little mother	father's younger sister, mother's younger sister, female child of grandparent's sibling younger than connecting parent
	řatika•hi•kʔih (natikaheki) adult spk.	my woman	mother, mother's sister, father's sister

Table I (con't.) [2]

Vocative	Non-Vocative	Translation	Relatives to which applied
wa•ciʔi•ʔi child spk	řatiwa•ciʔasʔih (natiwatsiossi)	uncle, my uncle	mother's brother, male child of maternal grandparent's sibling
ří•hasʔ adult spk	řatiří•hasʔih (natidihossi)	old man, my old man, uncle	mother's brother, male child of maternal grandparent's sibling
	řatiří•hasiwa•cʔih	my big uncle	mother's older brother
	řatiří•hasikicʔih	my little uncle	mother's younger brother
hiřca•ʔi•řaski male spk.	hiřata•ʔi•řaski (hantoeroski)	brother, my brother	brother, half-brother, male children of all father's and mother's terminological siblings
řatɛ•řa•ciʔi woman spk.	řati•řa•ciʔi (natirotsit.i)	brother, my brother	brother, half-brother, male children of all father's and
řatɛ•ta•ciʔi male spk	řati•ta•ciʔi (natitᵂtsii)	sister, my sister	sister, half-sister, female children of all father's and mother's terminological siblings
hařcaři•aciʔi woman spk.	hiařtaři•aciʔi (hantare1 eyatsli)	sister, my sister	sister, half-sister, female children of all father's and mother's terminological siblings
wíř ʔi•s		little girl	daughter when under 10-12 yrs. of age
wí•řikisʔ		little boy	son when under 10-12 yrs, of age
	řati•a•ʔi (nateoi)	my child	child, brother's child, great-grandchild, and sister's child woman spk.

	řati•wi•ca•ʔ	my grown male child	adult son
	řati•wica•ʔiřřaki	my, married son	married son
	řatí•ciɛ•řikicʔia•ʔi	My single daughter	daughter
	řatí•ackɛhɛ•ia•ʔi	my child who has children	married daughter
tu•řikicʔ male spk.	řati•tu•řikicʔih (natitorikitsi)	young man, my young man	my sister's son
řatɛ•cɛ•wa•ciʔi male spk	řatɛ•cɛ•wa•ciʔi (natltsewats^l)	niece, my niece	sister's daughter
i•wuwuʔ	řatiʔi•wuwuʔih (natiiwaworisi)	grandchild, my grandchild	grandchild, child of any classificatory child, child of a nephew or niece, spouse of grandchild

Affinal Relatives

řata•kʔi male spk.	řatia•kʔi (natiok'i)	wife, my wife	wife, wife's sister, granddaughter, grandmother
	hiřcia•kʔi (hirotsioki) male spk.	our wife	two brothers speaking of wife of one, grandson's or grandfather's wife
řatɛ•kiřʔih woman spk.	řati•kiřʔih (natikidi)	husband, my husband	husband, husband's brother, grandson, grandfather
	řatiɛ•kiřʔih woman spk	our husband	two sisters speaking of husband of one, granddaughter's or grandmother's husband
áckicsʔ	řatiackicsʔih (natiotsskitsi) (natitsitsi)	sister-in-law, daughter-in-law, (actually female-relative-in-law)	brother's wife – woman spk., wife's sister – man spk., son's wife, father's brother's wife, mother's brother's wife,
i•ʔɛ•s	řati•ʔɛ•sʔih (natiesi)	brother-in-law, son-in-law, (actually male-relative-in-law)	sister's husband – man spk, daughter's husband, father's sister's husband, mother sister's husband, granddaughter's husband
	řata•cʔɛca•ksʔih (natseiowksi)	father-in-law, mother-in-law	parents-in-law
hiřti•ciʔɛ•a•wi		my rival	wife's sister' husband, grandfather, grandson, granddaughter's husband
hiřti•ciřɛʔɛ•kicski		my rival	Husband's brother's wife, grandmother, granddaughter, grandson's wife

[3]

40

Table I (con't.)

Affinal Relatives

Vocative	Non-Vocative	Translation	Relatives to which applied
hiɾtì·cìʔeʔáˑwi male sp.		my rival	wife's sister's husband, grandfather, grandson, granddaughter's husband
hiɾtì·cìɾeʔéˑkicski woman sp		my rival	husband's brother's wife, grandmother, granddaughter, grandson's wife

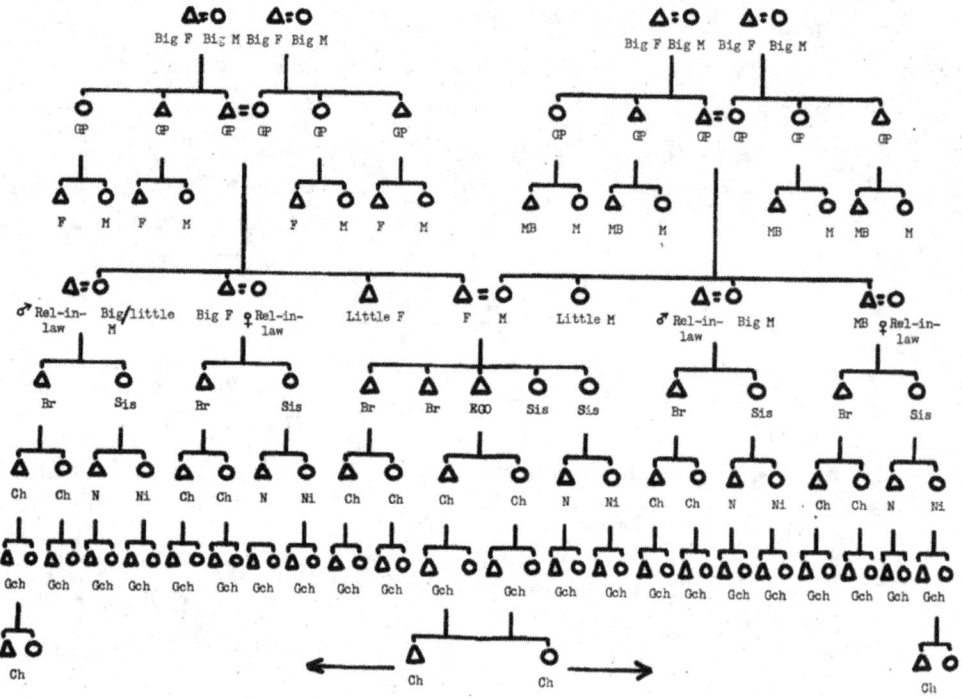

Figure 1
Older Wichita Consanguineal System

Note: Siblings of grandparents are big or little grandparents depending on the relative age of the connecting grandparent. Children of siblings of the grandparents are big or little father, mother, or mother's brother depending on relative age of connecting parent. For a female ego, children of both brothers and sisters are children.

[4]

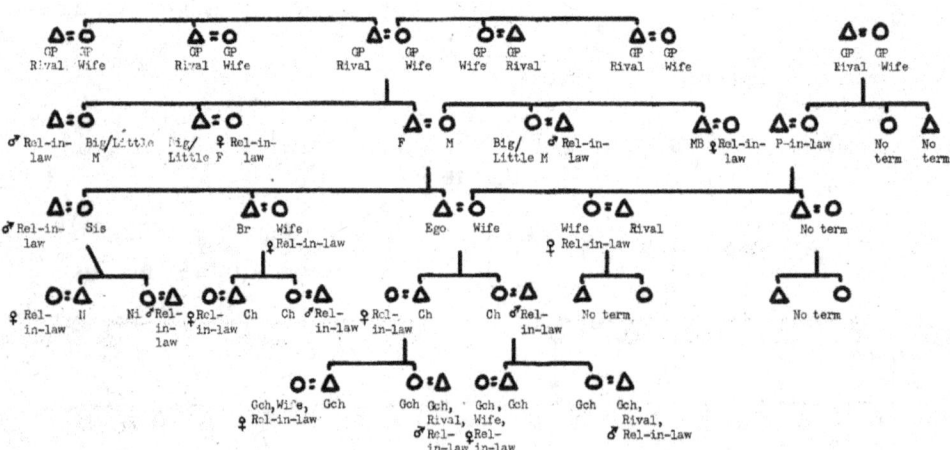

Figure 2
Older Wichita Affinal System

[5]

Consanguineal Relatives

When the older Wichita terminology is converted into conventional English terns and diagrammed as in Figure #1, most of the important characteristics of the terminological system are readily apparent. Complete reciprocity of terms is present; there are no non-logical differences from one generation to another. This indicates that the Wichita kinship system of the mid-nineteenth century was a stable type.

The terms are stratified by generation although several relatives may be distinguished in one generation. In the paternal generation male and female siblings of the father are <u>fathers</u> and mothers; the mother's sisters are <u>mothers</u>, while the mother's brother is designated by a separate term. Children of siblings of the paternal grandparents are also <u>fathers</u> and <u>mothers</u>, while children of siblings of the maternal grandparents are <u>mothers</u> and <u>mother's brothers</u>. In the second ascending generation all grandparents and their siblings and their cousins are <u>grandparents</u>. In ego's own generation all relatives are <u>brothers</u> and <u>sisters</u>. In the first descending generation a male calls his brother's children <u>our children</u> but his sister's children are designated by nephew and niece terms; in the same generation a woman calls both brother's and sister's children <u>our children</u>.[22] The terminology of this generation corresponds to the separation of the mother's brother and designation of the father's sister as <u>mother</u>. Relatives of the second descending generation are all <u>grandchildren</u>. With the third ascending and descending generations, the principle of alternation of generations operates; in the former, individuals are again <u>fathers</u> and <u>mothers</u> while in the latter, they are again <u>children</u>. Detailed information for these generations is lacking. It might be expected that a brother of a female great-grandparent would be called "big uncle" (older mother's brother) and that then a male would logically call his sister's great-grandchildren <u>nephew</u> and <u>niece</u>. This was not reported; ~~informants~~ merely stated that great-grandparents "go back to father and mother" and great-grandchildren are called <u>children</u>.

The generational character of the system is recognized by most Wichitas, as are some other general features; some individuals even come close to stating propositions of "equivalence of siblings" and "uniform descent."[23] While being questioned about terms for more distant relatives, ~~informants~~ would make statements such as "you never get any further away than a brother" or "you figure from a brother and sister always." Some ~~informants~~ would tell the investigator they called a certain individual brother but were unable to give the genealogical relationship. 'In situations like this, they considered satisfactory such explanations as "my father called his father 'brother', so I call him 'brother'."

It should be pointed out that the generational character is one of genealogical generation and not of relative generation. Occasionally, because of extremely disparate ages between siblings or half-siblings and their descendants, the normal age situation is reversed. Thus, ~~Informant~~ #B as a child called Tawakoni Jim, an adult, <u>nephew</u> and was reciprocally called <u>little mother's brother</u>.

Another characteristic of the Wichita system is the partial distinction by sex. In ego's own and in the parental generation, this distinction is made for all relatives. In the second ascending and second descending generations, relatives are <u>grandparent</u> and <u>grandchild</u>, with no sex differentiation. In the grandparental generation it is possible to make a sex distinction after ego becomes an adult; then one may call a grandfather <u>old man</u> and a grandmother <u>old lady</u>. In joking, grandparents are also called <u>husband</u> and <u>wife</u>, a sex distinction. In the first descending generation,

---

22 The "children" term is used for both real and extended siblings.
23 Tax, 1937, pp. 19-21.

the sex differentiation is only partially drawn. The children of sisters (male speaking) are distinguished by nephew and niece terms while one's own children and the children of brothers are called children regardless of sex. However, with one's children it is possible to make vocative sex distinctions, particularly when they are small. Then, one may use terms meaning little boy and little girl.

Partial recognition of relative age is another feature of the Wichita system. In the parental generation, one's own father and mother are designated father and mother. The father's brothers are called big father if older than the father and little father [6] if younger. Similarly a father's sisters are designated big mother and little mother with reference to the age of the father, and a mother's sisters big mother and little mother with the mother's age as the point of reference. Terms for mother's brothers are not as clear cut; two old ~~informants~~ said that big uncle was used for one older than the mother while little uncle was used for the mother's younger brother. Other ~~informants~~ stated that if the mother had several brothers, the oldest was big uncle while the others were little uncles regardless of their age relative to the mother. The age-distinctions for the mother's brother seem to have been used infrequently by the Wichita and this early resulted in uncertainty when the system began to change.

Children of siblings of the grandparents are also called big and little fathers, mothers, and uncles. These age qualifications are applied with reference to the age of the connecting parent; for example, the father's male cousin (his brother in Wichita thinking) is called big father if he is older than the father, and mother's female cousin is little mother if she is younger than the mother. Siblings of grandparents are also qualified as big or little depending on their relative age with reference to the connecting grandparent.

The feature of relative age is not carried to its logical extreme. In ego's own generation, all brothers and sisters are vocatively called by name and referred to ordinarily without reference to relative age. When there is some chance of confusion, it is possible to refer to siblings as my brother the older or my sister the younger, but these are somewhat awkward constructions in Wichita and used only rarely and not systematically as are the terms in the first and second ascending generations.

Some age distinctions are made in the first descending generation. Vocatively, children sometimes are called little boy and little girl until they approach pubescence, when this terminology is abandoned in favor of personal names. This, however, is not distinction by relative age. The latter occurs occasionally in non-vocative terms when confusion of children is possible. Then, qualifiers are added to produce such terms as my married son, my single daughter, and my married daughter. These latter terms are not often used and, again, are relatively awkward constructions. Nephews, nieces, and grandchildren are not differentiated by relative age.

Another prominent feature of Wichita kinship is the use of different terms by an individual as a child and as an adult. This involves partially the use of vocative and non-vocative terms and partially the increasing use of personal names as one grows older. An Individual learns vocative terms for father and mother when very young. As a child he uses the same terns non-vocatively merely by prefixing my. By puberty he learns to refer to his father by an entirely different term and to his mother by a term meaning my woman. A child may, and does, refer to step-parents by the same terms used for father and mother; at a later age he is taught to use a special term for step-parent which makes no sex distinction. Children refer to brothers and sisters of the father, and sisters of the mother, by terms meaning big and little fathers and mothers; on reaching adult status they may call these relatives by personal names. In a somewhat similar manner a mother's brother is called vocatively and non-vocatively by one term when ego is a child and by a different term when he reaches his teens. In the grandparental generation the situation is not clear; in addition to regular kinship terns, personal names are applied to grandparents and their siblings. The strong joking relationship between grandchildren and grandparents becomes somewhat tempered when ego acquires adult status and then there is an increased use of personal names. There was, and is, frequent use of nicknames between grandparents and grandchildren.

Another shift in terminology occurs when ego becomes an adult and has children of his own; then he may refer to both his great-grandmother and grandmother as old lady and to his father, grandfather, and great-grandfather all by a single term meaning real old man. These latter cases are the only instances where the Wichita merge consanguineal relatives of two adjacent generations. However, this usage for the father was quite rare and there seems to have been something rather disrespectful about it.

Certain vocative terms (those for siblings and spouses and one of the "father" terms) were used rarely and then in situations in which one had to attract the attention of the relative concerned. Most of our ~~informants~~ did not even know these vocative forms. Brothers and sisters were normally called by their personal names; husband and wife never called each other by name and appear to have usually attracted each other's attention with the Wichita equivalent of "Hey!"; children of any age seem vocatively to have called the mother *s•'ciɛ•* and probably also called the father *ta•'ta*.

Another feature in the terminology is the slightly greater emphasis on the mother's side of the family. The mother's brother [7] is separated out by an uncle term while the father's sister is a mother. Corresponding to this usage a male has nephews and nieces, who are a sister's children, while a brother's children are our children; for a female, children of both brothers and sisters are our children.

Affinal Relatives

Perhaps the outstanding feature of the affinal terminology is the treatment of persons who marry into ego's bilateral family; without exception they are accorded kinship terms. There is a strong tendency to distinguish them by sex and group them under two terms *i•'?ɛ•s* and *ackics'?*, which seem to correspond to "male relative-in-law" and "female relative-in-law".

Thus, spouses of mother's and father's brothers and spouses of male children and nephews are called female-relative-in-law, while spouses of mother's and father's sisters and spouses of female children and nieces are called male-relative-in-law. A male ego also calls his sister's husband male -relative-in-law and may call both his wife's sister and his brother's wife *female-relative-in-law* as a joke, though normally he would refer to them by name or as wife. A female ego calls her brother's wife female-relative-in-law and her sister's husband our husband. It might be expected that the latter individual and a woman's husband's brother could be called male-relative-in-law as a joke, but this was not reported. Spouses of grandchildren, even, could be called by the relative-in-law terms on rare occasions as a joke. Thus, with the exception of the use in joking of female-relative-in-law for the wife's sister, both terms are used only for individuals marrying into one's family. Even the one exception might be logical in that with the practice of sororal polygyny the wife's sister could be expected to marry into one's family. The in-group nature of ego's blood relatives and out-group nature of his affinal relatives is made distinct by non-reciprocal use of terms; a male ego calls his sister's husband male-relative-in-law; however, that individual cannot call ego by the same term but has to call him by name, or refer to him as my sister's husband, or say "I am his male-relative-in-law." Similarly a female ego calls her brother's wife female-relative-in-law and the latter individual, in return, calls ego by name, or refers to her as my husband's sister, or explains "I am her female relative-in-law."

The mother or father of either spouse is referred to as parent-in-law. No vocative term for these individuals was considered necessary since they were due extreme respect and seldom addressed directly; in the case of a man's mother-in-law and a woman's father-in-law this respect almost reached complete avoidance. Only under most pressing circumstances could a son-in-law and mother-in-law converse, and normally each withdrew from gatherings when the other approached. For a father-in-law and son-in-law, the avoidance was not so extreme; they could converse about hunting or horse-herding activities, but the father-in-law did not like to have the son-in-law initiate the conversation. For a daughter-in-law and her parents-in-law, the respect relationship also held, but here it was tempered by distance" since normally these individuals resided in different households. The parent-in-law term was reported as not being extended to siblings of parents-in-law.

The lack of kinship terminology for siblings of parents-in-law, a husband's sister, a wife's brother, and children of a spouse's sister or brother, illustrates the Wichita viewpoint that these individuals are not relatives. Indeed, even those in-laws who are accorded kinship terms are considered as outsiders and not real kinfolk; in Wichita thinking only those persons with genetic or "blood" relationship are really relatives. This does not minimize the importance of the in-laws; even a husband's sister and wife's brother, who are not designated by kinship terms, are placed in relationships with ego characterized by highly patterned joking and reciprocal duties.

Spouses have non-vocative terms for my husband and my wife. As indicated above, although vocative forms appear to have existed, they were little used. Husband and wife terms are applied to other relatives, both affinal and consanguineal, and are part of an Integrated joking pattern. Associated with these are two terms, one for male speaker and the other for female speaker, which are freely translated by Wichitas as my rival. A wife's sister nay be called by name or female-relative-in-law as a joke; she may also be referred to as wife. This last term is consistent with the former Wichita practice of sororal polygyny. If the wife's sister married another man, then ego and that man were in a special relationship; they called each other rival. With matrilocal residence the two men inhabited the same house and were in competition for favors from members of the household; and, since each could call the [8] other's wife, wife, they were in theoretical rivalry over spouses. In a somewhat similar manner, women called a sister's husband by name or referred to him as husband. This is part of sister-in-law and brother-in-law joking relationship but is also consistent with former Wichita practice of the levirate. Two women who were married to brothers likewise called each other rival. Although under special circumstances it was possible for them to live under the same roof, the main aspect of rivalry seems to have been that each married a potential spouse of the other.

The above terms for husband, wife, and rival are also utilized in the intense joking relationship between grandparents and grandchildren. A grandfather, real or conceptual, refers to his granddaughter as my wife and the reciprocal is my husband; a grandmother refers to her grandson, as my husband and the reciprocal is my wife. Theoretically, and in a joking way, grandparents and grandchildren of the same sex are in competition with each other for spouses, so grandfather and grandson, grandmother and granddaughter call each other rival. This terminology and the joking behavior also includes spouses of grandchildren and grandparents. All these relatives in the grandparental and second descending generations could also use the conventional grandparent and grandchild terms if they wished.

Discussion of Spier's Terminology[24]

Spier's ~~informant~~ for Wichita terminology was John Haddon, who was also one of our principal ~~informants~~. As might be expected, the terms given by Mr. Haddon in 1919 agree very well with those collected in 1949. Further work with Mr. Haddon and with other ~~informants~~ necessitates some minor revisions in Spier's schedule.

Spier was undecided as to whether or not the non-vocative term for father, *ratɛ•'?asi?i*, was used only for God. According to information given the writers, it is also the standard term for "my father" after ego has passed out of boyhood. Concerning the terms for "big father", *ta•'tasiwa•'c?*; "little father", *ta•'tasikic?*; "big mother", *ɛ•ciɛ•siwa•'c*; and "little mother", *ɛ•'ciɛ•sikic?*; the writer's older ~~informants~~ agreed that <u>big father</u> and <u>big mother</u> were the only terms used for great-grandfather and great-grandmother. None of the ~~informants~~, including Mr. Haddon, reported <u>little father</u> and <u>little mother</u> for these relatives.

Concerning the term, *řakiři•a•ckski*, which Spier gives for stepfather, father's sister's husband, and mother's sister's husband: our older ~~informants~~ gave this term for <u>stepparent</u> of either sex. When children were young they called their stepparents father and mother, but when older were instructed to refer to then, at least, by the term under consideration. Because of the possibility of the sororate and the possibility of adoption by the father's sister or mother's sister, the use of this term for the mother's sister's husband and father's sister's husband appears logical. Normally, however, relative-in-law terms were preferred for spouses of the parent's siblings.

Concerning the terms *ackics?* and *i•'ɛ•'s*; Spier reports several obvious variants and one term, *natıtsıtsi*, which appears to be a contraction of *řatiackics?ih*.

Statement of Classifications

In Spier's classification of kinship systems of North America, the Wichita are placed in the MacKenzle Basin type.[25] Although more than ego's own generation is considered as a basis for this, the most important feature of the type is the classing of both parallel and cross-cousins as siblings. Spier goes on to make, in effect, a subdivision of the type by pointing out the similarity of the Wichita and Caddo, who distinguish between parental siblings of different ages by calling them "older" or "younger" father or mother. He also points out that the Wichita, and many other tribes in the MacKenzie Basin type, use "son" and "daughter" for a man's brother's children and for a woman's brother's and sister's children.

Eggan places the Wichita provisionally in the Kiowa-Apache subtype of his "Generation" type when he classifies Plains kinship systems.[26] The "Generation" type [9]

> "is characterized by a simple and coherent organization in which generation is emphasized, lineal and collateral relatives are merged, the range of relationship is rather wide but indefinite, the duties and obligations between relatives are organized (largely in terms of familiarity and respect) and marriage is outside the circle of blood-relations, In most tribes having this general type of kinship organization, the domestic or household

---

[24] Spier, 1924.
[25] Spier, 1925.
[26] Eggan, 1937, pp. 90-93.

group is an extended family based on matrilocal residence."[27]

The Kiowa-Apache subtype differs from the Cheyenne and Arapaho in "their recognition of additional generations above and below the grandparental and grandchild generations and in their greater use of self-reciprocal terms and behavior." The Wichita and Caddo are provisionally placed in this subtype although the Wichita are noted by Eggan to "show some variation toward a "Hawaiian type". All this appears to be supported by our data on the Wichita, with the exception of the "greater use of self-reciprocal terms."

Murdock assigns the Wichita to the Hawaiian type and to the Matri-Hawaiian subtype.[28] This follows from his definition that Hawaiian cousin terminology (parallel and cross cousins called by sibling terms) along with bilateral descent constitute the Hawaiian type of social organization. Matrilocal residence among the Wichita results in the final classification of their system as Matri-Hawaiian. Murdock's classification is based "on male-speaking terms for female relatives" but for the Wichita consideration of female-speaking terms would not have changed the type or subtype. [11, blank 10]

OLDER KINSHIP BEHAVIOR
Social Setting

The Wichita were organized by villages and each village appears to have been an Independent unit. They were also grouped together into "bands," though it should be pointed out that present day ~~informants~~ use the latter form with varying meanings. Usually the word "band" is employed to denote the units making up the Wichita confederacy; the Wichita proper, the Waco, Tawakoni, and Kichai. It is also used at times to denote the village unit, as in speaking of three bands of the Wichita proper when that group was inhabiting three separate villages. Another usage of "band" is as an indication of a subdivision of a village. A Wichita village had dual chiefs, usually referred to as "first" and "second" chief; each of these chiefs, however, had his own following so that, for instance, one spoke of "Tawakoni Jim's band" and "Tawakoni Dave's band." With the continuing population decline of the nineteenth century, the village and larger band unit came to be the same; in 1870 the Wichita proper, Waco, Tawakoni, and Kichai inhabited four separate villages near present day Anadarko, Oklahoma.

Each village was composed of a number of large grass houses and their inhabitants. A strong tendency to matrilocal residence existed. From the standpoint of a young married woman, an ideal household would contain herself, her husband and children, her mother and father, her maternal grandparents, her unmarried brothers, her sister (who might be a co-wife), and the latter's children. Epidemics and population decline often upset the ideal residence pattern so that it is said that sometimes a girl would have to go live with the husband's family at marriage, or a man and wife would have to live in his sister's house. In Wichita thinking, houses were not owned by individuals but by families. Our oldest informant, however, speaks of the "mother of the house" or the oldest competent member of the female lineage living in that house. This individual to a large extent controlled activities of the female aid child residents and to some extent those of adult males. On death of the "mother of the house," her "oldest daughter" took over control.

Grass house villages were inhabited during spring, summer, and early fall, when the

---

[27] Same, p. 90.
[28] Murdock, 1949, p. 229.

women were busy tending or harvesting their crops of corn, beans, pumpkins, and melons. Late in autumn or in early winter, the villages were closed up and the people left for their "winter" buffalo hunt. At this time tipis were used. Since they were not as commodious as grass lodges, the larger family grouping broke up into a number of smaller units. Again, though tipis were not thought of as owned by individuals, each respectable married woman seems to have possessed one. Two sisters and their husbands could share the same tipi. Though the composite family of the grass house was split up during the winter hunt, the division was not one of major proportions since the members seem to have pitched tipis close together. During the winter hunt the organization was still by village. Although tipi groups were somewhat scattered through a sheltering belt of timber, they were still close enough together to be spoken of as the "Wichita village" or "Waco village," as the case might be.

It is thus evident that the Wichita individual lived his life in close proximity to a large number of relatives. Within the same grass house, or grouping of tipis, were relatives and in-laws covering three of more generations. In addition, since relationship terms were extended to anyone with whom a blood connection was traceable, relatives were also widely scattered throughout the village. In the examples of behavior to be cited, it will become apparent that kinship patterns operated not only at the time of major crises such as birth, marriage, and death, but also in many minor day to day contacts in the house group and village.

Kinship Practices of Larger Family Units

The fragmental treatment of kinship behavior by pairs of opposing relatives to be utilized below, while useful for analysis of patterned behavior, tends to obscure the important fact that much behavior was really that of the family as a whole or consisted of cooperation between nembers of several families. To remedy in part this deficiency, a brief consideration of such kin behavior follows.

Marriages were arranged between two families. Most often the young man's family Initiated proceedings through a go-between. Occasionally a girl's family spotted a desirable young man and started proceedings in a similar manner. Horses and buffalo robes were given to the girl's father or brother, when the union was between high status families, and a joint feast was held by the two groups. [12]

Dorsey gives the following summary concerning marriage arrangements.[29]

> During the early life of a girl she was closely watched, not only by the parents, but by relatives; as she grew older she was warned to have nothing to do with men, to keep away from them, and in the choice of a husband she was supposed to have no part. It being decided by the parents of some young man that a particular girl was desirable for a daughter-in-law, they asked some individual to go to the lodge to obtain the parents' consent. This go-between was usually a middle-aged woman and a relative of the boy. She asked of the girl's parents if they were willing that their daughter should marry, and in case of an affirmative answer the relatives of both families were called together. First, however, it was supposed that the parties had learned all about the boy, whether he was of good or bad reputation, and especially whether he was able to support a wife. The parents of the young man were informed that their proposition had been accepted, and the

---

[29] Dorsey, 1904, pp. 9-10.

young man himself went to the lodge of the girl next evening. Should the parents of the girl still favor him he remained. Then, after this, the girl was watched, that she might not associate with other men. Should she prove unfaithful at any time she was beaten with a stick by her father.[30] But should the parents of the girl at any time disapprove of their son-in-law they told the girl to send him home. This constituted divorce. The duty of the young man was to watch over the property of the family, and in the faithful fulfillment of these duties and in the providing of food rested his claim for favor with his wife's parents.

Again it might happen that the parents of a certain girl desired a certain young man for their son-in-law, in which case the girl's parents sent some middle-aged woman to ask the parents' consent for him.

As birth became imminent, a woman left the grass house for a tipi which was pitched close by. Wichita men feared contact with a woman in confinement and the mother-to-be thus removed the danger from her male relatives by going to the tipi. The husband did not stay; "he had to go home" to his mother's or sister's place. The mother's female relatives helped her in her confinement and one of the older women almost certainly was competent as a midwife and as a conductor of the necessary prayers. At this time, too, the husband's mother and sister were there to aid. Birth concerned women of both families and only if a specialist doctor was needed was there a man present. The baby could be brought into the family grass house immediately after birth but the new mother had to stay in the tipi "about a week;" she then was purified by bathing and smoking and allowed to return home. Sanctioned behavior associated with pregnancy and child birth is illustrated in a myth in which Coyote turns himself into a woman, marries, and has a child:[31]

Some time afterwards the Coyote woman told her sister-in-law that she was pregnant, "for, "'said she, "my mother has told me that when a woman is in my condition she is pregnant and must not sleep with men any more. My mother and father no longer sleep together when a child is in my mother's womb. Moreover, before any brothers and sisters are born, my father cuts twenty-four dogwood sprouts to make a cradle, and other material that is used in making a cradle." The woman listened attentively to all that the Coyote woman had to say about the handling of a child after it was born, and it sounded strange to her. When the brothers came home she repeated all that she had heard; how they were not to sleep any more with the Coyote woman, and how they were to cut dogwood sprouts to make a cradle for the child. She told them they could sleep with the Coyote woman once more, but after that the two women would sleep together.

After the child was born:

"Now," said the Coyote woman, "my mother has told bib that whenever a child is born it is the rule that men may not enter the lodge until four days have elapsed. So we must not allow the men to come in, but let them remain somewhere else until after four days." The woman kept watching for her brothers to come home, so she could "tell then about the child, and tell them to remain somewhere until after four days should pass.

---

[30] This punishment sounds extremely severe, since ideally a father should _never_ physically punish a child.

[31] Dorsey, 1904, pp. 78-9.

After this the Coyote woman would remain at home with the child while the other woman did the work. This is the way they did things around the lodge.

An excellent example of interaction between families concerns the manufacture of a cradle. The mother of the new father picked an old man[32] to gather the material for the cradle; both the selecting of the old man and the gathering of cradle material were done with much ritual activity. The old man and the women of the husband's family then cooperated to complete the cradle, again with much ritual designed to promote the welfare of the new baby. During the wife's pregnancy her mother and female relatives braided a sash, which she wore as a belt before the birth of her child. Then, after, the child was born the sash was used as a necessary part of the cradle equipment. The cradle as such could easily be interpreted as symbolic of the cooperation and union of the two families. At birth the child went through no formal naming ceremony. When it was two or three months old, the new mother's parents arranged for an old woman who had raised a family without loss to perform a blessing ceremony for the new child.

A son-in-law performed duties for all his wife's family; the most important of these, when he was young, was to help herd their horses and to contribute the game that he killed. His warfare activity added to or detracted from the prestige of his affinal family as well as his own. Matrilocal residence and a husband's duties are illustrated by this mythological reference:[33] [13]

> Early the next day he started out to hunt and kill game for the whole family. It was a custom that any man marrying a young woman should at once begin to support the family by going hunting, or on the war-path to bring home a scalp for the family. So this became Man-having-greater-Powers-than-any-other-Man's duty, for he was a great warrior, and a great hunter.

A daughter-in-law prepared special dishes for her mother-in-law and gave bundles of fire-wood to her husband's family. In return the girl's mother-in-law gave her presents and her husband's sisters donated fire-wood to her family.

Both girls and boys who belonged to respectable families had their names formally changed during their early teens. Such procedure could be initiated by a father, grandmother, grandfather, or even some other relative, but the cooperation of the whole family was necessary to feed and show respect to the old successful warriors who had been invited to suggest suitable names. When a daughter of a "high-class" family was tattooed, the specialist who carried out the process was similarly feted.

While a man was on a war party, his wife had to dress in ragged clothes, lead an inactive life, and particularly shun any sort of social gathering. An example of mythological sanction for this type behavior is as follows:[34]

> On their return from the war-path, the one who had scalps would present them to his people. If a man was married he would present the scalp to his wife. When the brothers were out on the war-path together their people at home would keep the wife of the married brother and help her in the lodge at all times. A woman had to wear moccasins at all

---

[32] Same, pp. 11-12, says the new father cut the material and picked an old woman to aid in the manufacture. However, his and .and our data agree that it was the duty of the father's family.

[33] Same, p. 174.

[34] Same, pp. 300-1.

times during the absence of her man. She would have to go to the creek for an early morning bath. She was not to look around, but to look straight ahead. While going to or coming from the creek she was never to speak to anyone, especially to the men folks, until her man came back from the war-path. By doing all of these things a woman gave good luck to her husband who was gone on the war-path. When a woman did not do these things something often happened to her husband.

If the expedition was successful, and the wife had behaved well, then the husband's female relatives came in and washed her and clothed her in fine attire. During the festivities following the return of the party, the man's female relatives — particularly his "sisters" — and his wife sang in his honor. The older women of both families gave away property in his honor, and if he had taken a scalp his mother and mother-in-law could strip their families of nearly all their possessions.

When a person was sick and appeared in critical condition, word was sent to all blood relatives to assemble. When death occurred all the relatives were supposed to be present before the body was buried. "They have to wait until all relatives arrive; maybe (a) day before some cousins come. When they come, it won't be long before they bury it." Non-relatives had charge of the actual burial, a fact which ties in well with the Wichita belief that the spirit of the deceased often tries to entice close relatives to accompany it to the afterworld. Relatives cut their hair in mourning, and the amount cut varied with the closeness of relationships distant "brothers" or cousins cut less than a blood brother. After death the members of the deceased's family were visited by many non-relatives, who came to mourn with the family. The visitors had their faces washed by the female relatives of the deceased and were given presents. A family which followed ideal patterns would finally give away everything in the nature of horses, bedding, and utensils. During the period of mourning, their blood relatives of other households supplied their daily needs. When the family of the deceased thought the surviving spouse had mourned enough, they sent word that they were coming on a certain day. At this time the female relatives of the deceased cut a little more of the hair of their relative-in-law, bathed him (or her), dressed him in new clothes, and formally "turned him loose." Ceremonies included prayers and talks by the mother-in-law and a grand-mother-in-law of the surviving spouse. The family of the deceased was re-equipped with household necessities by blood relatives. A bathing and smoking ceremony was also held for all close relatives, including the spouse, of the deceased so that they could stop mourning and so that they would not dream of the departed and waste away. Dorsey describes death customs as follows:[35]

Should the young husband die the girl's parents cut her hair, the length being determined by the favor in which they held the young man. The parents of the deceased husband might also visit her from time to time and cut off a portion of her hair. The girl remained single for a certain number of months, during which time she kept secluded and permitted her hair to remain uncombed. During this time she wore old clothes. After the requisite number of months had passed, the parents provided new clothing for the daughter. The parents of the deceased husband now went to the young widow's lodge. She, having been forewarned, had carefully swept the lodge. Upon entering, they washed her face, combed her hair, and painted her face, and then placed upon her, her new clothing. They then began to talk to her, telling her that they thought as much of her as when their son was alive, and now they had come to tell her that the period of mourning was over; that they

---

[35] Same, p. 10.

had given her the things that they had brought; that she might laugh, eat heartily, and that now she might marry anyone she pleased. The woman, having her liberty, after the requisite period, might meet with some man whom she conversed with and who desired to marry her. She then reported the fact to her parents and to the parents of the deceased husband, in which case she was usually told that she might do as she liked. Should she have been faithful to her former husband during the time of mourning, her husband's parents then said that they thought just as much of her as when her husband was living, and they might take her and her new husband into their lodge. [14]

Economic activities included much cooperation between extended relatives. Building a new grass house involved the male occupants, who split cedars for the framework and cut poles for the supporting posts, and the women, who gathered grass and elmbark for the covering. When the time came for the erection, distant "sisters" of the females in the household assembled to help with the work or with the cooking which was necessary to feed the crowd. Similarly at planting and harvest time all the women of one household worked together; at times, related households aided one another in these tasks. Ceremonies were almost always initiated by men, but an important part of any ceremony was serving food to the participants. This was prepared by the female relatives of the man, or men, sponsoring the rite.

Respect and Joking

In Wichita thinking, one possible manner of classifying people was on the basis of being or not being a relative. Relatives were those to whom one was joined by a blood tie. This excluded individuals who in our society are called "affinal relatives" from being real kinfolk in spite of the fact that there were highly patterned attitudes and behavior between these people. Wichita thinking also categorized people on the basis of respect and joking relationships. Some blood and some affinal relatives were in each of these categories. The alternation of generation principle evident in the terminology correlates with the respect and joking behavior: individuals of adjacent generations respected each other, individuals of the same or alternate generations exhibited joking behavior. Respect and joking varied in intensity and ranged from the extreme respect of almost total avoidance to the milder form of behaving in a decorous manner, and from extreme sexual joking, or joking about 'witch' relatives, to a mild twitting concerning innocuous subjects. It should be pointed out that respect and joking behavior does not always correlate with the terminology: joking between siblings and between conceptual siblings (both were called brothers and sisters) varied markedly in intensity, and a man and his sister's husband joked while a man and his father's sister's husband could not; yet both the sister's husband and the father's sister's husband were called by the term male relative-in-law.

While there was, and is, a definite pattern to the joking relationships, there was individual variation in practice. Some individuals are known as "hard teasers" and about them more moderate individuals say, "they don't care what they say!" At the other extreme are individuals who react adversely to joking, taking it seriously instead of retaliating in kind. While the "hard teasers" are recognized as deviating from the great run of people, there is no formal social pressure for them to change their ways. They appear to be acting within the accepted pattern, and one's only recourse is to tease back. However, those who resent teasing and show it are considered somewhat abnormal, and there is a definite mechanism for resolving the situation, as indicated by the following examples:

~~Informant~~ #E says, "If somebody gets mad, that cuts off teasing. I made up a story about old man who teased me. (It was) about woman and him doing business in bed. He saw me in Cashway; came straight to me; said I told a lie on him. He got mad. I said, 'I'm going to tell you you must quit. You can't stand that! I don't want you to tease me any more! Never did tease me anymore." (These individuals were distant brothers, about third cousins.)

On another occasion a Wichita said of another individual:

"He used to be my grandpa, but he said cut it off. Now he's just plain #F."

No corresponding example of disrespectful respect relatives was encountered. However, a girl's family could break up her marriage if the husband was, in their opinion, not acting correctly.

Respect Relationships

Parent~Child

Both the mother and father were important figures in the physical and social development of the Wichita individual. For the first few years of a person's life, however, it was primarily his mother and her female relatives who were responsible for his care and education and whom he associated with such physical necessities or comforts as food, water, warmth, and dryness. Often the help of a woman's mother or grandmother was greater than her own efforts in caring for her child. The father had no obligation to assist. To be sure, he contributed to the child's psychological welfare by picking it up from time to time, fondling it, or playing with it; but such things as feeding, bathing, dressing, or going to it when it cried were definitely beyond his line of duty.

As a matter of fact, the father was with the child much less than the mother. This was true from the very beginning of a [15] child's life, for, in accordance with Wichita customs, he was absent at the time of his baby's birth. A woman in confinement, like a menstruating woman, was considered dangerous, and so when birth became imminent the father took off for his parent's or sister's home. He would return when his wife's lying-in period was over but was not expected to have anything to do with the baby's care as that was in the hands of his wife, her female relatives, and his mother and sister.

A man's duties, which would include such activities as hunting, going on the warpath, tending horses, and participating in the ceremonial and political life of the group, took him away from his home much of the time. Even a considerable part of his leisure time was spent elsewhere in visiting or gambling. The mother, however, was always at hand to attend the child until he was two or three years old. When the baby was not being actually handled by his mother, he was placed near her either in his cradle or on a pallet on the floor. She even brought cradle and baby to the field and kept him there while she worked, so that if he needed her she would be immediately available. At night she took the child to bed with her and if he woke up and started crying, she would nurse him. A Wichita woman would never allow her baby to cry for an extended length of time; in fact, if a woman was rather slow in going to her baby, she could be scolded by her grandmother or reminded of her duties by her husband or mother. The Wichita explained a baby's crying as being indicative of hunger, thirst, sleepiness, wetness,[36] or of a desire to be taken out of the cradle or put back in. With regard to the latter, infants did cry to get back into the cradle when they were tired and sleepy in spite of the fact that the cradle was tight and constricting.

One can only conjecture as to how much the baby was in actual physical contact with his mother. In morning when the baby was placed on the pallet to play, he was picked up and fondled not only by his mother but by the other members of the family as well. In the words of one informant, the baby went "from one set of arms to another." Other times when the baby was held and petted by his mother were probably at the morning and evening bath periods and when he was removed from his cradle to be dressed in dry clothes. Extensive contact with his mother was limited by the very nature of the cradle in which the baby was kept so much of the time. The cradle, as mentioned above, was very constricting[37] and prevented the baby from snuggling up to his mother or wrapping his arms or legs around her. The baby was even kept in the cradle while he was being nursed. At night the baby was taken to bed with his parents and was laid beside them at the back of the bed but he was either in a cradle or swaddled in a blanket.

A woman nursed her child until he was two or three years old, or until she became pregnant again. In the latter ease, weaning was apt to be sudden and of a rather severe nature. Ordinarily, however, weaning took place mare or less gradually as the child learned how to eat. The mother started the process by feeding the child broth or dipping bread in broth and giving it to him. In the old days, according to our eldest informant, the mother would chew meat soft and feed it to the child, but this method was subsequently frowned upon. When the child was older the mother would fix a little dish for the child with various kinds of soft food, such as pounded and cooked corn, or stewed pumpkin, that he could eat with a spoon.

If a child insisted on clinging to the breast, more drastic methods were resorted to. Sometimes the mother would go off for a few days, leaving the child with her female relatives. Another method was to make the breast unattractive to the child by rubbing a bitter tasting preparation around the nipple.[38]

Toilet training was not deliberate but, rather, casual and without much stress involved. Children went about the house with the lower parts of their bodies naked. If a child urinated or defecated on the floor, the mother was not particularly bothered; she would simple clean the place up and remind him that he should have gone to the woods. Physical punishments were never inflicted. Training was evidently started quite early and sometimes was well along before the child could even talk. It appears that the child was not impressed with the "dirtiness" of excrement but rather with the fact that going to the brush was the grown-up thing to do.[39] [16]

Sex education was of an informal nature. In the words of an informant, children "learn pretty young by seeing things; just grew up knowing." This is understandable in view of the

---

[36] Diapers were not worn; instead cloths were placed behind the baby and this padding had to be changed from time to time.

[37] The baby's body was completely wrapped until he was 5 or 6 months old, at which time his hands were freed. A cloth on the back of the cradle was pulled down over the baby's face when he was asleep and fastened near his upper leg.

[38] 3r{ok}The preparation was made from roots or, in later times, quinine was used. One instance was given of a mother putting an ugly worm on her breast and thus scaring her child.

[39] Adult Wichitas were and are modest concerning bodily functions and such attitudes may have been instilled at an early age. Although no direct statements were heard, there is some indirect evidence that body products were disposed of carefully to prevent their possible use in witchcraft.

close quarters in which the family lived, the fact that young children slept with their parents, and the considerable amount of sexual joking to which the children were exposed. It was not considered out of the way for a child to ask questions concerning sex, though ordinarily it was the grandparent, not the parents, who answered.

In general, parents were quite permissive in their attitude toward a young child's behavior. Our ~~informant~~ said, "Child can do pretty near anything it pleases around home." However, there were a few prohibitions. A child was not supposed to pick up things when visiting in another family's home. He was also told not to do anything that would hurt him, such as playing with an axe or fooling with fire. Children were also warned to stay away from the father's shield and sacred bundles. Grabbing for food was frowned upon; if a child reached out to get something from the big pan rather than being content with what was in his own container, his mother would slap his hand gently. In general, however, children were not physically chastized <chastised> for spilling food or for their eating habits.

When a child became old enough to know right from wrong,[40] his parents began to discipline him. Since the young child was with his mother more than his father, much discipline of the early years was in the hands of the mother or older sister. If a child misbehaved, the mother would scold him or perhaps switch him. When she was scolding she would say things like "Why you're not human!" or "Don't you have any ears?". The latter would be accompanied by a vigorous poking or twisting of an index finger in the offender's ears. While scolding the child, the mother might call him "child chief" or "child death"[41] — Wichita terms of derision.

The mother could and sometimes would call in another person to assist her in disciplining her son; this person very rarely might be an older brother, a grandparent, or a mother's brother, but a non-related individual was preferred. Often this person was an ugly old man who would pretend he was going to eat the child or would scare him in some other way. One way of punishing a small boy was to throw him in the creek. If the boy did not stop crying after the latter treatment, the punisher would throw him back and continue the treatment until the child quit crying. Older boys could be given the "knife treatment" by whomever the parents had called in: this consisted of sticking the point of a knife in the boy's leg or scratching his legs with a knife. If the punishment method was particularly harsh, the parents might develop misgivings but were not free to interfere. In the words of an informant, who had been punished both by water and knife treatments, "When parents give child to someone like that to punish, they can't do nothing, no matter what the man does to the child!"

The amount of attention given children by mothers lessened as the children grew out of babyhood and new siblings arrived. This was at least partially counter-balanced by the fact that in the typical Wichita household there were other relatives, notably the mother's mother, mother's sisters, and older siblings, from whom the child expected and did get attention. Tantrums are reported to have occurred with children at the weaning period and in some cases to have persisted several years thereafter. We have no way of evaluating the extent of submerged sibling rivalry in the older culture. Actual fighting was contrary to the mores and most overt rivalry appears to have had expression in conventionalized joking and, to a lesser extent, in the punishment which an older brother could administer.

Thus it will be seen that the mother was a primary figure in the life of the small child, and

---

[40] We could get no precise definition as to an exact age but it could be as early as three or four years.

[41] The Implication of "child chief" is that of "Who do you think you are, acting like that, a chief's son?" No satisfactory explanation for "child death" was obtained.

she continued to be very important in the development of her daughters. As a boy grew older, however, his father gradually assumed the chief role in his education. A man's main duty to his son was to prepare him to be a good Wichita male. He lectured to his boy on such Wichita virtues and ideals as bravery on the warpath and in the face of hardship, modesty, getting along peaceably with other Wichitas, being good to one's family, being a good hunter, and controlling one's emotions — particularly anger. He told him stories about scouting and going to war, tales of daring and bravery. He taught his son how to look after horses, shoot a bow and arrow, hunt, and play boy's and men's games. He saw to it that his son took his daily morning bath in the cold river water, participated in the annual young men's footrace, [17] and generally became physically hardened. Sometimes a father would call in an older man with more experience in life to talk to his son; this individual would be feasted by the father for his service. A chief would take his son to councils with him so that he would learn how things were done. While in theory chieftainship was not hereditary, chances were that a man would succeed his father as chief, if he possessed the necessary personality and war record, because of the training received from his father. Power and medicine bundles could be inherited from a father by a son, as the following mythological excerpts indicate:[42]

> This young man having power to travel fast by the gift of his father, the Wind, finally overtook the two women again. Not knowing what else to do with him, the two women took him on to their home.
>
> The following day Bad-Boy was rather quiet. He asked his father to instruct him regarding the war bundle that he had always offered to give him. The old chief took down the bundle, with everything in it, shield, quiver, bow and arrows, tobacco-pouch and war-club, the whole bundle being called War-Secrets-Bundle (*Narwitstanaseh*). Everything was spread before Bad-Boy. The thing that was spread before him was a shield, and in this shield was a stuffed hawk, in each of whose feet was a scalp; one white soft feather, and tobacco-pouch with black stone pipe in it, this pouch being a stained skunk hide.

A father theoretically could "talk to" or correct his children. He would lecture his sons more vigorously than his daughters, but in any event was not supposed to lose his temper. The following excerpt from a myth illustrates a father gently scolding his errant daughter by telling a story with a moral:[43]

> The woman's father said to her, "Let me tell you a story." He then commenced to tell her the story about a chief having a daughter who married and left home for the sake of keeping her husband, when the old folks did not want her to keep her man. The chief told her the whole tale of her life while out by herself and with her man; how her man lost his arrow; how they soon ate up everything; how greedy her man became after losing his arrow; how some one came to notify her that her life was threatened; that in a short time on that day she should be killed by her husband; how she was compelled to make her escape by various means, in order to prevent her man from catching up with her; how she traveled fast, and what hard times she had had.

As a rule, he "talked to" his daughters in only a mild way; it appears, however, that in

---

[42] Dorsey, 1904, pp. 133 and 258.
[43] same, pp. 238-9.

families in which there were no sons and the daughter was particularly unruly, the father took a firmer hand. Other people would still be critical of his conduct, though. A father was not supposed to inflict physical punishment on his children; a man who whipped his children was open to severe criticism. He could, however, call in the "ugly old man," referred to above, and ask him to scare his son or take him down to the creek or give him the "knife treatment."

Complementary to the father-son relationship in the elementary family was the mother-daughter relationship. A mother's chief obligation to her daughter was to teach her the behavior and duties expected of her as a Wichita woman. Under her mother's tutelage, a girl began at an early age to learn the various aspects of women's work; gardening, cooking, food preservation, and making skin and cloth apparel.

A woman had control over her daughter. She was "boss" of the household and as such told her girls what to do around the house and superintended their work activities. For example, along in the evening, when it was the best time to cultivate, a woman would tell her daughters to go out and hoe till sundown. If it had been raining and the weeds were growing fast, she would instruct her daughters to go out at daybreak, before eating, and hoe. She would probably tell one daughter to stay home and fix breakfast for the men and for the women when they returned from the fields. In a similar way, the mother would supervise all the other work around the house. It was the daughter's duty to learn how to perform the various women's duties and to follow her mother's work orders. However, often a maternal grandmother was vigorously present in the household and then she would be "boss."

A woman's control over her daughter would continue to a considerable extent even after her daughter's marriage. This was particularly true if the latter and her husband continued to live with her parents. In this case, the older woman remained "boss" of the household and her married daughter was expected to follow her instructions just as before. When the couple became parents, the girl's mother helped with rearing the child and could advise her daughter on various aspects of child care. Sometimes the older woman would correct or scold her daughter for such things as nursing a child too long, or for failing to go to a baby immediately when it cried. If a baby should die of "summer complaint," his parents would be blamed[44] and his mother's grandmother would severely reprimand the two. [18]

Occasionally a woman would break up her daughter's marriage. If a husband did not measure up to what he should be (was not a good hunter, did not treat his in-laws right, etc.), the mother would "get after" her daughter and cause the couple to separate.

The mother was a major disciplinarian of her daughter; the father, as we have seen, would only mildly "talk to" his daughter. However, the older brother of a girl was the strongest disciplinarian and in addition to chastizing her verbally could physically punish her. Scolding was a woman's primary instrument of disciplining her daughter, though she would sometimes resort to whipping with a switch.

Parent's Sibling~Sibling's Child

In general, this was the same type of respect relationship as that between parent and child with similar prerogatives <prerogatives > and obligations. The terminology correlated with the behavior here in that parent-type terms (big mother, little mother, big father, little father) were

---

[44] It was believed that sexual intercourse during the nursing period resulted in a baby's illness with "summer complaint." Seminal fluid was thought to go directly into the mother's milk and to be the cause of illness.

applied to siblings of the parents, the mother's brother excepting. The latter was given a separate term and this appears consistent with the fact that there was some behavioral differentiation between mother's brother and father's brother and some emphasis on the maternal side.

Siblings of the parent were expected to be mindful of the general welfare of their nephews and nieces and assisted in the parental functions of training, correcting, and disciplining. The role of being "second parent" was probably more closely approximated by the mother's sister than any of the other parental siblings. Two women who were sisters often lived in the same household after marriage and helped take care of each other's children. Thus an individual grew up looking upon his mother's sister as another mother. This was particularly true in those families in which two sisters were married to the same man; the children of the two sisters would then have the same father and would refer to both women as $\varepsilon\cdot'ci\varepsilon\cdot$" (i.e., the simple term for mother, without the qualifying "big" or "little".)

The maternal character of the mother's sister's role held even in more extended relationships. ~~Informant~~ #A was a distant "sister" to #B's mother and to this day treats #B as a "son" (this, in spite of the fact B is 80 years old). #B is a diabetic who does not adhere too strictly to his diet at times. In the summer of 1948, A was observed telling him; "I'm going by Wichita rules — your mother told me her boys was my boys, not to be afraid to talk to them, tell them what to do." A then told B to stick to his diet. That her admonition had the desired effect, for a time, at any rate, was attested to by B's wife.

The mother's sister assisted greatly in the informal training of her nieces in various phases of women's work and behavior. Special skills, such as midwifery, were also often learned from aunts.[45] Because of matrilocal residence, the father's sister probably figured less prominently in a girl's training.

Uncles helped instruct their nephews in the various men's duties, such as hunting and fighting, and the correct behavior, attitudes, and Ideals of men. Again, because of matrilocal residence, the mother's brother's role was more intensified than that of the father's brother. The mother's brother also served as disciplinarian to his sister's sons. If a boy got too far out of line his mother called upon her brother to lecture to him concerning the proper way to behave.

Further emphasis on the maternal side of the family was evident in the ideal adoption practices described by our eldest informant. In the old days orphaned children were taken to be raised by maternal relatives — frequently, the mother's brother.[46] If the father was living, the maternal relatives would ask him for the children and he was expected to relinquish them. If the father died, and the mother was having a difficult time with the children, she would ask her brother to take them. Sometimes, even if the father was living but the mother was having trouble controlling her child, she would turn him over to her brother.

Evidently, however, in the latter half of the neneteenth <nineteenth> century, the ideal situation was breaking down and orphan children were being adopted by both maternal and paternal relatives. There are living today several older Wichitas who represent both types of adoption: ~~Informant~~ #A, as we have mentioned, was raised by her maternal relatives; #B, on the other hand, was brought up by his father's sister. In this latter case it was not possible to ascertain whether or not the mother's family gave its permission. [19]

---

[45] A modern Wichita woman, who still delivers maternity cases, states that she learned her art from her aunt.

[46] ~~Informant~~ #A herself was taken by her mother's brother after the death of her mother. Her mother's brother's mother-in-law did not treat her right, however, and so her mother's brother gave her to his sister (A's mother's sister), who raised A to adulthood.

Inferences may be drawn from myths as to the importance of the mother's brother. In one myth, Thunderbird and his nephew are first and second chiefs of a village.[47] In another a powerful man names and passes power on to his sister's son:[48]

> In this village was a man known as Wearing-Flint-Stone-on-top-of-Head (*Tahadiidakotskitiwe*), who afterwards became the Great-South-Star, as we call it. This man was famous in all ways. He was the leader of war-parties and had many followers who always followed him whenever he sent out war-parties. In his home his father was the chief of the village. He also had a mother and a sister. When he had become famous and a great warrior, his sister got married to a famous warrior. Once upon a time, before he undertook to leave home, his sister became pregnant. He told his sister that when the child should be born they should call him Flint-Stone-Yelling-Boy (*Tahanitsiaskase*). He also said that this boy would follow the footsteps of his uncle and be a great warrior.

All relationships between parental siblings (both maternal and paternal) and their nephews and nieces were characterized by marked respect. This respect was manifested in certain prescribed rules of behavior:

> 1. Behave with decorum and do not say "anything out of the way" in front of an uncle, aunt, nephew, or niece. Refrain from talk of a sexual, critical, or teasing nature. Do not address one of these respect relatives by his nickname.[49]
>
> 2. If present while someone is criticizing or teasing a respect relative;
>
>   a. Protest verbally with: "He's a good man, don't say that" or something of a similar nature,
>   b. Do not laugh or join in the mirth.
>   c. Refuse to listen and walk off.
>   d. Retaliate by saying something of a derogatory nature about one of the teaser's respect relatives (providing the latter is not also your respect relative or a respect relative of the person you are defending). Although these rules of behavior are old in tradition, they also exist today and we have seen them demonstrated again and again.

A few illustrative examples are given below:

> When #G's teasers tried to induce the investigator to call her uncle (#F) by the name of the latter's 'witch' relative, she protested with, "He's a good man!"
> On other occasions, #F was heard defending his "witch" uncle.
> At the urging of H's teasers, the investigator called #H a name having the connotation "woman chaser." H's niece then shook her head rather sadly and said, "You shouldn't say that, he's a good man. He's got a name — a pretty one. You call him that."

---

[47] Dorsey, 1904, p. 106.

[48] Same, p. 52.

[49] Nicknames often are salacious in nature or have sexual connotations. They are usually bestowed upon individuals by grand-parents; no individual would think of giving his nephew or niece such a name.

While dining with a Wichita family, the investigator was teasing #C about looking at pretty girls in swim suits. His niece, who was serving the food, said in an irate tone of voice: "You better stop making fun of my uncle, or I won't feed you!"

The investigator was telling an amusing story he had heard about #F getting stuck while creeping through the small south door of a grass house to keep a romantic rendezvous. F's niece interrupted: "He's a good man, don't believe those stories. He wouldn't do anything wrong."

Stories of #J and his extra-marital affairs were being told by the teasers of his nephews. The nephews tried to hush up the stories, said the teasers were not telling the truth, and that J was a good man. One of the nephews then went on to retaliate with a story about the uncle of one of the teasers: how the uncle would get money and go around giving it to women, that if his nephew (F) were to ask him for a dime he would not get it. While the latter story was being told, F, now on the defensive, kept saying: "K is a good man. He is good to give money to kids for pop and ice cream and to poor people."

G and her "mother's brothers," #L and #H, were riding to town with the investigator. L and H are teasing relatives and L is known for his hard teasing. However, on this occasion, they teased each other scarcely at all—indeed, only to the extent that H called L, who weighs 260 pounds, "Slim." Their subdued behavior no doubt was due to the presence of their niece.

In addition to this attitude of respect, the relationship between an individual and his parent's sibling was characterized by a feeling of pride in each other's abilities, achievements, and assets. In a myth, Coyote once went with his uncle to play the hand game: "When they were seen the Coyote was in the lead, and felt proud because his uncle was there.[50]" Pride in an uncle's or nephew's war service has continued to the present day. ~~Informant~~ #G told us of how she and other female relatives danced at a Turkey Dance held in honor of her mother's brother, returned from World War I. The membership of several women in the Wichita Service Club is based on the fact of their having or having had nephews (or "sons" in Wichita terminology) in the service. According to ~~Informant~~ #A, in the old days, a man's special possessions — bow, shield, spears — were frequently inherited by his nephew,[51] "more so than own son." [20]

Corresponding to this attitude of pride is a, feeling of shame over the shortcomings or failures of one's respect relative. Apparently, the respect relatives of the one who had erred frequently would refuse to admit the fact. This is illustrated by some of the previous accounts and excellently by the following:

#J was having dinner with a woman not his wife at a restaurant in Pawnee. His nephew H came in and saw his uncle with the woman. <u>Both uncle and nephew were greatly embarrassed</u>. Later when #H was asked whether he had seen his uncle in Pawnee, he denied that he had. He even tried to deny he had been in Pawnee at all.

That an individual had considerable influence with his parent's sibling is indicated by our informant's statement that a man whose wife was leaving him might ask his wife's nephew to talk to her, to persuade her to reconsider. For this service, the man would give his wife's nephew a horse.

---

[50] Dorsey, 1904, p. 103.

[51] #A said this could be either brother's or sister's son.

Spouse of Parent's Sibling~Spouse's Sibling's Child

These relationships all fall under the respect category and in the case of the cross-sexual relationships, i.e., male ego and his mother's brother's wife and father's brother's wife and female ego and her mother's sister's husband and father's sister's husband, behavior was of a near-avoidance nature. Spier secured similar information: "Neither a man nor a woman could talk much to their parents-in-law or the brothers or sisters of these parents-in-law, nor to the <u>wife's or husband's nephews and nieces.</u>"[52]

Once upon the mere mention of the relationship between a man and his uncle's wife, a seventy-year old male ~~informant~~ volunteered: "That's just same" as the behavior between a man and his mother-in-law. To him this meant a disinclination to be in the near company of his mother-in-law or uncle's wife and possibility of speech only when there was absolute need.

Sibling of Parent-in-law~Sibling's Child's Spouse

Relations in this category are also of a respect nature, and the cross-sexual relationships seem to approach near-avoidance.[53]

Parent-in-law~Child-in-law

All ~~informants~~ were agreed that this was a relationship of marked mutual respect. A person would not "talk or do anything out of the way" in the presence of his or her parent-in-law; joking between an individual and his parent-in-law was unthinkable. The cross-sexual relationships, i.e., <u>mother-in-law ~ son-in-law</u> and <u>daughter-in-law ~ father-in-law</u>, approached complete avoidance. These relatives did not talk to each other, except under the most pressing circumstances, and avoided being near each other:

> "Mother-in-law see son-in-law coming, she manage to make some excuse — move so she wouldn't be near son-in-law — same for father-in-law and daughter-in-law."

They were careful not to offend each other in any way. An example of such consideration was the behavior of mother and son-in-law as regards "hinting for a gift." According to Wichita custom, if a person verbally admired some personal belonging of another individual, the latter would immediately give the coveted article to him. A woman, however, was not supposed to express a desire for anything in front of her son-in-law; if she did, even in the very slightest, way, "he would get right up and go get it if he possibly could — would do anything to get it." Mothers-in-law would be particularly careful to keep from saying anything in the presence of their sons-in-law that could possibly be interpreted as hinting for something.

Two illustrations of this type of behavior from the modern situation follow:

> A man living with his wife's people inadvertently made the observation that eggs would certainly go well with some food that was being served. There were no eggs in the house. The next day his mother-in-law made a special trip to town and returned with two dozen

---

[52] Spier, 1924, p. 261, italics our own.
[53] *same.*

eggs. She put them on the table and told her daughter that "he had better eat them all up!"

On another occasion a family was camping at the "Indian Fair" in Anadarko. A man smelled meat broiling over coals in a neighboring camp and commented on the good smell. His son-in-law immediately went "to town without saying a word and returned with two large steaks. The mother-in-law told her husband he would have to eat every bit of them.

In general, if a person wished to communicate with his parent-in-law, he would do so through a third person, usually his spouse. Similarly, a parent-in-law might "talk" to his child-in-law through the latter's spouse, i.e., his child. Talking restrictions were less rigid in the father-in-law~son-in-law and mother-in-law~daughter-in-law, relationships than in the cross-sexual relationships. A man and his father-in-law could and did converse about matters of "business," such as hunting and herding horses, [21] but a man was supposed to let his father-in-law Initiate conversations. This is also illustrated by the instructions given, in a myth, to a man whose wife died and who visited her people in spirit land: "On entering you must get along the best you can and seat yourself somewhere apart from your wife, and wait until your wife's father speaks to you. The very first thing he will ask you will be, if you can shoot good.[54] Similarly, some talking between a woman and her mother-in-law was probably permitted and expected.[55]

Besides the taboos against talking, joking, physical proximity, and saying or doing anything of an offending nature, certain other kinds of obligatory behavior characterized the parent-in-law~child-in-law relationship. Among these was a person'" obligation to defend verbally a parent-in-law or child-in-law who was being criticized, teased, or insulted. ~~Informant~~ A told us of how once she said something slightly critical of her husband in front of her foster mother, Aunt Fanny. Then, "Aunt Fanny jumped right in and said 'Don't say that about him'!"

Certain specific services were expected from parents-in-law or children-in-law:

Son-in-law~Parent-in-law. As we have seen above, many of the services which a man rendered his parents-in-law were, in effect, services for the entire household. According to ~~Informant~~ #A, his "biggest job was looking after horses," for the Wichitas believed horses had to be watered three times a day, at morning, noon, and night. A man would also take game he had killed to his mother-in-law. Occasionally a man who thought well of his son-in-law might pass on to him possessions, ceremonial knowledge, or political office as illustrated in the tale of an old chief:[56]

He said to the chiefs: "Head warriors, and all you leaders, I tell you what I want done. Since I am getting old and am not able to remain always as your head chief, I will now appoint my son-in-law to be your head chief hereafter, and I will remain as a common man hereafter. My son-in-law is yet a young man and he will be a good head chief and a

---

[54] Dorsey, 1904, p. 302.

[55] This statement is conjectural, we have no direct statements from our ~~informants~~ concerning the amount of talking in this particular relationship. However, in the summer of 1948, while talking to #A of a present day case in which a couple were living with the man's mother, we asked about the possibility of the talking tabu there. #A said that the talking restriction was observed by these people: "...if #M (the young woman) wanted the old lady to do something, she told her husband, who then told the old lady."

[56] Dorsey, 1904, pp. 111-112.

good leader in all things." This was all the head chief had to say.

Son-in-law~Mother-in-law. - A woman would prepare special dishes for her son-in-law as a gesture of her respect attitude toward him. Also, if he returned from a successful war party, she would give things away in his honor.

Daughter-in-law~Mother-in-law. - A woman was expected to help her husband's mother and sister cultivate their crops and work for the family in any way she could. A common way for a woman to demonstrate her respect for her mother-in-law was to prepare some food, most often a large pot of corn dumplings or a pan of corn bread, and take it to her mother-in-law. The latter would "think it was a grand thing, an honor, for the woman to do that" and would give her daughter-in-law presents in return. A woman would also sometimes take a bundle of wood she had cut to her mother-in-law, and again the older woman and others of the husband's family would be pleased at the gesture.

A woman's mother-in-law was supposed to be present and ready to help during the woman's confinement at child birth. She assisted in making the cradle for the new-born child. She also served at other life crises: if her son should die, she and her female relatives looked after her son's wife and at the end of the mourning period would hold a ceremony in which they "would turn her loose." Of course, if a woman did not behave with proper decorum after her husband's death, this ceremony might not be held.

A girl's mother-in-law and her sister-in-law administered to the girl at the time of her husband's return from the warpath. These relatives would take the girl down to the creek and give her a medicated bath and then dress her in a clean, new outfit and give her fine gifts. They honored her for behaving as she should while her husband was warring against the enemy, that is, for living a secluded life away from all dancing and gaiety and other men.

Great-Grandparent~Great-Grandchild

This relationship could be considered a special variant of that between parent's sibling and sibling's child, and, like the latter, was one of respect. Great-grandparents were called big father or big mother; great-grandchildren were called children. Because of the greatly disparate ages, most behavior seems to have been that of aiding in child care on the part of the great-grandmother, and the exhibition by great-grandparents of pride and satisfaction at having great-grandchildren of either sex. [22]

Friend~Friend:

A special type of sibling relationship was that between two friends of the same sex. The formation of such a bond was much more common between two men than between two women. Dorsey's ~~informant~~ interpolated an ideal behavioral pattern for such friendship in myth:[57]

Once upon a time there were two young men who had grown up together and were of the same age. In their early days they were playmates, and the older they grew the better they liked each other. When they became grown, they went with war-parties like other men. They then became real friends, for they had made an agreement that each should

---

[57] Same, p. 300.

share the home of the other. They offered their homes to each other's people and they lived as one family, simply because they were fast friends. By their agreement they were both to die at the sametime. If one of them was killed in battle, the other was to die, so that both should die at the same time, instead of one having to mourn for the other. They were always together, and whenever there was a war-party sent out they would go to war. According to Indian custom, any persons making this kind of an agreement were called brothers, and this is the way people regarded them. One of these brothers got married, but that did not have anything to do with their friendship; the other one always remained single.

In those times there was a good many men who world get up a war-party and stay out on the war-path, one party after another. The two brothers would always be in the same party and world never part from one another, on account of the agreement they had made between them. While out on an expedition, whatever they did in time of battle they would be together, and would not leave one another, and if they killed any enemy, the one who did the killing would present the scalp to the other. In those times a scalp was a fine gift, and many men made friends by presenting scalps to one another.

The story of Old-Age Dog illustrates the same pattern operating in a mythological situation.[58]

Chief's-Son began to tell all about his journey; how he was betrayed by the woman; how he had been captured; how she had abused him and danced around him with her man, the chief of the Trickster tribe; how he had been burned to death; how on the next day he had been restored to life by White-Dog, who was now before him; how he had resolved from this time on to call White-Dog his brother, and that they should look upon the dog as his own brother; that the dog was now to be the chief's son; how he was going out in search of the Trickster-Spies who had put him to death; that he was going to take his life and that of the woman; how he and his brother White-Dog were going to send out a war-party against the Trickster-Spies, with whom all who wanted to might go.

~~Informant~~ #A had the following to say about the friend-friend relationship:

When two men is on scouting trip and both happen to run on to same victim. Them two, after that, whatever was done both had a hand in it. Them two is true friends for life. Them two had stronger tie than brothers (or) blood kin. They act kind of special friends — always together, work together, inseparable, more than what a brother would be. Brothers can argue, friends can't. Brothers can disagree, it natural. But, them two who have cemented their friendship in war — what one says is law to other one. Pretty near same what one owns, other owns, (But they) don't take advantage of each other. I have heard that if one of them had a wife that other wanted, he give her up to him.

Concerning the terminology for friend, #A volunteered:

Another word takes in whole business. Men used to bunch up, ten or twelve or more,

---

[58] *same*, p. 158.

and go on scouting trips. There's something that binds them together, $\tilde{r}a\bullet'wa\bullet'\tilde{r}^?$ means friend when there's more than two — among men. Old man can use when he sees another old man an' say, 'This here's my $\tilde{r}a\bullet'wa\bullet'r\tilde{r}^?$ or my friend.'

#E's father and another man were "warfare partners" and were considered to be brothers. There is a possibility that they had been "distant brothers" before they became warrior friends, but following formation of the war partnership the relationship became highly intensified. Once while on a scouting trip, the two were subjected to danger from white soldiers and the friend "made medicine with his shield," causing a large rain storm to hide them from the soldiers. Later the friend taught E's father how to make rain.

People considered friends as brothers. As Dorsey's ~~informant~~ indicates, kinship behavior and terms were extended on the basis of this relationship to both families so that parents of a <u>friend</u> became <u>father</u> and <u>mother</u> and his siblings became <u>brother</u> and <u>sister</u>. ~~Informant~~ #A was most positive that incest taboos also were extended and that marriage of a man to his friend's sister was unthinkable.

Behavior between friends seems to have been of the respect variety, another discrepancy between behavior and terminology since other brothers could be joked. The author and #H are in a joking relationship and have come to use Wichita nicknames for each other which are somewhat salacious. Once when the investigator used the nickname and said, "He's my friend," another older man spoke up, "If you were his friend you wouldn't call him that!" Other ~~informants~~ cite examples of men defending their friends when stories are told about the latter by saying such things as, "Don't say that, he's a straight man. He wouldn't do anything wrong." This behavior is quite similar to that of uncles and nephews when defending the reputation of one another.

Women also made special friends, though this may have been a later development among the Wichita. ~~Informant~~ #A says that [23] they were "not as close friends as men .... now women have special friends among other tribes, especially among Comanche. They're called $ha\bullet c$ (a Comanche word) or if the friends are among the Caddo then they use the Caddo word for friend."

The friend~friend relationship across tribal boundaries was connected with trading practices. A related how her family had "special friends" among the Kiowa and how they looked forward to "annual trade day" when the Kiowa came to the Wichita villages. The Kiowas brought dried buffalo meat and pounded mesquite beans, which were traded to the Wichita for corn, beans, squash, and melons. Women carried on the trade and exchanges were between individuals in the friend relationship. Wichitas also had special friends among the Comanche and similar trading practices existed. Friendships, too, were reported with the Pawnee and the Osage.

The Wichita also possessed a ceremony similar to the Pawnee Hako; this was called by a term meaning <u>Baby Dance</u>. A central feature of the ceremony was the dressing of a boy and girl from another tribe in Wichita clothes and ritually adopting them as Kichitas and as children of the person sponsoring the .ceremony. The parents of the adopted children and the sponsor of the ceremony seem to have become ritual friends.

It is not certain that the friend-friend relationship between members of different tribes was thought of as a special variant of the sibling relationship; but in the light of Information given by, and practices of, the middle-aged and older living individuals, it seems highly probable that such was the situation.

Joking Relationships

Brother~Brother

Wichitas extended the brother term to include half-brothers and the children of parent's siblings and the children of anyone when a parent called brother or sister. Thus relatives known in the English system as second, third, or distant cousins were brothers to the Wichita. Behavior, however, was not identical between "blood" brothers and between classificatory brothers.

Real or blood brothers exhibited only a mild joking relationship. "Real brothers can tease each other but don't do it often." One female informant said that "generally the younger brother, tease the older one." The younger might ask the older brother to loan him some arrows and not get them. Then the younger brother would tease the older by saying, "You let Ruth's brother borrow those arrows!" This combined a mild teasing of the brother over his interest in a girl with mild censure at favoring an outsider over one of the family. A male informant said that brothers would tease each other about "just little things; about what I had done and what he hadn't done." Joking between brothers could lack the competitive motive and be just "fun." Sometimes they "joke around, tease about some girl. Boy tickled to death when say flirtin' with girl." Teasing or joking of blood brothers was, as we have said, relatively mild. While one could mention the other's interest in a girl, it was not considered proper to describe or to elaborate on a brother's escapades for the amusement of others.

Real brothers had duties beyond joking with one another. The oldest brother was responsible for much of his younger brothers' education, teaching then such skills as riding and shooting the bow and arrow.[59] Brothers cooperated in herding the family horses, a boy's job. The oldest brothers had disciplinary duties to the younger; this was most often verbal and consisted of advice as to what was right and wrong, administered when the younger had done something considered mildly antisocial. For repeated offenses, such as not minding the mother, the older brother could "switch" the younger. If behavior was repeatedly bad then the parents could tell the older brother to impose the more harsh punishments, such as throwing the boy in the water or sticking a knife in his legs. This last seems to have been quite rare; harsher punishments were most often threatened or administered by some older non-relative, at the bidding of the parents.

Real brothers could borrow each other's property almost at will. Our oldest male informant said, "I had Indian saddle ...... young brother everlasting borrow that to ride horses!" In turn this man would borrow leggings and moccasins from his older brothers. There was a definite feeling that real brothers were close and that they should share and cooperate with each other. Brothers were not completely equal in status however, since the oldest was to a great extent the disciplinarian of the family. This fact seems to correlate with the very mild form of joking characterizing the brothers relationship. Discipline ordinarily is not consistent with familiarity. [24]

Male cousins of varying degrees of relationship were also called "brother." These included "first cousins" in the English system and anyone on ego's generation to whom there was a remembered relationship. Often the connecting line of relationship was not known thoroughly but the proper term would be deduced from terms used by the parents. Thus, "I call him brother because my father called his father brother." An intense joking relationship existed between these more distant brothers and was often of a strong sexual nature and of the practical joke type. This kind of behavior is greatly in force at the present date. Several examples of such behavior follow:

---

[59] One male informant's older brother taught him how to ride a buffalo horse during one of the last hunts conducted by the Wichita.

#H and #N are "brothers" though the actual blood connection is not known to them. Once while attending a meeting N gave H a small piece of chocolate laxative. H thought it was plain candy and said, "Aren't you my brother? Why are you so stingy?" Then N gave him another piece of candy and again was chided for being stingy. Finally N gave H all the laxative. "It really made him sick!" N and other joking relatives of H think this story is extremely amusing.

#O and #E are "brothers" though in the English system they are distant cousins. On one occasion the investigator was talking with a group which included these two men. E told the investigator to call #O *so•'diwa•'c* which was a manner of teasing the latter and got a large laugh from the group. When the investigator asked what the word meant E said:

"I'll tell you, I was sleeping up at #O's arbor the other night. You know how a horse, when it pull hard, lets go sometimes? Well, I was awake and O and his wife were lying in bed. All of a sudden O let go with one. It made the bed springs go down and touch the ground. O's wife woke up and made a noise '*whiiiiiii*'. Then she said, 'Must be some mosquitoes around here!'"

This story illustrated the meaning of *so•'diwa•'c* ("big voiced" with flatus understood). This highly exaggerated story told at the expense of a "brother" caused much amusement. #O himself obviously enjoyed the story and did not deny it had happened. On another occasion in a similar gathering, #B teased #O by telling the following story:

Once I was wandering around. It was night, I got lost. Finally I came to a house on a hill and yelled, 'I'm lost, come help me!' The door opened and a woman came out and took me by the arm. She squeezed my arm, I like it. I sort of squeeze back. I said, 'I'm a poor Indian, I'm lost.' She took me in the house and when she looked at me, she threw my arm away and said, 'I thought you was #O!' She mistook my voice for O's, white woman too. He's a real Kidia'.[60]

This story, which may or may not have been true, was told as good-natured teasing over O's sexual escapades. The latter made no effort to deny it and was obviously pleased when the story was told.

The more distant brothers were expected to joke and tease each other whenever they met. Such behavior to them was evidence of good fasting, and contrary behavior would have bean interpreted as evidence of dislike, a feeling that relatives should not exhibit. In addition, such brothers were supposed to cooperate; they were relatives and should work together for the beat interests of the family. If an individual should do something contrary to such interests, a brother could publically censure him for it. At a tribal meeting in 1949, #C rather harshly criticized #P for blocking the use of some money available for the Wichitas at the agency. #C said, "I can say this because he's my brother." #P made no reply and showed no emotion. This sort of behavior is obviously related to that exhibited by the boy who teased (censured) his older brother for loaning his arrows to a girl's brother.

---

[60] A "sheik" or "sport". Such individuals used to ride horse-back and sing with girls at night.

Brother~Sister

This relationship seems quite similar to that of brother-brother. Real sisters and any female relative of one's own generation were called sisters. Real sisters and brothers were in a mild joking relationship while classificatory sisters and brothers engaged in moderate joking. Our oldest female ~~informant~~ said, "A boy could tease his own sister, but didn't much." With more distant sisters the joking was more pronounced. Our oldest male ~~informant~~ said, "A boy could tease his girl cousin (sister) about another boy. He would notice things that she do and say, 'I saw you noticin' that boy!" The sister could retaliate by teasing her brother about his interest in a girl. Such behavior was expected behavior and when done made the recipient "feel good."

While the brother-sister relationship was, and is, thought of as one of joking, other duties involving discipline and mutual obligations appear to have been at least equally important. Our oldest male ~~informant~~ said:

Sometimes girls just won't mind nothin', want to use own head! Then brother (real) takes board (a little heavier than a shingle) and gives 'em good boardin'! He can use a switch, too.

This same man said of his own younger sisters:

If don't mind mother, they been thinking they don't have to mind, then I get after then. Tell then to mind mother, not to argue around! [25]

Our oldest female ~~informant~~ told a story of a drunken night of terror, in the Wichita village of the 1870's, which included a man's whipping his sister.

She saw he was getting drunk and hid it (whiskey) on him. He asked her where it was and she wouldn't tell. He started whipping her. His brother-in-law came by and hog-tied him.[61] That man loved his sisters tool That one thing Wichitas had a rule about! Nobody supposed to interfere with brother and his sisters. Sisters supposed t o do what brother said. Outsider wasn't supposed to interfere - was bad to do so!

A brother's authority over his sister was also manifested in connection with the girl's marriage. Wichita marriages mere arranged between families and a brother could exert much influence in the choice of his sister's spouse. Dorsey's ~~informant~~ said:[62]

Occasionally a man might wish to marry a woman who had a brother, and who had been separated from her first husband by death, in which case, the suitor went to the brother and asked him if he might have his sister, taking with him a present, such as a robe or a bow and quiver full of arrows, on his pony.

The following two excerpts from the mythology indicate that a man could also play the major role

---

[61] This was highly atypical of behavior between brothers-in-law. The woman's husband was doing something very un-Wichita in physically disciplining a brother-in-law. Even verbal criticism ordinarily would have been considered highly insulting. Insanity, including drunkenness, in the Indians' conception, and witchcraft activity were the two factors which negated ordinary rules of behavior.

[62] Dorsey, 1904, p. 10.

in a previously unmarried sister's marriage:[63]

> These were times when young men would ask the chief's son if he could let them marry, his sister.

> The people came to the chief's place, and some of the leading men asked him why he had called the people together. The chief replied that since some one had favored the people by restoring the lives of their warriors and had killed their enemy, he wanted to appoint that one head chief over him; that he wanted them to build for that one a new dwelling placer that it was only right that some of the men who had been at the dangerous place should offer their sister to the man who had restored their lives.

In reference to marriage and the brother's duties to his sister, our oldest ~~informant~~ said:

> Some cases girls wouldn't put up with parents' choice. Then, usually has beau picked out. Had to be punished for that! Sometimes it work, sometimes not. Sometimes she leave home and go to other relatives. Oldest brother one to correct his sisters, Girls marry young, generally to older man. Sometimes girl don't want to marry that old man and run away from home. Brother has to whip her. Sometimes the girl wins out, sometimes they force her anyway.

The same ~~informant~~ also said:

> Even if brother was younger than sister, she supposed to do as he said. A brother didn't punish or talk to his sister just to be mean. If he had reason, sister supposed to mind. Specially if brother older, the mother and father couldn't stop him, couldn't say nothing.

Occasionally the situation was somewhat reversed: "If a sister was a lot older than her brother, then she could get after him if he tried to be bossy." Our older male ~~informant~~ also said, "Sometimes older sister switch or board younger brothers when they don't mind nothin'."

Brothers and sisters had the right to censure each other's actions. This was often exercised by an older brother when he lectured or physically disciplined a sister. A sister, on the other hand, could criticize a brother. Our oldest male ~~informant~~ told us that once his father, a chief, hit him with his hand and that then the chief's half-sister lectured to her brother thus; "You whip kids, they run off, afraid to come back, go to other relatives!" Physical punishment of a child by a father, particularly a chief, was anti-social behavior.

At a tribal meeting in Anadarko in 1949, a woman stood up and reproved a man for actions which she considered contrary to the tribal good. At the end of her talk she said, "I can say this, he's my brother." The man who was criticized received it with complete silence and no show of emotion.

Brothers and sisters also had mutual obligations which did not fall under categories of joking or discipline. They were supposed to be considerate and helpful to each other and to have a strong bond between them. A man was a protector of his sister's reputation. He did this by telling her the proper way to act, and implemented talk with physical discipline if necessary. Also if "some young man hadn't been trained right — no parents — (he) might make remarks about a girl. Girl's brother settle with that man! He tell man to stop it." The inference here was that the

---

[63] *same*, pp. 234, 256.

offender was shamed by the girl's brother and not manhandled. But, ~~Informant~~ #A says that when a certain well known chief severely beat his wife, the people thought it-was disgraceful and said, "It's a good thing she didn't have a brother, he would have killed him for that." [26]

A man seems always to have been welcome at his sister's house. Our oldest ~~informant~~ said, "When man and woman split up — man often go to live with sister." Our oldest male ~~informant~~ was raised by his father's sister and his father lived at the latter's home for a while until he remarried. The father's sister had no children of her own, so she asked her brother for one of his and the request was granted. Our eldest female ~~informant~~ was raised by her mother's sister, and she remembered that her mother's brother came to visit often.

Women looked after their brothers. "In olden times one girl was left behind to fix breakfast for father and for brothers when they (other women) went to hoe gardens." A woman would make shirts and moccasins for her brothers. When a man went on the warpath and returned successfully, his sisters and other female relatives were expected to be out singing in his honor. If a sister was bashful and did not do so, she was dragged out by the other women and made to participate. A woman also honored a brother by giving presents to his wife and mother-in-law. A man "who is splitting up with wife would send a sister after things his wife had kept."

A man in turn helped his sisters. A man did not spontaneously give things to his sister. However, she was free to ask tea-things she wanted and would not be refused. Other specific details are lacking, though we were told our eldest male ~~informant~~ helped his younger sisters make moccasins — he brushed yellow paint on them to color them properly. A woman could and did call on her brother to help with her child training problems. A man's lecturing to his niece and nephew on good behavior and the right way to live seems to have been very effective due to the respect relationship between the man and his sister's children.

Wichitas did not seem to worry greatly over possible breaches of incest regulations between brothers and sisters. There was no rule against their being alone together. Although boys and girls tended to separate at early ages and young boys in a family slept together in one bed and young girls in another, occasionally young siblings of opposite sexes slept together. Our oldest male ~~informant~~ slept with an older sister (cousin) who was about seven years older than he. However, he said, "Have to be small brother to sleep with sister."

Sister~Sister

Sisters were thought of as joking relatives though joking behavior between real sisters was very mild. Sisters could tease each other but "not so much as brothers" could. As with brothers, generally the younger teased the older, and about interest in members of the opposite sex.

Sisters were supposed to be close; "they didn't fuss among themselves." In the old days sisters stayed together, even after marriage. Once, when we asked about inheritance of land, our oldest ~~informant~~ said that when the "mother died, the daughters take over" and that the oldest one had charge. Sisters were expected to cooperate in obtaining wood and water for the household, in cooking and cleaning, and in working the fields. With the practice of sororal polygyny, sisters shared a husband. In one case of sororal polygyny, a man's first wife asked her husband to take her younger sister as a second wife and he did so.

With classificatory sisters the cooperation motive also was evident. Particularly at planting time, at harvest, or at a house-building, female relatives, including distant sisters, assembled to aid in the tasks. Such sisters also teased each otter about men and apparently more extensively than did real sisters.

Grandparent~Grandchild

This relationship, between real or classificatory grandparents and their grandchildren was and is considered to be one of "rough" joking. When a grandchild was born, the grandparents were teased by their joking relatives about the new arrival. If it was a boy, the new grandmother was teased about getting a new husband and the new grandfather about losing his wife. If the child was a girl, then the joking was reversed; the grandfather was teased about his new wife and what was going to happen to the poor old woman who had been his wife, and the grandmother was teased about being thrown away for another woman. When grandchildren were old enough to talk, they could learn to refer jokingly to the grandparent of the opposite sex as husband or wife. Grandparent and grandchild of the same sex called each other by forms meaning my rival; they were theoretically rivals for the grandparent's spouse and perhaps later for the grandchild's spouse. #E said:

> At the time of a young man's marriage a grandmother would act like she was going to get mad, and she would say, "If you and that girl get married, she and me going to fight; If she whips me she win you. If she whip me, I say 'He belong you; you took my man away from me.'" [27]

There is no evidence that such fights actually took place.

Teasing or joking between grandparents and grandchildren was in the spirit of fun. Our oldest male informant, #B, said of his "grandfather" (actually grandfather's brother), "He won't get mad, he's tickled to death, he liked it!" Most teasing seems to have concerned hypothetical sexual activity. #B said that he would "Tease grandfather about a woman or something like that." In return his grandfather would twit #B about looking at girls. The sane individual said of his grandmother, "She all time joke around. She say, I think you fix to love that woman over there'." Teasing about sexual matters seems to have been an informal method of teaching the "facts of life." In response to the question of how Wichitas learned about sexual matters, our oldest female informant responded "Grandmother always joking with grandchildren, both boys and girls. They learn from that, just tease them. Don't seem like there was anything old people wouldn't tell children."

Joking was not only about sexual activity, but also about anatomical characteristics. One older Wichita woman has a name meaning "Dirty Crotch Woman." When we inquired how one would get a name like that, our informant replied, "When somebody has a name like that, you can be sure that a grandmother or grandfather gave it. If an aunt gave it, it wouldn't be like that. Grandparents and grandchildren tease each other like that; the name just stuck." During the summer of 1949, while the investigator was working with some Wichitas, he noted a grandfather and grandson teasing each other about the size of each other's penis. For the rest of the afternoon the grandson called his grandfather "Chief Pumphandle."

Joking also could be about non-sexual matters. #B teased his grandfather about falling off a horse and was teased in return about missing the morning bath in the creek. In the summer of 1949 during the butchering of a yearling at a ceremony, a young man told the following story about his grandfather:

You should have seen him butcher. Once he came home drunk and decided to go out and butcher. Pretty soon he came running in holding his hand. He cut his finger off. There it was on the ground with the rest of the meat.

The grandfather smiled and laughed and said, "Yeah, I wanted to use it with the rest of the meat, but they wouldn't let me."

Joking of a corrective or censuring nature was practiced. This stemmed largely from the grandmother and seems to have been particularly directed toward a granddaughter. Wichitas were ideally supposed to be even-tempered and considerate. However, the ideal was not fully expected of women, and older women could be quite aggressive verbally. Our eldest informant said, "Two women have to be quarrelsome to get into word fight. If only one quarrelsome, the other just listen, do nothing. Then, old grandmother (of quiet one) hear about it and say, 'Why didn't you let me know about it, I talk back to her!'" Grandmothers were privileged to correct their grandchildren. B's grandmother corrected him when he made too much noise about the house, when he stole watermelons, when he stayed away from home too long, and when he brought puppies into the house. This woman even punished #B on a number of occasions by throwing him in the creek. Informant #A says, "When a girl begin to get about nine or ten years old, they kind of act silly. Grandmother sure get after her! Talk to her and tell her to be modest."

When a girl was married and had a baby of her own, her grandmother not only helped greatly with its care but often told the woman how and when things should be done. If the baby should cry and the mother was slow in answering, the grandmother would reprimand her. A says, "If (they) hear child cry, (they) don't let it cry! Oh! It made them sick to hear child cry! If mother isn't quick enough, grandmother tell (the) mother to go to child." Or, if a woman nursed a child too long, her grandmother would censure her for welcoming the interruptions to get out of working. A says, "grandmother can do this, she can tease, mother can't." Grandmothers would also berate granddaughters and their spouses when unweaned babies got sick; such sickness, as indicated above, was attributed to sexual intercourse, which was not supposed to be practiced until a baby was weaned. Such corrective joking could also be used by grandfathers, as when B's grandfather teased him about missing a bath in the creek. This type of joking seems to parallel that of the censuring kind permitted between brothers and sisters.

Information concerning disciplinary functions of grandparents is conflicting. All Informants agree that verbal corrections, though largely in a joking vein, were made by grandparents. Concerning actual physical measures, our two oldest informants are in disagreement. A says, "Grandfather and grandmother could scold, that's all." #B's grandfather reportedly inflicted knife and water punishments, though only very mildly, while his grandmother also threw him in the water and occasionally spanked him. The latter statement seems at variance with the pattern as stated by most Wichitas and these individuals appear to have been extreme deviants. [28] #B once said of his grandmother, "She cranky, guess all grandmothers are." Our other informants felt that the harsher punishments should not be administered by grandparents, or even by any relative.

Grandparents also helped look out for the education and welfare of their grandchildren. Grandfathers would teach boys how to make and shoot bows and arrows; tell them stories of hunting, war, and tribal lore; and in general were informally responsible for much of a boy's education. A grandfather could also advise that it was time to change a boy's name. Grandmothers, in addition to assisting in small child care, looked after the welfare of their older grandchildren.

"One old woman went to one of the chiefs and cried and pleaded and begged so hard not to send her granddaughter to school. Her mother (had) died and grandmother had to raise her — couldn't stand losing her! That woman is living today, never went to school!" Little girls were called *wiร̃?i•'s* but when they reached ten or eleven years of age the grandmothers would say, "Why call her that? I saw her looking at the boys!" This combined teasing and social recognition of the girl's new age-status. Grandparents helped in the formal name-changing ceremonies, either by suggesting it was time to do so, or frequently by putting up the necessary feast themselves. In later days, from about 1885 on, grandmothers often gave grandchildren, both boys and girls, their formal adult names by announcing the new names publicly.

Sister's Husband~Wife's Brother

A sister's husband, male speaking, was called <u>male relative-in-law</u> or by name while a wife's brother was called only by name. This was, and is, a highly patterned joking relationship. No specific information, beyond statements that such relatives could tease each other "hard", was obtained concerning the earlier culture. However, again, illustrations can be drawn from the present day behavior of a number of older Wichita men who are brothers-in-law in this fashion (although the connecting relative in some cases is a distant sister). #C, #F, and #H are three such men. #C and #H invariably call #F by his "uncle's" name; the "uncle" is reported to have been a witch and to have died of a venereal disease. #C and #F often call #H by the name of his "uncle" who was shot as a witch. #F and #H tease #C by calling him by the name of an older female relative who is also said to have been a powerful witch. On one occasion #F teased #H by telling a story about purported sexual behavior of a living "uncle" of #H. #Q, who is also a brother-in-law of #H, teased him with a tale of a romantic escapade of the same "uncle." H teased F back by telling a story about the latter's nephew's supposed excessive interest in women.

Joking here appears to follow a pattern of teasing about each other's respect relatives. By mentioning the name of a respect relative who was well-known to have done some reprehensible deed, or by telling a story which places such a relative in a sexual context, one can tease a brother-in-law. The person who is teased does not get angry, but tries to hush the story up and to defend his relative by saying, "Don't say that, he's a good man!" This often is followed by teasing the teaser with a story about the latter's respect relatives. Joking in these situations does not appear to utilize incidents in the sex life of the person being teased, although an individual will obviously greatly enjoy and appreciate such stories when told by someone else about a brother-in-law.

Husband's sister~Brother's wife

A brother's wife, female speaking, was called female-relative-in-law, or by name, while a husband's 'sister was called only by name. This was also, and is, a patterned jolting relationship. We have only general statements concerning this relationship: individuals could tease each other, though we can cite no specific instances. In former days there also appear to have been mutual obligations other than those of a joking nature. These two women were supposed to help each other in their work, such as hoeing in the gardens and carrying wood. ~~Informant~~ #A says, "She (a man's wife) help his mother and sisters cultivate their crops. She just works for family anyway she could. The young women get together and cut wood. The wife take hers to in-laws' home." A husband's sister looks after her brother's wife; and helps take care of her brother's wife when he is out on a raid. No examples of 'witch-joking', as between brothers-in-law, was recorded for this relationship.

Brother's wife~Husband's brother

Two brothers, even classificatory brothers, refer to each other's wife as our wife. Similarly other people can ask the whereabouts of a man's brother's wife by saying, "Where is your wife?" People will also ask a woman about her husband's brother by [29] saying, "Where is your husband?" This correlates with the former practice of the levirate. Lesser[64]1 reports that brothers could have sexual intercourse with each other's wives even for a life-time. In the modem situation, three cases of brothers sharing wives were recorded. Mores of "white" American culture apparently have influenced the Wichita on this point, since our oldest ~~informant~~ denied that such a practice had ever existed. In the mythology several references to "fraternal polyandry"[65]' occur, such as in the tale of The Seven Brothers and the Woman:[66]

> The woman told Big-Belly-Boy that where there were people, man and woman became husband and wife. Big-Belly-Boy told his brothers of this, saying that people ought to increase in number, and so in the night, the oldest brother did the same as the young boy had done, and he told the rest of his brothers about it. Altogether, the woman had seven men to whom she was married.

This relationship is one of "hard" joking. One illustration will suffice. #O and #H are distant "brothers", so H is a husband's brother of #O's wife. In 1949 a handgame broke up early because #H as "dance chief" wished to go home to bed. Other people wanted to keep on playing. O's wife finally told H, "You're too old; you quit that sexual intercourse!"[67]"

Wife's Sister~Sister's Husband

A wife's sister could often become a second wife, either through the practice of sororal polygyny or through the operation of the sororate at the death of the first wife. This correlates with the terminology in that people spoke of a man's wife's sister as your wife and of a woman's sister's husband as your husband. Such terminology was extended to classificatory sisters of a wife and to husbands of classificatory sisters. Vocative terms for husband and wife were seldom, if ever, used.

This relationship also was, and is, one of hard joking. When our oldest ~~informant~~ was a girl, her sister's (cousin's) husband was a "big tease" and was continually joking. One evening he came into the grass house and said, "You'd better look out, that old man (who had been shot as a witch) coming down the draw."' It scared the girl so, that she took her small male cousin and went to be with other kinfolk who were living in the center of the village.

Only one case of sororal polygyny came to our attention among living Wichitas. A man married the elder of two sisters and had one or more children by her. Our ~~informant~~ said that his

---

[64] Lesser, 1930, pp. 99-100.

[65] Murdock points out that use of the tern "fraternal polyandry" is not correct for temporary unions of the type under discussion. 1949, pp. 25-26.

[66] Dorsey, 1904, p. 67.

[67] Original statement was in Wichita. The on-the-spot translation by a bystander has been paraphrased.

"sister-in-law teased him. He teased back. He took it serious and the first thing you know she had a baby by him — then had several more."

In 1949, while the authors were visiting #N and #S, who are husband and wife, S, who was there, made several derogatory remarks about N. We asked whether N and S were related. S said, "No, I wouldn't be related to him!" Then she pointed to #R and said, "She's the one I'm related to, we're sisters." R said, "He's our husband — he needs two wives." Whereupon N retorted that he'd rather have a "better looking one" than S.

Rival~Rival

Two unrelated men married to two sisters called each other <u>my rival</u> and two unrelated women married to two brothers called each other by a similar term. Grandparent and grandchild of the same sex also used the terms. This relationship appears partially to be connected with operation of the sororate and levirate. Since a man's wife's sister was a potential wife and was referred to as wife. Her marriage to another man brought the two men, at least theoretically, into competition for the same woman. In addition, ~~Informant~~ #C pointed out that with the old pattern of matrilocal residence, the two men were also in competition for food and favors around their wives' household. Such Individuals could joke — indeed were supposed to — though not to the extreme to which grandparents and grandchildren did. Also, as sons-in-laws in the household, they were expected to work together in such activities as herding horses.

The term for male rivals is of psychological interest. One older man volunteered that there were two ways to translate it into English. One was as <u>my rival</u> and the other was as <u>like getting another son</u>. This could be interpreted as recognition by the Wichita of the rivalry present in the ambivalent father-son relationship. [30]

Two unrelated women married to two brothers were <u>rivals</u>. This relationship appears to be connected with possible operation of the levirate. A husband's brother was also a potential husband and referred to as <u>husband,</u> so each-woman would in effect be married to a husband of the other. Such women carried on joking of moderate intensity.

Husband~Wife

Wichita spouses were supposed to be even-tempered. Ideally, marriages were arranged between families, at least in the case of "good families". Couples from families of lesser social standing might elope and marry without formal ceremony and exchange of property. Actually, marriages appear to have been quite brittle. Our genealogies indicate that over a majority of individuals had two or more spouses during a lifetime and that separations were frequent. On the other hand, cases of enduring affection also occurred.

In Wichita thinking the husband-wife relationship was a joking one only because it was not one of respect. Actually spouses did a relatively small amount of joking and that was of a mild nature. Spouses were not demonstrative toward each other and this would seem to have precluded hard or even moderate joking'. Wichita men were not supposed to show emotion in public toward their wives; this included most overt expressions of affection and displeasure. The same was ideally true of women, but because they were women, in actuality they could lose their tempers and express displeasure with their husbands.

A full treatment of the husband-wife relationship would include consideration of economic activities of the household. A wife helped the other women in hoeing fields, tanning hides, cooking, preserving food, tending children and other duties; a man hunted and protected the family and tribe. Most ~~informants~~ considered this aspect of the relationship self-evident so that little information of this nature was volunteered. The following excerpt from the tale of "Trouble Among the Chief's Children" illustrates the ideal division of labor as well as the fact that the social status of the wife was partially a reflection of that of her husband:[68]

> Here they lived the woman fixing up the place, building their grass-lodge and shed to dry meat, Man-fond-of-Deer-Meat doing all the hunting. The woman remained at home by herself, for there was no sign of any people living near them. She sometimes thought that hers was the kind of a man she wanted, one who would make a living, so that she would never be hungry, instead of having a man going out on the war-path and becoming a famous woman, the wife of a warrior. They lived here a good long while, the woman remaining at home, the man going out hunting every day. They always had plenty of meat, and the woman raised corn, so that they had plenty to eat.

Sexual behavior between spouses was one area of life on which we had little opportunity for and almost no success in gathering data. There is present a decided reluctance to verbalize on this subject. From the tremendous amount of sexual joking going on between certain relatives and the manner in which respect relatives almost completely overlook sex, one gathers that there is something almost of a "forbidden fruit" nature in sexual relations. Although this could be the result of influence of white American values, there is high probability that it was true of the time before intensive white contact. Spouses theoretically owed each other marital fidelity, though in practice a tendency toward the "double standard" existed. A respectable woman, if alone in a house when an unrelated man stopped by, would take off immediately for the home of some kinfolk. Women in such a situation could not "trust" a man. Such behavior is strong inferential evidence for a philandering pattern among men. Other evidence indicates men seem to have been excused their deviations from the ideal if their outside activity was carried on in relative secrecy.

Much of our information on marital affairs, though not all, stresses difficulties which sometimes arose between spouses. According to ~~Informant~~ #A:

> Girls were married off young, about fourteen years; this helped to keep them from running around. Older man pick a certain girl, young girl. Sometimes man quit his family to marry young girl — pretty mean thing! Girls married young, but men were middle-aged lots of time. (Then) husband wouldn't let her run around with young people. Only chance young bride have to see young people was 'festival time'.

A also says, "If couple have family, never supposed to separate. Before they have kids, they separate a lot. His people mistreat her people, some disagreement between families." Sometimes a younger man would run off with another man's wife. Then the action taken depended on the families concerned.

> "A man whose wife is stolen go to home of other man, take anything he want, horse or anything, can't stop him. Take that and relinquish rights to wife. The Comanches would cut off a woman's nose who ran away with another man (but) the Wichitas wouldn't abuse a woman. The affair was between two men."

---

[68] Dorsey, 1904, p. 235.

However, sometimes if "man heard another man was stealing out with his wife, (he would) beat her and disgrace her and then turn her [31] out. It was pretty hard on man losing his wife, especially if he was man of distinction — couldn't do anything and keep respect of people." A chief once severely beat his wife after she ran off with another man. The people "sure did ridicule him — him being a chief was very disgraceful for him to act like that. He used to have influence over Wichita, but after that he didn't, people say, 'He was like a dog!'"

#A reports:

If a couple splits up, he goes away, takes little individual belongings; shield, bow and arrows, quiver, best suit of clothes, (for dancing and ceremonies), skunk blanket (stroud with white stripe), leggings, bone breast-plate. In old days you could tell when a couple split up — Shield have to be outside tipi (or grass house) on west side, on stand. When man left he took his shield, stand and all.

Separated couple rarely go back together again. If wife told her husband to leave and he really didn't want to, he would leave, but give his wife's nephew a horse to talk to his wife to take him back. If husband one that caused separation (by running after another woman) and he start to leave, she (wife) wouldn't let him have none of things back.[69] That's the way they did long time ago. He (husband) might send his sister to get things." (This might or might not be successful.)

As mentioned above, our genealogies and the extensive data on marital difficulties indicate that the marriage bond was of a brittle nature. Conflicting obligations to one's blood kin and one's in-laws could create stress and in the end one's blood relatives were more important. To counter this, the Wichita seem to have developed highly rigid patterns for dealing with in-laws. If these patterns were adhered to there was no overt friction. Of course, birth of children tended to cement the relationship of a Wichita couple and their families. However, another factor tending to make for brittleness of the marriage bond was the philosophy of how a man should behave and of the nature of women. Men should not show emotion over women. As ~~Informant~~ #E said, "Daddy told me no use beating woman, they won't tell what they done. They's plenty womens, get another one."

Residence after marriage was ideally matrilocal. If, however, through ill-fortune a girl was an orphan, or nearly so, she might go to live in her husband's, home. Concerning matrilocal residence and problems of newly-weds. ~~Informant~~ #A once volunteered, "Lots of times husband, if his parents is living, wouldn't quit home. (He would) live back and forth." On another occasion she related:

The young man stay with his family. He would take only a few things to wife's place after marriage. Husband only stay evenings in wife's place. Maybe he would go over

---

[69] One of the older living Wichita men has a name which means "He just got his things there yet." ~~Informant~~ #B says this name came from a situation like the following: "When man got married and left his wife, went home. People say, 'He's not living there anymore, he just got his stuff over there.'" {Cf Newcomb noted above (p54, p79) that husbands moved out during a wife's menstruating and when giving birth.}

late in evening (night) for matrimonial business and leave early in morning when it was still dark.

Then, as the couple got older, and after they "have family of own," the man went to live permanently with his wife.

Wichita spouses slept in the same bed in a grass house or in a tipi. Before the couple had children they might share a tipi with other members of the family during the winter camping period. After they had children, the woman got a tipi of her own, which was made by her mother and mother-in-law. If a younger sister of the girl married another man, then the older sister and husband could leave and establish a home of their own — "younger sister is old enough to look after old people."

When a man's wife was ready to have a child, "husband don't stay there, has to go home! There are two things Wichita afraid of about a woman — monthly period and confinement." Although informants said there was no confinement of women to a menstrual hut or tipi at the time of menstruation, husband and wife slept apart because of the fear men had of menstrual blood. Even today, some women are reported to keep separate food dishes for use at this time. Dorsey's informant reported:[70]

> During the period of the woman's monthly sickness the husband did not sleep under the same roof. She did not prepare food for him; otherwise he would suffer illness. Having recovered, the woman went at once to the river and bathed, and her relations with him were resumed as before.

Husband and wives could tease each other moderately. They could also censure one another's actions. Such criticism could be made only by those in a joking relationships ideally it was unthinkable for respect relatives to notice, or admit, deviations from ideal behavior, but parents and the mother's brother might do so in the case of younger children. H says that his wife teases him if he does not call his nephews and nieces by the right terms, and he retaliates when she has similar lapses of memory. Joking between spouses appears to have had little sexual connotation, though privately such joking may have been practiced. Of course, joking between a man and his wife's sisters and between a man and his brother's wives did get roughly sexual in nature. [32]

By no means was all behavior between spouses of a frictional category. Men could show some affection for their wives. #A said, "Man, if thoughtful of wife, cut meat for her. Woman didn't have hunting knives. They have big butcher knives." A man would cut a chunk of meat several times, "not all the way through, but almost," so that his wife could bite off pieces easily. "Old Man Kiowa (a Wichita chief) do that for his wife many times. Other woman say, 'My man don't think enough of me to cut my meat for me!'"

#A also said she had heard from the old people:

> When a young married couple was moving around — camping during the winter, every young man have his favorite horse. When they are ready to break camp and move to another place, a young husband would curry his horse, clean it, fix it up pretty, saddle it up. His wife would be packin' up in another family — he would be with his family and she with hers. The husband send his younger brother or his younger sister to take horse

---

[70] Dorsey, 1904, p. 11.

down to wife to ride. When group is moving the young wife ride that horse. When they pitch camp again, she send horse back to her husband — by younger sister.

Wives, of course, could also demonstrate their affection for their husbands. This was best done by being a good housekeeper, gardener and cook, and by keeping her husband neat and looking well. Also, when her husband was out on a raiding party, a woman dressed in old clothes and shunned all festivities. After the return of the war party, her husband's folks world wash and dress her in new clothes because she had shown the proper respect for her husband and their son.

Some folktales tell of the regard and affection of men for their wives. One such tale is the wide-spread one of a man mourning faithfully at the grave of a dead wife. Finally his wife cones back on the condition that he cannot sleep with her or look at other women. Later she hears that two girls are after him, gets jealous, and goes back to her family in the village in the sky. Another relates of how a Wichita woman was captured by the Osages. Her husband hears where she is and the detailed circumstances of her life. He disguises and acts like an Osage, kills her Osage husband, steals many horses, and returns with his wife to the Wichita village. Other folktales include situations involving unfaithful spouses.[71] [33]

RESPECT AND JOKING: PROBLEMS OF CLASSIFICATION AND THEORETICAL CONSIDERATION

Wichita joking and respect behavior categories are summarized in Table II. In this list we have elaborated upon the Wichitas' oral two-fold classification by subdividing the joking category into plain joking and obligatory joking, by subdividing the respect category into ordinary respect and avoidance type respect,[72] and by adding a category of relationships which involve features of both joking and respect.

Table II
Classification of Respect and Joking Relationships

Avoidance	Respect
Mother-in-law~Son-in-law	Parent's sibling~Sibling's child
Parent's sibling's spouse of opposite sex~Ego	Father-in-law~Son-in-law
Parent-in-law's sibling of the opposite sex~Ego	Mother-in-law~Daughter-in-law
Father-in-law~Daughter-in-law	Parent's sibling's spouse of same sex~Ego
	Parent-in-law's sibling of the same sex~Ego
	Friend~Friend
	Parent~Child

Joking tempered with Respect	Joking	Obligatory Joking
Brother~Brother (real)	Brother~Sister (classificatory)	Brother-in-law~Sister-in-law
Brother~Sister (real)	Sister~Sister (classificatory)	Brother-in-law~Brother-in-law
Sister~Sister (real)	Sister-in-law~Sister-in-law	
Husband~Wife (real)	Brother~Brother (classificatory)	

---

[71] Dorsey, 1904, pp. 155, 161.

[72] As indicated in the section on kinship behavior, avoidance among the Wichitas at the 1850-75 period was not as complete as it was in tribes such as the Cheyenne.

Grandparent~Grandchild

The four relationships with features of avoidance represent an extreme of respect behavior for the Wichita — one characterized by a minimum of social' Interaction and an intense attitude of respect. The emotional intensity of the mother-in-law~son-in-law relationship is closely followed by that between ego and a parent's sibling's spouse of the opposite sex. Our data on the behavior between ego and his parent-in-law's sibling of the opposite sex are meager but seem to indicate that it is close to that of the last relationship. The father-in-law~daughter-in-law relationship appears to have the least intensity of the four and here the fact that normally there is little possibility of face to face contact apparently is a related factor.

Concerning the next category, that of plain respect, there are a number of uncertainties in scaling the relationships. All relatives involved here are due respect behavior but the kind of behavior varies with the relationship. It would be quibbling to say on the basis of our evidence which of these respect relationships is of the greatest intensity. If they are ranked on the basis of intensity of interaction, then the parent-child, friend-friend, father-in-law~son-in-law, and mother's brother~sister's son seem most important. But difficulty of scaling is encountered here; frequency of interaction changes with age, so that in childhood the parent~child relationship would be ranked first while in adulthood the father-in-law~son-in-law relationship might be. As for emotional intensity, the relationships between friends and between parent's sibling and sibling's child appear to generate the strongest personal feelings; emotional Intensity of the latter is often forcefully verbalized while that of the former is seldom talked about. In the category of plain respect, there is no particular gradation away from avoidance toward joking, or vice versa, except that one avoids talking about sex with all but a friend. [34]

In the case of the relationships permitting joking, there seems to be a gradation along a scale from mild joking to that of an obligatory nature. That this is so is not surprising; joking behavior is mostly verbal as contrasted with respect behavior, which may or nay not be verbalized. Thus it is much easier to judge the intensity of joking behavior. The relationships between real siblings and between husband and wife have very mild joking and marked overtones of respect. While the details of respect and joking differ some between these sets of relatives, similarities as to the relative amount of joking allowed and the nature of the joking indicate that they belong in the sane category.

The relationships between classificatory siblings permit quite rough joking, often of a sexual nature. Particularly, distant brothers tease each other hard, and the compulsiveness sometimes exhibited indicates this relationship may be closer to the obligatory joking type than other sibling relationships.

Sisters-in-law tease each other much as distant sisters do. Grandparents and grandchildren can joke in very rough terms and do so at most opportunities; though their joking at times is quits mild, at other times it appears almost compulsive in nature, suggesting that this category edges on that of obligatory joking.

The two obligatory joking relationships present another problem of grading: which, if either, is the more intense? That between brother-in-law and sister-in-law permits rough sexual joking and even occasional sexual liberties, the latter not being obligatory. That between brothers-in-law takes the form of teasing each other about reprehensible behavior of respect relatives — such as witchcraft — but forbids mention of each other's sexual activity. By American-European standards, the coarse sexual joking with occasional liberties would appear more extreme. Our feeling, however, is that since a Wichita's emotional involvement with his respected uncles and nephews is of such great intensity, and since witchcraft is the most socially disapproved activity a Wichita can practice, joking between brothers-in-law is the more intense.

The Wichitas' own explanations of joking and respect behavior are largely in terms of ideal patterns, of how aunts and nephews or grandfathers and grandchildren should behave — though they partially realize that there is some variance in actual behavior, that some individuals, for example, are known as "hard teasers" while on the other extreme are people who do not take teasing graciously. Wichitas are satisfied with this first level of analysis, they are content with explaining joking and respect behavior in-moral terms: certain relatives are treated thus and so because that is the right way and to do otherwise would be wrong.

In anthropological literature there are a number of theoretical conceptualizations which aim at a better understanding of respect and joking behavior. We have chosen here to consider the Wichita data in the light of those of Eggan and Murdock.

Eggan sees respect and joking as alternative mechanisms for regulating social conflicts.[73] There are certain weak points in a social structure at which there are possibilities of strain, and conflicts arising at these points tend to be resolved in terns of respect and joking. This approach is inclusive as compared to that of Murdock, who says that no single hypothesis can explain the behavior associated with the various respect and joking relationships.

Eggan's hypothesis is that the intensity of the joking~respect relationship is correlated with the inevitableness of the conflict. On the basis of his Cheyenne and Arapaho material, he thus defines four joking and respect categories:[74]

1. Respect relationship — where there is some possibility of conflict and the social necessity for avoiding it.

2. Mild joking relationship — where there is some possibility of conflict but no particular necessity for avoiding it.

3. Avoidance relationship — where the conflict situation is inevitable, where there is the social necessity for avoiding it and where generation differences are present.

4. Obligatory joking relationship — where the conflict situation is inevitable, where there is the social necessity of avoiding it, but where no difference of generation is involved.

In the following paragraphs, we shall briefly examine the Wichita respect and joking relationships and indicate to what extent Eggan's definitions seem to apply.

The Wichita respect relationships, not including those of the "avoidance type," are: parent~child, parent's sibling~sibling's child, father-in-law~son-in-law, mother-in-law~daughter-in-law, ego~parent's sibling's spouse of the same sex as ego, parent-in-law's sibling of opposite sex~ego, and friend~friend. These all fit Eggan's "respect" category in that in each of them some [35] possibility of conflict is involved; but the other criterion, "the social necessity for avoiding conflict," is not always apparent.

The situation involved in the Wichita parent-child relationship is much the same as that found in the Cheyenne-Arapaho relationship, being the ambivalent one so prevalent throughout the world. The parents are providers of food and other physical necessities of their children as well as givers of affection; but they are also their children's main educators in the Wichita way of life, and as such must exercise authority and exact obedience. Like the Cheyenne-Arapaho parents,

---

[73] Eggan, 1937b, p. 80.
[74] *same*, p. 79.

they are the chief persons responsible for "transmitting the social heritage"[75] and there is thus "a social necessity for avoiding conflict."

The parent's siblings are in a position similar to that of the parents. Their attitude toward their nephews and nieces is one of fondness and concern for their welfare, but at the same time it is their duty to help educate them and verbally discipline the young folk. Since they are not the primary figures in the individual's socialization, however, there would at first seen to be "no particular social necessity" for avoiding conflict. This by definition should place them in Eggans' "mild joking" relationship; however, joking of any kind is unthought of between an individual and his parent's sibling. It should be pointed out, perhaps, that in former times (if our hypothesis about former matrilineality for the Wichita is correct) the mother's brother probably was a very important person in a boy's education) in such a case it was certainly essential that conflict be avoided. The present respect attitude toward all uncles may be an extension of this earlier attitude toward the mother's brother. Also, it should be remembered that the brother's sister, though not the primary figure in her sister's children's rearing, nevertheless was a very important assistant to the mother and, indeed, a veritable "second mother." Furthermore, with ego and his mother's sister and mother's brother (until his marriage) being members of the same household, conflict would have to be minimized for the efficient running of the household.

This latter explanation does not hold in the case of the father's sister, or the father's brother, who lived-in different households, but, again, perhaps the respect attitude was an extension of the behavior toward mother's sister and mother's brother. A further reason for avoiding conflict with any of the parent's siblings could be the possibility of adoption by them. The Wichitas have been markedly declining in population due to wars and plagues for at least 150 years and considerable family reorganization must have been necessary. Since any parent's sibling was a potential foster parent, a necessity for avoiding conflict could be said to have existed.

In the case of the father-in-law~son-in-law relationship there is possibility of conflict but probably not an inevitability of such. The son-in-law is an outsider to his wife's family, yet must live in that household and cooperate with his father-in-law in various economic activities. Since the father is not the dominant ruling figure in the household, the possibility of conflict between father-in-law and son-in-law is not as great as in the mother-in-law~son-in-law relationship. Furthermore, there is the tempering factor of their being of the same sex. Again the avoidance of conflict is necessary for the functioning of the household.

With regard to mother-in-law and daughter-in-law, there is some possibility of conflict between the husband~wife relationship and mother~son relationship.[76] Since the mother-in-law and daughter-in-law live in different households, however, there is not as great a necessity for avoiding conflict as in the case of mother-in-law and son-in-law. There is still a great desirability for avoiding conflict, though, for strife between mother-in-law and daughter-in-law could have serious repercussions on the husband~wife relationship.

Our data concerning the relationships between ego and a parent's sibling's spouse of the same sex arid between ego and a parent-in-law's sibling of the same sex are very minimal and not suitable for testing Eggan's hypothesis. The only apparent sources of conflict are; in the first ease, the parent's sibling's spouse is an outsider to ego's family and, by virtue of that, in an ambivalent position, and, in the second case, ego is the outsider. Because of generational differences, respect behavior, rather than joking, is chosen to minimize the conflict.

---

[75] *same*, p. 76.

[76] After he is married, the son still has a strong attachment to his mother's household and returns frequently to visit.

The friend-friend respect behavior is difficult to interpret since it runs somewhat counter to the conception of their being siblings. A possible source of conflict lies in their opposing loyalties to their families and to each other. We can only conjecture as to why respect, and not joking, behavior characterized the relationship. Since Wichita joking has elements of criticism, there is at least a slight possibility of offending with the joking itself. Friends are in a very close, emotional bond, and [36] any such possibility of conflict is avoided by emphasizing respect behavior. This does not explain the necessity for avoiding conflict} beyond the social need for cooperation and intense loyalty on dangerous war-parties and hunts, there undoubtedly is some deeper psychological explanation for the relationship.

The Wichita mother-in-law~son-in-law relationship fits Eggan's "avoidance" category very well. The son-in-law is placed in an ambivalent position: he is an outsider to his wife's household but also an important member economically of the household. Then there is the rivalry between the husband~wife and mother~daughter relationship: the mother, as head of the household, retains authority over her daughter and this clashes with the husband's interests. Conflict is inevitable. But as with the Cheyenne-Arapaho, this conflict must be avoided in order that the household may operate smoothly and efficiently – hence, "avoidance", or as Chapple and Coon would term it, an abnormally low "rate of interaction."[77]

The father-in-law~daughter-in-law relationship is one of avoidance, but Eggan's criteria for "avoidance" are not altogether present here. There is tension between the father-son and husband-wife relationships, and avoidance of conflict is desirable in order that the marital union may not be endangered. However, since father-in-law and daughter-in-law are not occupants of the same household, opportunities for conflict would not be as numerous as in the mother-in-law~son-in-law case and the necessity for avoiding conflict not as great.

The avoidance-type behavior between ego and a parent's sibling's spouse of the opposite sex, and between ego and a parent-in-law's sibling of the opposite sex (from ego), appear to be of a highly similar nature, but to be somewhat difficult to explain by Eggan's hypothesis. Some relationships in this category have strong, if not inevitable chances of conflict. Between a man and his mother's brother's wife and a woman and her husband's uncle there could be said to exist a conflict of interest. A man would owe certain obligations to both his wife and nephew; from the nephew's standpoint his uncle's wife is similar to a mother-in-law. A man's wife and his maternal uncle would also be relatives in conflict: a man would owe duties to both wife and uncle. Prom the woman's viewpoint, her husband's uncle is much like a father-in-law. Similar arguments could be set forth for other relatives in these categories. In applying Eggan's formulation, we have difficulty at times in deciding whether there is inevitable conflict or merely a possibility of such. Also, the necessity for avoiding conflict is not always apparent.

The Wichita siblings relationships (brother~sister, brother~brother, sister~sister) in the Indian's conception are all of a mild joking nature. These relationships meet partially, but not altogether, the definition of Eggan's "mild joking" category. There is possibility of conflict involved in all. Siblings of the same sex are equivalent in the kinship system; there is no distinction between them or between their offspring. At the same time, however, the older sister and brother do have authority over the other siblings. As for brother and sister — they have mutual affection and respect for each other, but the brother has very definite disciplinarian rights over his sister and both have the privilege of correcting and criticizing each other. Since all are members of the same household for a while — and sisters often stay together even after marriage — and all must

---

[77] Chapple and Coon describe the conflict as one due to "overlapping of the parental and male sets." Chapple and Coon, 1942, p. 314.

cooperate for the economic welfare of the household, an avoidance of conflict would seem almost mandatory. Thus, while the first part of Eggan's definition of mild joking is fulfilled, there is some question about the second part, "no particular necessity for avoiding conflict."

It should be observed, however, that the social necessity diminishes as the sibling relationship becomes more distant and the siblings are no longer members of the same household. Correspondingly, joking increases and the respect factor disappears. Mildest joking is that between real brother and sister and this amounts only to very innocuous twitting; in this relationship there is an appreciable respect factor because of the sex difference. It could be that, though in Indian thinking the real siblings relationships are of a joking type, that actually and objectively they belong more in a joking-respect category.[78]

Obligatory joking behavior between siblings-in-law is of two kinds. That between a sister-in-law and brother-in-law can be very rough and often consists of verbal obscenities (from an American value orientation) and sexual play; while that between brothers-in-law is most intense but avoids references to each other's sex activity. These relationships fit Eggan's definition of obligatory joking. Here we have the inevitable conflict between the strong siblings relationships, on the one hand, and the husband~wife [37] relationship on the other. The siblings relationships, as we have seen, are ones of great affection and solidarity, characterized, too, by the privilege of mutual criticism and the duty on the part of the older sibling of instructing and disciplining the younger? The conflict of a sibling's rights and privileges with a spouse's interests is obvious.

In these siblings-in-law relationships, the necessity for avoiding conflict is quite strong. Because of matrilocal residence and the occasional practice of "fraternal polyandry" these two kinds of siblings-in-law can be found in one household. The need for economic cooperation between these relatives means that conflict must be kept at a minimum. Also, the importance of a man's wife's brother to the man's son in the old days made avoidance of conflict between the two brothers-in-law necessary.

Eggan's analysis does not bring out the qualitative difference between the two kinds of siblings-in-law joking. Elsewhere, however, Eggan indicates that the "behavior of siblings-in-law of the opposite sex centers around obscene jests and sexual play, in addition to ordinary joking."[79] The apparent correlation between rough, sexual obligatory joking and a relationship 'in which the individuals are potential spouses or sex partners has been noted by a number of scholars and most lately by Murdock.[80]

The grandparent-grandchild relationship, on the whole, is one of ordinary joking, albeit it is often couched in very rough terms and sometimes is of a compulsive nature. However, individuals in this relationship often do not joke, but sit quietly together or discuss everyday subjects in an unemotional way. Although grandparents and grandchildren belong to different generations, the Wichita alternation of generations can be said to "equalize" them in a sense. At the same time, however, because of the child-rearing duties of grandparents, and because they occasionally inflict punishment, there is a good possibility of conflict in the relationship. Since the grandparent's role in the life of his grandchild is an important one, there can be said to be a desirability approaching necessity of avoiding conflict. In view of this and the sometimes compulsive nature of joking, the grandparent~grandchild relationship does not fall squarely in the mild joking category but edges on obligatory joking.

---

[78] As in the authors' classification, Table II, where real siblings relationships are placed in a special "joking tempered with respect" category.

[79] Eggan, 1937b, p. 79.

[80] Murdock, 1949, p. 276.

The difference in behavior between grandparents and grandchildren when the latter are young and when they become adults tends to corroborate Eggan's hypothesis. When the grand children are young, there is more likely to be conflict, but when they become adults and socialized, the possibility of conflict lessens. Also the social necessity to avoid conflict may be said to have been removed since the training is now complete. Thus there develops a milder type of joking relationship after the children have settled down into adult life.

The Wichita kinship data, on the whole, support Eggan's hypothesis concerning respect and joking behavior very well. This should be expected since Wichita kinship behavior patterns are quite similar to those of the Cheyenne and Arapaho. A more exacting test might be found in the analysis of data from tribes with more divergent behavior, such as the Lipan Apache, who have a generational system but joking between some members of adjacent generations[81] and the Osage, among whom all relationships are reported to be of the respect category.[82] Difficulties encountered in the brief Wichita testing were due to a common problem of the social sciences, inexactness of terminology: the question arose as to precisely what constituted "inevitability" and "social necessity for avoiding conflict." Concerning the latter, an argument could be put forth for a near-necessity, at least, of avoiding conflict in all Wichita relationships. In Wichita thinking, having many relatives was a good thing and a person who did not was poor, with few people to help him. Cooperation of relatives at times of crisis was needed and thus keeping on good terms with one's relatives was very important.

Murdock feels that no single hypothesis can explain the behavior associated with all respect and joking relationships. Rather, he says "different explanations are probable for different relatives."[83] He tends, however, to see the incest tabu as a common factor to the behavior patterns associated with several relationships, though he also allows for other factors.

So far as the mother-in-law avoidance is concerned, Murdock apparently explains this restriction entirely in terms of the incest tabu. He says; "The sex taboo between man and mother-in-law probably thus derives from an exaggeration of the same forces [38] which have everywhere produced ultra-family incest taboos, and the widespread prevalence of mother-in-law avoidance is readily understandable as a social device to prevent violations." This explanation of mother-in-law avoidance at first impression seems to differ from that of Eggan, and yet it appears to the writers that the two theories are not incompatible; as a matter of fact, both are at least partially anticipated in Freudian theory.[84] Could not the "forces" which Burdock speaks of as producing incest tabu be the sane forces which work generally to minimize disruptive disturbances in the household? So far as the Wichita are concerned, at least, it appears that the mother-in-law tabu can best be interpreted as a means of preventing or resolving several kinds of conflict, including both the disturbance which would develop out of an incestuous relationship and the conflicts of interest involved in the mother-in-law~son-in-law relationship.

Murdock considers the parent~child and sibling~sibling relationships as governed by universal conditions of the nuclear family and that the other relationships are governed by conditions which differ from society to society. He says, for example, that cases of respect or avoidance toward the mother's brother's wife occur mostly in societies in which cross-cousin marriage is the rule and the mother's brother's wife is equated with mother-in-law. Murdock rightly recognizes that this is not true of the Wichita and infers that another explanation would be

---

[81] Opler, 1936.

[82] Nett, 1951.

[83] Murdock, *Op. Cit.*, p. 276.

[84] Freud, 1919.

necessary. We have suggested that the mother's brother's wife is really somewhat like another mother-in-law because of the social structure of the Wichita which includes matrilocal residence. It might be a possibility that another conflict exists in the situation: the maternal uncle~nephew relationship is one of great intensity and demands that one refrain from seeing or hearing anything "bad" about the other after the nephew becomes an adult. This coupled with the Wichita feeling that there is something not right about sexual intercourse may explain the extreme reserve between a man and his uncle's wife, or his nephew's wife. The very proximity of an uncle's or nephew's wife might inevitably make for mental conflict between the ideal of a man who is always "good" and the actuality of one who indulges in sexual intercourse.

Murdock says the distribution of behavior toward father's brother's wife is like that of behavior toward mother.[85] In other words, in most societies father's brother's wife is treated like a mother. Among the Wichita, though, you get the same extreme respect or avoidance treatment of father's brother's wife as of mother's brother's wife. This, we think, is a function of the tendency to equate the mother's brother and father's brother when the system became bilateral.

Murdock, along with other authorities, believes the obligatory joking behavior between siblings-in-law of the opposite sex to be definitely connected with the sororate and levirate.[86] The Wichita, who practiced both of these, are one of the many cases supporting this. Murdock, like Eggan, considers conflict to be at the basis of the sibling-in-law joking relationship. His emphasis is somewhat different, however as he traces the coarse jesting to the frustration resulting from the fact that sex relations between the siblings-in-law are only semi-sanctioned. Eggan, as we have seen stresses the conflict of interest between the different kinship relationships involved. We do not feel that the Wichita data contradict either of these views.

Murdock notes that the relationship between brothers-in-law is frequently one of respect or reserve, particularly characterized by a "marked tendency to avoid mentioning matters of sexual import."[87] He explains the character of the brothers-in-law relationship as stemming from the incest tabu between brother and sister. He says:[88]

> ...with respect to the same woman one of the two men enjoys unrestrained sexual freedom whereas the other must observe one of the strictest of incest taboos. Any allusion to sex by the former is likely to arouse unconscious anxieties in the latter, whereas an allusion by the latter might imply to the former a lack of respect for the woman who unites them or even suggest the possibility of an unpardonable incestuous connection with her.

The Wichita brother-in-law relationship is a joking one but the jesting is of a non-sexual type. Murdock's reason as to why brothers-in-law avoid references to sex might apply in the case of the Wichita relationship, but we would still be without explanation as to why Wichita brothers-in-law joke. For the latter, Eggan's hypothesis must suffice at present. [39]

Joking behavior between grandparent and grandchild, such as found among the Wichita, has a high frequency, according to Murdock's recent study. Murdock's explanation for this is: "Grandparent and grandchild are drawn together by the fact that each can expect from the other an unconscious sympathy for his own dissatisfactions with the intervening relative (that is, the child

---

[85] Murdock, Op. Cit., p. 277.

[86] *same*, p. 281.

[87] *same*, p. 279.

[88] *same*.

of one and the parent of the other, toward whom both have ambivalent feeling)."[89] Murdoch goes on to say: "From this basis of warm congeniality it is an easy step to a mild joking relationship."

The authors have no quarrel with Murdock's theorizing concerning the development of a "warm congeniality" between grandparent and grandchild. We have already indicated the ambivalent quality of the Wichita parent~child relationship; that the warm, affectionate character of the grandparent~grandchild relationship could stem from the very ambivalence of the relations with the connecting relative seems not unplausible. We are not satisfied with Murdock's dismissal of "mild joking" simply as "an easy step" from the "warm congeniality." The question of why permissive joking is often found in the grandparent~grandchild relationship remains essentially unanswered by Murdock. One wonders why the "easy step" is made in a good many cases, but not in others.[90]

The answer may very well be in the presence or absence of the social situation which Eggan theorizes as being correlated with "mild joking" relationships in general: "The possibility of conflict but no particular social necessity for avoiding it." As we have seen above, this theory stands up in the case of the Wichita grandparent~grandchild relationship. This explanation still does not answer the question of why the joking is mostly of a sexual nature. We can turn to Murdock here for a partial answer: He points out that the sexual joking "doubtless provides both (grandparent and grandchild) with some substitute gratification."[91] So far as the Wichita are concerned, we can point out, too, that joking about sex has important educative aspects.

At this point we should like to make some further comments concerning the function of joking and respect on the basis of our experiences with Wichita culture. Such behavior seems deeply involved in total Wichita life; it is not a superficial aspect of their culture. Obviously it is used to resolve conflicts in personal relationships with relatives, but the Wichita carry it further and prefer to resolve conflicts in new relationships, such as with anthropologists, in the familiar patterns. This, of course, is not solely true of the Wichita. In Linton's terminology this behavior is like putting on a suit of ready-made clothes[92] and enables them to solve difficult situations with a minimum of mental effort. When this feature of the culture was understood, our rapport with Wichitas increased immeasurably. Most Wichitas took the joking mode of behavior, and perhaps "naturally" by Wichita values since we were not relatives of the certain kinds that are due respect behavior. The male investigator feels that he is in a respect relationship with only three Wichitas; one elderly woman treats him somewhat like a son, one older man also like a son, and one middle-aged man like a nephew; the rest with whom he has dose relationships treat him with behavior closest to that of a distant sibling, or perhaps a grandson. It appears that our experience, in a way, lends support to Eggan's hypothesis; there is always potential conflict with a white person, and possibilities of conflict seem greater when that person is an anthropologist who remains in extended contact and engages in activity not fully understood by many Wichitas. These conflicts were much lessened when we fitted {them} into Wichita patterns of joking, or occasionally of respect. [41, no 40]

---

[89] Murdock, 1949, p. 278.
[90] For example, see Whitman, 1937, *The Oto*.
[91] Murdock, *Op. Cit.*, p. 278.
[92] Linton, 1945, p. 104.

MODERN KINSHIP TERMINOLOGY

The present day situation is difficult to ascertain and perhaps more difficult to present coherently. While the older terminological system was internally consistent, and the teen-age generation of today uses a near-English system which approaches such consistency, the schedules reported by the great middle-aged group are variable. However, the individual variations and inconsistencies with reference to the "old" and the "new" are not unintelligible and in their totality indicate the direction and some of the manner of change.

For the total kinship study, fourteen complete genealogies and terminologies were collected.[93] Four individuals reported schedules which conform, in so far as they possess the necessary relatives, with what has been presented as the Wichita system of 1850-75. This, as has been pointed out, has the appearance of a stable system in that there are no illogicalities in the terminology. Three individuals of the young English-speaking group have also reported schedules which are completely reciprocal in so far as they go but which differ from the older system. Younger Wichitas, although they may understand Wichita, only rarely use Wichita words in conversing. Other individuals who are in the intervening age groups converse freely in Wichita and use Wichita kinship terms, but can also converse in English and use English kinship terms. The Wichita schedules of the latter individuals show deviations from the older pattern, while their English schedules are very close to those of the younger generation. All these variations of kinship schedules appear best explainable as examples of change from the "older" type toward that used by the younger generation Wichitas. Although this latter type is internally consistent in terminology, it almost certainly is not the end product in the changing Wichita system. It should be pointed out that relatives in the first and second descending generations are almost lacking for teen-age Wichitas and a crucial point is whether children of cousins will be nephew and niece, to conform with the many aunts and uncles of the parental generation.

For clarity of presentation, the system used by younger Wichitas will be considered first. This system is diagrammed in Figure #3. Since younger Wichitas, for the most part, do not speak Wichita, the terms given are the actual terms used by ~~informants~~. The essential features of the system are as follows: Vocatively parents are <u>Daddy</u> and <u>Momma</u>, or <u>Mom</u>; non-vocatively they are <u>my daddy</u> or <u>my father</u> and <u>my mother</u>; vocatively parents' siblings are most often called by name and non-vocatively referred to as <u>my uncle</u> and <u>my aunt</u> (often qualified "by marriage"); grandparents, their siblings, their cousins, and spouses of all are vocatively and non-vocatively-called <u>grandfather</u> and <u>grandmother</u>, depending on sex, or by name; in the third ascending generation relatives are non-vocatively <u>great-grandfather</u> and <u>great-grandmother</u>; in ego's own generation siblings are non-vocatively <u>brother</u> and <u>sister</u> and children of all uncles and aunts are non-vocatively cousin; ego's children are hypothetically son and daughter and children of brothers and sisters are hypothetically <u>nephew</u> and <u>niece</u>. The affinal terms, <u>brother-in-law</u>, <u>sister-in-law</u>, <u>son-in-law</u>, <u>daughter-in-law</u>, <u>mother-in-law</u>, and <u>father-in-law</u> are of conventional American usage. In addition, <u>wife</u> is sometimes used for a wife's sister or a man's brother's wife, and <u>husband</u> for a woman's sister's husband or a husband's brother. The outstanding feature of this system is the wide lateral extension of terms, a characteristic it shares with the older system. This lateral extension is learned from parents and other relatives, who often say such things as, "So and so is your <u>uncle</u>, he's a cousin of your mother", or "So and so is your grandfather, he's a cousin of your grandfather."

---

[93] Numerous partial genealogies and schedules were also collected.

It should be stressed that the English terminology is used by younger Wichitas almost entirely non-vocatively. Only for the parents are the terms often used in direct address, and even they may be called by name. Aunt and uncle may be used vocatively hut individuals report they rarely, if ever, do so. Brothers, sisters, cousins, grandparents and grandchildren, brothers-and sisters-in-law, and even sons- and daughters-in-law are addressed by personal names or by use of nicknames, a very prevalent practice.

The terminological schedules in the Wichita language of the middle group exhibit small variations. However, in many respects they closely resemble the older system. Such features as the wide generational extension of brother, sister, grandparent, and grandchild terms and the alternation of generation feature, according to which relatives of the third ascending generation are big fathers [42]

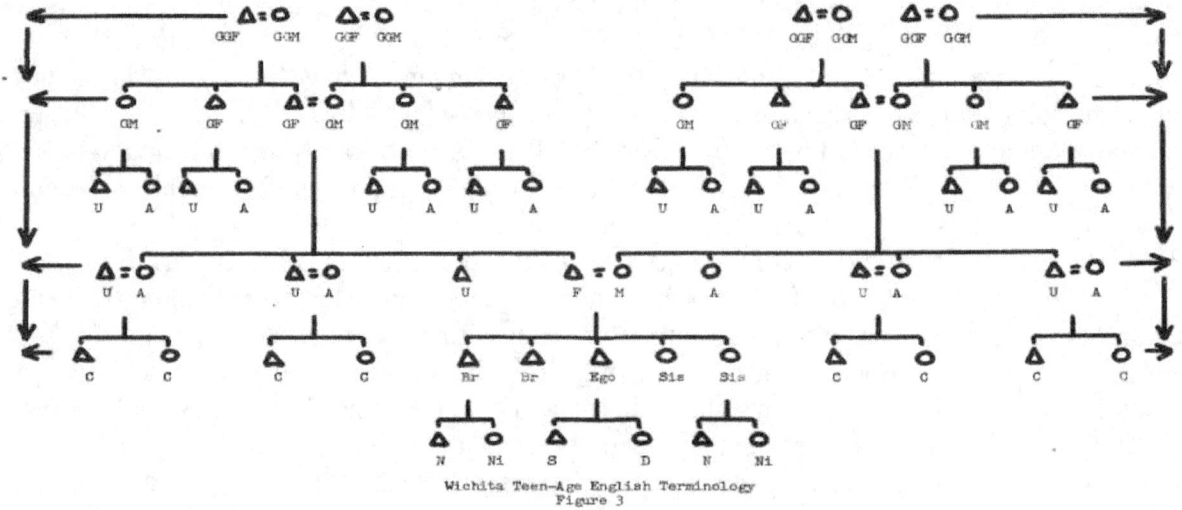

Wichita Teen-Age English Terminology
Figure 3

and relatives of the third descending generation are children, are points of close relationship. Most confusion arises in the treatment of relatives in the parental and first descending generations. In the former a number of variations have been reported:

(1) When a parent has two or more siblings of the same sex, they are called big father and little father or big mother and little mother, or big uncle and little uncle with reference to relative age of each other and not to relative age of the connecting parent as in the old system.

(2) When a parent has siblings, they are called little father and little mother regardless of whether they are older or younger than the parent. Sometimes the older relative age distinction is made correctly for big father and little father but not for aunts who are all classed as little mothers. A common reported reasoning is that little mother is for aunts and big mother is for the great-grandmother.[94] Here there appears to be a case of loan translation based on equating little mother and little father with the English aunt and uncle. (See Figure 4). [43]

---

[94] The Wichita term for great grandmother is ε•'ciε•'siwa'c? or translated "big mother".

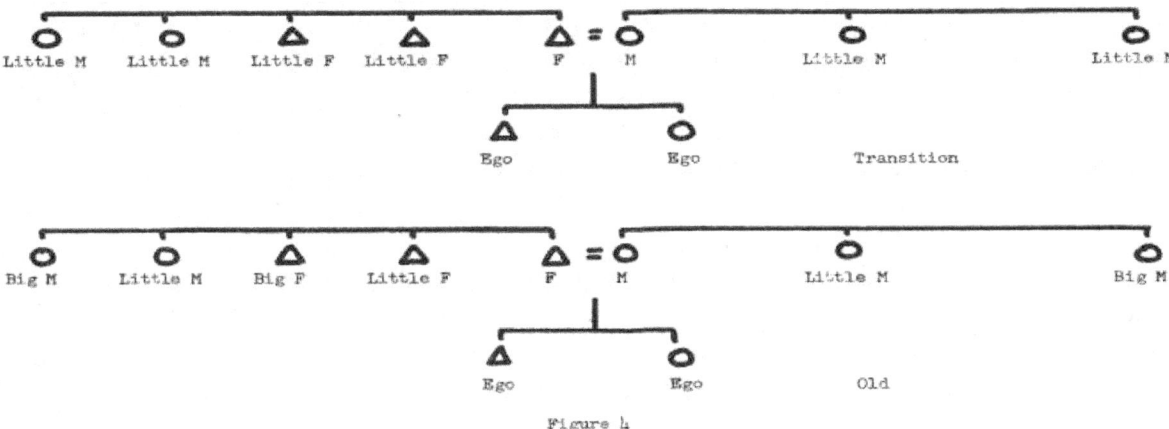

Figure 4

(3) When a father has brothers, they are called the old term for mother's brother. This could be called a loan translation based on the substitution of the mother's brother term for the English uncle. (See Figure #5).

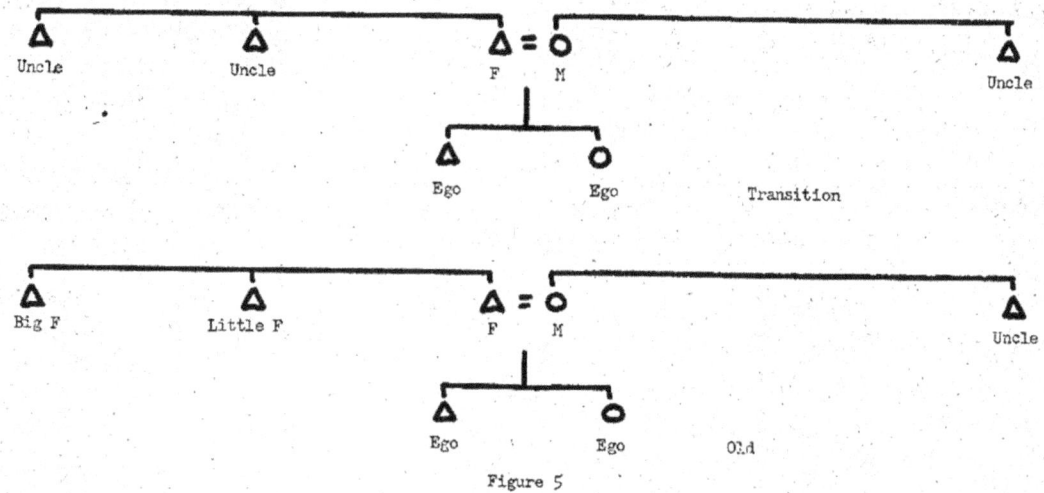

Figure 5

(4) The term little mother is used for spouses of the parent's brothers instead of the older term female-relative-in-law and the terms little father or uncle (mother's brother) are applied to spouses of the parents' sisters instead of the older term male-relative-in-law. All Wichitas, with the exception of those reporting the older system, gave such variations. Again, these variations involve loan translations; the substitution of little mother for the English aunt (by marriage) and of little father or mother's brother for the English uncle (by marriage). (See Figure #6).

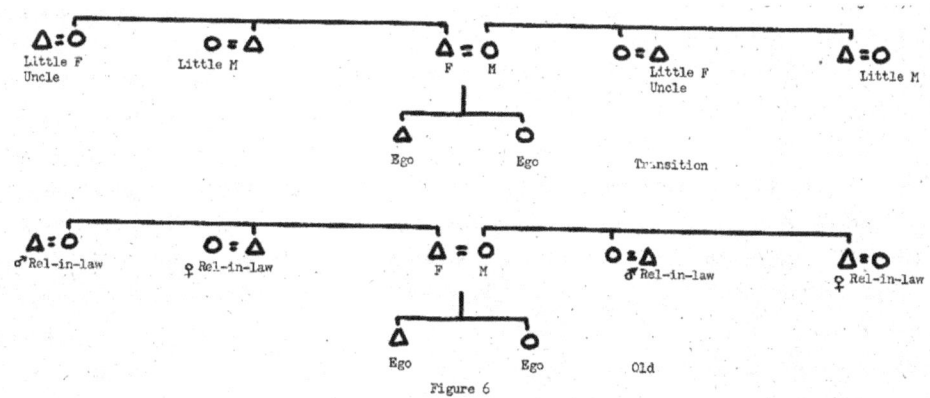

Figure 6

A similar confusion exists in the first descending generation. In the old system a man called his sister's children nephew and niece and his brother's children our children, while a woman called both sister's and brother's children our children. In the modern situation, some men will refer to a brother's children as nephew and niece and some women will refer to a brother's or sister's children by the same terms. This appears to be a loan translation based on the substitution of the older terms for a sister's children, male speaking, for the English nephew and niece. (See Figure #7).

Another obvious loan translation occurs in the occasional use of the older term big grandparent (older sibling of a grandparent) for relatives of the third ascending generation. This is greatly facilitated by translation of the Wichita suffix *wa•c?* as "big" or "great," resulting in great-grandparent. A very similar case is the occasional use of the older term big uncle (older mother's brother) for a male sibling of a grandparent. Here the English great uncle coincides nicely with Wichita big uncle. (See Figure #8). [44]

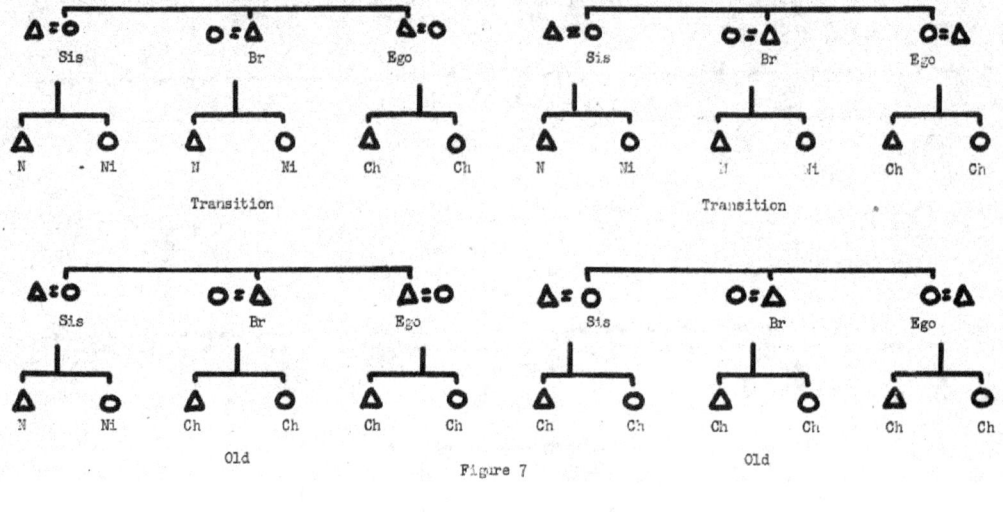

Figure 7

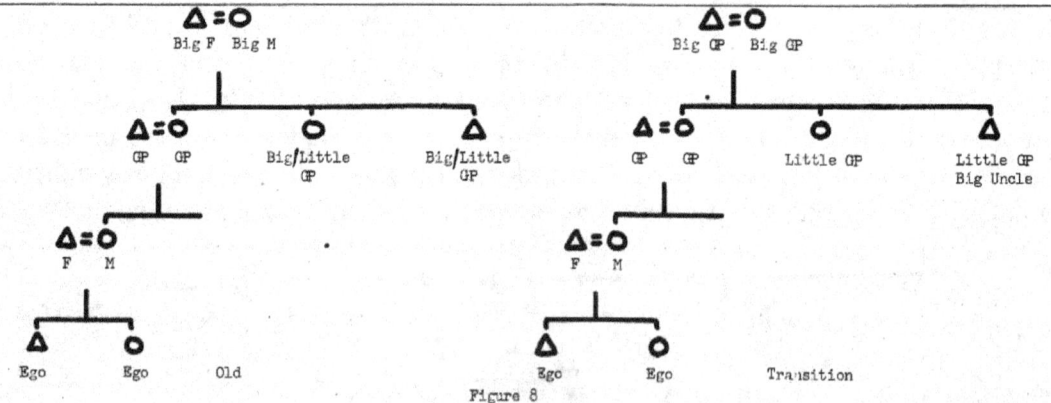

Figure 8

Further change revolves around the use of *ackics?* and *i•ɛ•s•*, the older terms which were used for female relative-in-law and male relative-in-law, respectively. Most Wichitas translate these terms into English as daughter-in-law or sister-in-law and son-in-law or brother-in-law even if they know they were also used for spouses of parent's siblings. Concerning ego's own generation, the following uses of female-relative-in-law and male-relative-in-law by Wichita speakers of the middle generations were noted:

(1) A woman preferring to call her sister's husband <u>male-relative-in-law</u> or <u>brother-in-law</u> instead of husband as in the old system. Some ~~informants~~ reported they could call such individuals, either husband or brother-in-law.

(2) A woman calling her husband's brother <u>male-relative-in-law</u> instead of <u>husband</u> as in the old system.

(3) A woman calling her husband's sister <u>female-relative-in-law</u> or <u>sister-in-law</u> instead of calling her by name or saying <u>my husband's sister</u> as in the old system.

(4) A man preferring to call his brother's wife <u>female-relative-in-law</u> or <u>sister-in-law</u> instead of calling her wife as in the old system. Such a use of female-relative-in-law was present in the "old days" but was considered to be a joke. Today the reverse appears to be true, the use of <u>wife</u> is now a joke.

(5) A man calling his wife's sister <u>female-relative-in-law</u> or <u>sister-in-law</u> instead of <u>wife</u> as in the old system. Here again, both terms were used in the "old days," but whereas the use of <u>wife</u> was not a joke, today it is.

(6) A man calling his wife's brother <u>male-relative-in-law</u> or <u>brother-in-law</u> instead of calling him by name or saying <u>my wife's brother</u> as in the old system. [45]

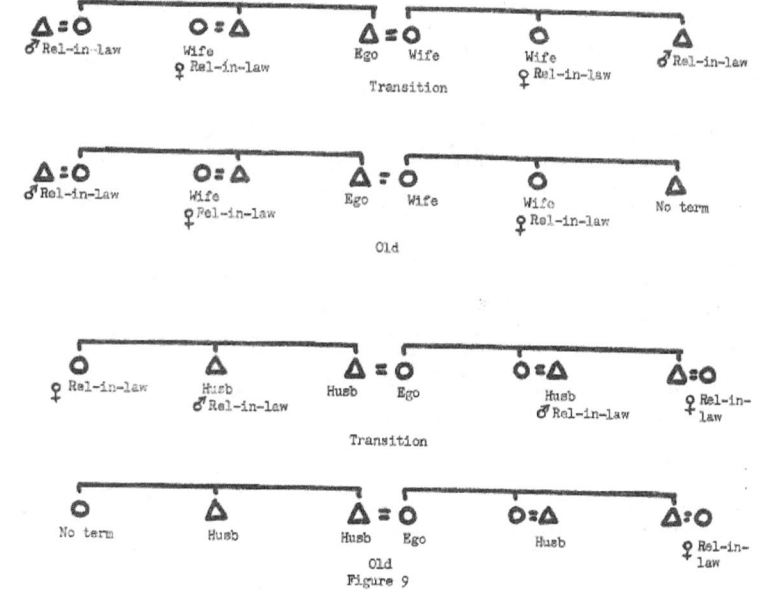

Figure 9

This present use of *ackics?* and *i•ε•s•* for all brothers and sisters of spouses appears to be a loan translation based on the substitution of these terms for the English sister-in-law and brother-in-law. (See Figure #9). However, at the same time, Wichita speakers can still use the same terms for spouses of sons, daughters, nephews, and nieces and translate them as <u>daughter-in-law</u> and <u>son-in-law</u>.

Treatment of the parents-in-law and their siblings is variable but there is a marked tendency to apply the <u>little mother</u> and <u>uncle</u> terms to siblings of the parents-in-law; this is another instance of the loan translation based on equating these Wichita terms with English aunt and uncle. In the illustration below, the ~~informant~~ called her mother-in-law mother Instead of the older Wichita <u>parent-in-law</u>.

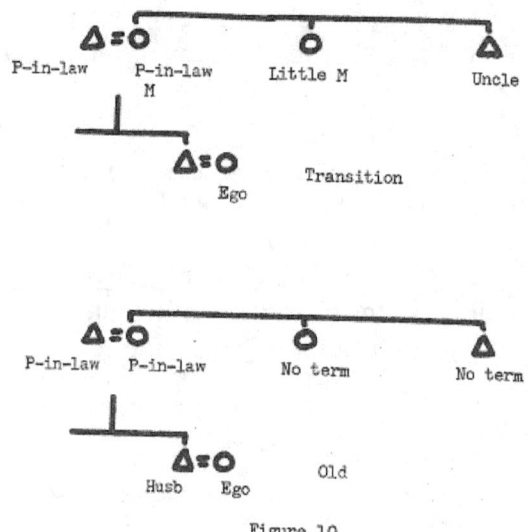

Figure 10

Statement of Classifications

The individual schedules reported by the bilingual middle group of Wichitas would still fall within the MacKenzie Basin Type of Spier[95] since both parallel and cross-cousins are classed as siblings. In Murdock's classification they would be of the Normal Hawaiian Type,[96] since there is Hawaiian cousin terminology, bilateral descent, and bilocal residence, even though matrilocal residence may still have been the ideal. Present during the early days of intense Wichita-American acculturation was a slight tendency toward [46] neo-local residence. This was also true in the "old days" since the elder sister and her family could establish a new home when a younger sister married. However, the hone was almost always near that of her mother or her sister, so the matrilocal theme was still present.

The terminological system of the young English-speaking Wichita would belong to Spier's[97] Eskimo Type since parallel and cross-cousins are classed as cousins and are separated from siblings. In placing it in Murdock's classification there is some difficulty because of the indefiniteness of the residence pattern. It belongs in Murdock's Eskimo type[98] because of bi-lateral descent and Eskimo cousin terminology, but the sub-type might be classed by one as Bi-Eskimo, by another as Normal-Eskimo, and others might not like to choose either. The young Wichitas are just reaching the marriageable age. The information to be desired is whether at marriage they will still live with older kinfolks or will establish new residences. [47]

---

[95] Spier, 1925, pp. 76-77.
[96] Murdock, 1949, pp. 228-9.
[97] Spier, *Op. Cit.*, p. 79.
[98] Murdock, *Op. Cit.*, pp. 226-8.

MODERN KINSHIP BEHAVIOR
Present Social Setting

The present Wichita live primarily north and east of Anadarko, Oklahoma in the Sugar Creek valley. Some individuals live in the vicinity of nearby Ft. Cobb, and others live in the town of Anadarko. A few individuals who are still considered members of the tribe reside in Oklahoma City and Tulsa, Oklahoma; in Wichita, Kansas; and in California. In 1902 Wichitas were each allocated 160 acres of land and the remainder of their reservation was sold to whites. Since that time many allotments-have been sold to whites, other allotments have been divided among heirs, and still others have so many heirs that they cannot be equitably subdivided. Most Wichitas lease their land to whites and many tenants or "renters" live on Indian land. Thus, the population distribution is that of whites and Indians Interspersed over the old Wichita allotment areas.

Modern residence is determined by a number of factors but apparently does not include preference for patrilocal or matrilocal variety; residence can be at the home of either spouse, with relatives of either spouse, or of the neo-local variety. Family composition often is larger than that of the elementary family; two or more such families, related by kinship bonds, ordinarily reside in one house. This is particularly true of houses on old allotments; in town there are many more neo-local families.

Subsistence is gained from garden plots, tended chiefly by women, and by income from leased land, agricultural labor, and miscellaneous odd jobs. Many, particularly men and older women, have much leisure time. Centers of interaction for modem Wichitas are the towns of Gracemont and Anadarko, the Camp Creek community house and dance ground, the Rock Springs Baptist Church, the Wichita Mission, meetings of the Native American Church, and — particularly for the younger generations — the Camp Creek country grade school, Riverside Indian School, and public schools in Gracemont and Anadarko.

There is a tribal organization with elected officers, but attendance at meetings is sparse and there is considerable bickering over what has been done or should be done. The limits of tribal membership appear well marked; there is little trouble in determining who is, or is not, a Wichita. However, there are many factions within the group and these center primarily around religious affiliation. Furthermore, there are divisions within larger factions and the difficulty in planning tribal business is apparent.

Behavior based on kinship ties, is one of the most noticeable aspects of modern Wichita life and appears to be the most important mechanism for maintaining what solidarity there is for the total group. One of our younger informants said, "Wichitas just one big happy family — cousins in all families." Bonds of kinship cut cross the obvious factions: one man is a leading church figure and for a time would not set foot in the Camp Creek area while his wife is a leading figure at Camp Creek, where "old" ceremonies are held; another man is a member of the Native American Church while his wife belongs to the Church of Latter Day Saints. At church a person will speak up in defense of a respect relative who belongs to the Camp Creek faction; and brothers-in-law in opposing factions will joke each other roughly, and with great glee, in what is considered the correct manner.

Similar to the problem of presenting modern terminology, is that of presenting modern behavior, living Wichitas include members of five generations, and behavior ranges from that considered "old-time Wichita" to that of the English speaking high school group. Fortunately for our problem, no really great differences in the kinship behavior of the throe older generations were perceived; and from statements of our oldest informants, such behavior appears to have been very close to that of the Wichitas for the 1850-75 period.

As has been discussed before, older Wichitas classify relatives as to whether they fall into "teasing" or "respect" categories. Even teen-age individuals are well aware of this, but for them the boundaries between the two categories have become somewhat clouded in practice.

Respect Relationships

Parent~Child

This relationship is still one of "respect." Parents and children are not supposed to "tease" or "joke" one another. Parents are very permissive with their children. Small children are nursed apparently on demand[99] and they often are given soft [48] drinks, cold cuts, fried bread, meat, or whatever food takes their fancy. Children from the age of almost three years are allowed to play relatively unsupervised, often for hours at a time if they so desire. At church or at Camp Creek, children run in and out of ceremonies almost at will. However, women scold and verbally threaten their offspring a great deal. Even though some ~~informants~~ say that Wichitas now spank their children, a practice reported to have been learned at Indian schools, we have never witnessed such punishment. We have also never observed fathers scolding their children — an obvious similarity to the reported older pattern. Punishment, though often threatened, appears to be rarely administered and considerable criticism was heard of some individuals who supposedly had been harsh with their children. Older forms of punishment are still threatened; at a New Years Eve celebration in 1919 one mother told her small boy repeatedly to stay away from the drum and dancers' bench; when he failed to do so, she told him that a certain old man would take a knife and cut his leg. This quickly brought about the desired behavior. On another occasion, at a tribal meeting in 1950, an older woman took a pocket knife from her purse, sharpened it and said she was going to cut the same boy, who was climbing on seats in her vicinity. We, however, have no evidence that these punishments are actually administered in the modern situation, though it would be no surprise to find occasional occurrences.

Old-time Wichita cradles are no longer made or used; however, very young children are still swaddled and often sleep with parents. "Indian cradles" made with a blanket, two short sticks, and a rope tied to two trees or other supports are extensively used to rock small children to sleep. Some baby carriages have been noted.

Instruction of children appears somewhat haphazard; children acquire much knowledge informally and just by continual association. "Baby sitters" are rarely, if ever, used. If so, they almost always are close female relatives. Instead, children are taken to dances, meetings, and church services, and thus have much opportunity to learn by continued observation. Children of five or six years and up are expected to help in family activities such as gathering firewood and picking or "chopping" cotton. Much of the instruction is now left to the school systems where, in addition to conventional subjects of English, geography, etc., students may learn cooking and farming techniques and even Indian-lore. Formal teaching by parents, observed or recorded, consists of fathers teaching sons and daughters how to "war dance," parents instructing children as to who their relatives are and how one should behave toward them, and mothers instructing girls in child-care. Probable areas of instruction, though not recorded, are those of cooking techniques for girls, and "cotton chopping" and "snapping bolls" for children of both sexes. There is obviously no longer a need for instruction in horse-herding, warfare practices, hunting, house-building, and

---

[99] One woman of 20 plus years was observed feeding her child by means of a nursing bottle in 1949; but, as a rule children are breast fed.

many other former activities. Men's activities are more affected — though only relatively more so — since horses, hunting, and war were the earlier Wichita man's main concern. ~~Informant~~ #A recognized this when she said of the days of her girlhood, "Their (the men's) business just about played out. There was too much civilization and the hunting grounds (were) restricted." But women still cook, have and care for babies, and do some gardening.

Children are supposed to look after aged parents and frequently do so. When an old person has no living children, this often becomes the duty of grandchildren, or even some more distant relative.

The older relationship of respect is still supposed to exist; parents and children should show respect for the desires of each other. In actuality this is only relatively the case. Women scold and threaten punishment often, and children frequently disobey. At later ages children often cause their parents worry by staying away from home or by minor brushes with the "law." An example of lack of proper respect is that of #T who reports he never calls his father or mother by the Wichita kinship terms, but by their personal names:

"If you call *ta•ta•*, then you have to mind him. If you get older and don't want to mind him, then call him by name. Same rule for mother. If love her, have to do anything she say."[100]

Parent's siblings~Sibling's children

This is still a respect relationship. Middle-aged and younger Wichitas speak up quickly to defense of respect relatives with statements such as, "Don't say that he's a good man!" Teen-age individuals know that they are not supposed to joke with relatives in this category and only occasionally forget this restriction — at least when they are around the older folk; when they do so their elders resent the in-propriety. Parents' siblings may correct their nephews and nieces when there is cause to do so. There is no obligatory [49] usage of the kinship terms; instead personal names are preferred in direct address and the kinship terns appear to be limited to situations in which a third person does not understand the relationship involved. No apparent difference between mother's and father's sisters or between mother's and father's brothers was noted. All are accorded equal respect and all seem to show equal pride in the accomplishments of their nieces and nephews. No distinctive duties, beyond those of mutual respect, defense against slander, and help in time of stress were ascertained.

Examples of behavior in a modern setting, but in line with old patterns, are as follows:

#E's sister's child became very ill and he became very concerned. He got #H, a classificatory brother, and they went off and prayed for the boy — with success.

On the occasion of a program at Rock Springs Baptist Church another uncle had been telling people what his nephew was going to do — "You know how uncles are." Then when the time came for the boy to perform, he could not say anything; then the uncle could not say anything either, he was so shamed.

---

[100] This could easily have been older behavior also. #T's father is apparently the most conservative Wichita alive. #T, though young, knows more of older Wichita culture than many middle-aged ~~informants~~.

An example of conflict arising out of the modem situation follows:

A young man in his early twenties worked for over a year in a bus station in a town near Anadarko. There he said he got used to joking with everybody. When he returned to Anadarko he saw those "old men," his father's brothers, on the street and joked with them. They did not like it, and when he tried to explain why he acted in that manner, "They just couldn't understand."

Also indicative of change in the modem situation is the different behavior at school. There a chronological age-set includes not only <u>cousins</u> but <u>uncles</u> and <u>aunts</u> as well. A teen-age girl volunteered that at school "Whole bunch of kids be kin"(and) not supposed to tease. But, don't take it that way any more — <u>tease anybody at school</u>." Here, the inference is that such behavior is not permitted around Wichita adults.

Parent-in-law~Child-in-law

The behavior associated with this relationship appears to have changed as much or more than that in any other category. Spier, collecting data in 1919, states that communication with parents-in-law was usually carried on through the spouse and that "This taboo is rigorously followed even today."[101] In 1950 this is not the case. We observed one instance of a woman living with her mother-in-law in which the two conversed through the connecting man; and, we suppose, there are a few other similar cases. On the other hand, however, we had one informant, #U, older than the woman keeping the taboo and in some ways more conservative, deny that such a taboo ever existed. ~~Informant~~ #G said there was no mother-in-law avoidance among the Wichitas. She had heard of it among the Sioux, but "Wichitas didn't have it." The same woman in speaking of parents-in-law said that one should "respect them, don't tell them anything in a teasing way." They act in the same way toward ego. "Like if there was a crowd and mother-in-law there, and some one teasing me. She'd turn around and say some good about me." This woman calls her mother-in-law "mother". #G says one also has to respect the siblings of a parent-in-law. In speaking of her husband's mother's sister, #G said, "In Wichita way, she's my aunt."
    #T's mother-in-law is dead but when she was alive he had been told they should not converse. His father-in-law is still living and is called by his "given name, he don't care." However, again #T had been told that in the old days "they didn't talk, unless pertaining to business."
    At a New Years Eve ceremony in 1949, #F appointed four women as waiters to serve food. After they had started the distribution his daughter-in-law got up to help. As she passed her father-in-law she said, "You didn't appoint me a waiter, but I wanted to make sure these dancers got served."
    Although our information is sparse, it appears that reticence to talk to parents-in-law is fast disappearing among present day Wichitas and that the behavior is coning to be like that accorded "uncles" and "aunts," one of a little less rigorous respect than in the old days.

Friend~Friend

This institution exists in the modern situation though it appears to be more prevalent

---

[101] Spier, 1924, p. 261.

between women than between men. Friends are considered by their relatives to be brothers or sisters and relationships are extended on this basis. Boys who grow up together and appear inseparable are thought of as friends and are welcome as siblings in the households of both families. Many friendships, particularly of women, start at government schools and operate across tribal boundaries. The great number of such friendships [50] begun at school seem to have an element in common with old warfare practices: as on war parties, people going to school together leave home and share an experience which is strange and which appears initially dangerous.

The friend-friend mechanism for extension of kinship across tribal boundaries is a most interesting phenomenon. In the old days Wichitas had out-of-tribe friends for trading purposes — particularly among the Kiowa, Comanche, and Pawnee. In the present, the friends relationship serves no such obvious purpose; but as a mechanism for diffusion of kinship practices and leveling of differences in systems, it seems highly significant. An individual becomes aware of different practices in the tribe of his friend and when in the company of "kin" of the friend's tribe, tends to behave in the particular manner acceptable there. One of our Caddo friends saw an old Wichita man on the streets of Anadarko and made a joking remark to him and he returned in kind. After our inquiry, she explained that, in a way, he was a grandfather and among the Wichita grandparents and grandchildren tease each other. This is not true among the Caddo. The Wichita man was a grandfather because one of her kin had established a friend relationship with a Wichita.

Another example of such inter-tribal extension came to our attention when we went to visit #U, a Wichita woman, and took a male Caddo friend with us. We started to introduce the two, but #U interrupted by saying, "I know him, he's my son." #U and the man's mother had been friends at school, so each had taken the other's children as sons and daughters.

Joking Relationships

Sibling~Sibling

The sibling relationship is one of importance to Wichitas today. Large families are common, and for a child whose family lives outside of town, siblings are frequently the only playmates available. The oldest sibling occupies an important position: to this individual much of the supervision of the younger ones is delegated. Siblings can joke with each other, and do so in a mild way. It is also permissible to laugh when someone teases a sibling. One middle-aged informant said that if someone teased her brother about being drunk and being with a woman, she would laugh a little but she would not join in the teasing. An individual is not obligated to laugh at such 'stories about his sibling: we have noted occasions when the sibling of a person present is criticized for having performed some reprovable deed, and the latter to all intents and purposes will ignore the talk and launch into a discourse which in reality is a defense of the accused sibling. In such cases behavior of brothers is full of overtones of respect and is not unlike that of the uncle~nephew relationship.

The siblings relationship is a close one. At gatherings it is common to observe siblings of the same sex sitting together for long periods of time: one does not see siblings of the opposite sex do so because there tends to be a separation of sexes at Wichita gatherings. However, brothers often visit their sisters' homes and even yet may go to live with their sisters during periods of adversity. Siblings should help each other out when there is need. Those who do not follow this are considered to be acting in an abnormal way. Confidence in a sibling is shown by the following story, which was told about a Pawnee by a Wichita, but which was also supposed to be illustrative of Wichita behavior. The incident happened in 1949. The Pawnee said to #F:

#F, you have treated me fine. I have stayed at your arbor. You have fed me well. You know that if you come to Pawnee, I can't do the same for you. I'm not married, I haven't got a wife. But, I've got a sister. When you come to Pawnee, I want you to come to her house. She'll look after you, treat you well.

Cousin~Cousin

This is still an out and out joking relationship. All manner of verbal horse play goes on between cousins and some practical joking. The older generations, of course, consider this a variant of the sibling~sibling relationship and use such terminology in Wichita. The middle-aged groups bridge the gap between the very old and the new since they can also use English cousin terminology. The younger generation, however, seems to consider the cousins relationship separate from that of siblings. Examples of behavior between living cousins of the middle-aged and older groups have already been cited as examples of older patterned behavior. Younger individuals carry on the joking behavior but often phrased in good American idioms. The cousin term is widely extended, and cousins of different degrees of relationship can almost always be observed joking with another at Camp Creek, at church, in town, or at school. Once at church we heard three teen-age girls teasing a young man-in a most persistent fashion. After, this had gone on for some time, one of the girls said, "I'll bet you sure wish you were our uncle, instead of our cousin!" [51]

Grandparent~Grandchild

This relationship is still one of rough joking and also one of indulgence. Grandparents of both sexes obviously show much pride in their grandchildren and greatly enjoy being around them. A common sight today is a grandparent fondling infant grandchildren. Grandparents often take care of children for extended periods of time. #C and his wife kept one grandson for over a year and at present have had another grandson for nearly that long; #V and her husband had her granddaughter for the summers of 1949 and 1950; U took care of her classificatory grandchildren when their mother recently died; #W keeps one of her grandsons permanently even though the child's mother is alive and well and the elementary family structure is otherwise Intact. In the older system it was the "old grandmother's duty" to help take care of children. This appears to be true today; grandmothers are often seen tending the various wants of small children.

As children become older, grandparents — particularly grandfathers — tease them, sometimes very roughly. #X, a girl of about fifteen years, states that sometimes this teasing is "so hard it makes them cry." Many of our teen-age ~~informants~~ when asked whether a certain individual (real or classificatory grandparent) teased them would reply with such a statement as, "Oh, he teases too hard!" Younger individuals seem often to come out the loser in a joking session though this is not always the case. Teasing still seems to revolve largely around hypothetical situations involving sexual behavior. One teen-age boy said of a grandmother, "She teases me — not too much. About old lady — marrying her and things like that." Another form of joking is in the use of "funny" nicknames, such as "Popcorn," "Manhead," "Warhead," which were recorded as used for grandchildren of a certain individual, and "Doughnut" and "Chief Pumphandle," recorded as applied to grandfathers of other individuals.

Grandchildren, after they are grown, are expected to help their grandparents. One boy in his late teens cones hone periodically to help his grandparents and is criticized for not staying around Anadarko so he can be of greater assistance to them. Grandparents may criticize and do so; usually it is the grandmother who does so, and sometimes in an angry fashion; grandfathers also correct, but in a more even-tempered manner.

This relationship appears to correspond closely to that reported for the older days. Joking, mutual help, and mutual regard still seem to be the ideal in behavior. Actual practice of this is sometimes not carried out and failure to do so may well be correlated with cases involving monolingual Wichita grandparents and essentially monolingual English-speaking grandchildren. Some younger ~~informants~~ have stated that their grandparents tease them, but they cannot understand what the old people are saying, and they make no attempt to tease back.

Sibling-in-law~Sibling-in-law

This relationship is still one of intense joking and one of the most noticeable among the Wichita today. Behavior seems to have changed little, if any, from what was considered ideal in the older pattern. One major difference is in the terminology: where-as in the old days a wife's sister or a brother's wife, male speaking, was properly referred to as wife, now the tendency is to call each of these relatives _áckics?_ and the use of the term <u>wife</u> for her is a joke in itself. Similarly the use of husband for a husband's brother has become a joke. In view of this terminology indicating possible sororal polygyny, levirate, and/or a type of fraternal polyandry, it should be mentioned that older marriage practices have not entirely disappeared. One man is reported to have practiced what was essentially sororal polygyny within the last forty years. He married one sister legally and later also lived with his wife's younger sister and had families by both. One man, now near thirty-five years of age, married his older brother's wife shortly after his brother's death. Three examples within very recent times of an older brother allowing a younger brother sexual access to his wife were reported. One of these cases involved distant brothers, or cousins in English terminology.

Subjects of joking between relatives in this category are not restricted, though sexual topics appear to be favored. Any shortcoming, real or fancied, can be utilized. However, there is individual variation; some individuals tease much harder than others, "They don't care what they say!" The younger monolingual, English-speaking generation is just arriving at the marriageable age and their behavior in this category is not known.

Husband~Wife

This relationship is most difficult to characterize because of the wide divergence of behavior. Genealogies indicate that [52] broken marriages are very common in "the modern situation, and this has been the case for over seventy-five years. On the other hand, several instances of long enduring marriages have been noted. Most troubles seem to arise because of extra-marital romances but the latter do not necessarily lead to terminated marriages.

Pride in the accomplishments of spouses is often noted. Verbalizations of such feelings most often come from women while men tend to remain silent.

The relationship is thought to be one of mild joking. Such behavior seems most characteristic of long established marriages and presumably is a reflection of the secure union. Spouses jokingly call each other "old lady" or "old man" and even tease each other about the possibility of lovers in an easy, bantering fashion. A possible contributing factor to such relaxed behavior is the older cultural pattern of allowing women more freedom of expression after reaching middle age.

Spouses cooperate in securing a living, often working together in the garden patches, in drying corn, at "chopping" cotton and corn or "snapping bolls" for wages. Indeed the whole family often cooperates in such tasks. Either spouse may take on a job as the occasion arises. Ordinarily the wife tends the children, but this can easily be turned over to ah older child, a mother, a sister, or some other woman of the extended family. Cooperation between spouses is maintained even when they belong to different factions. As mentioned above, one man is a leading church official while his wife is an ardent Camp Creek participant, and this seems to occasion little serious strain, even though many Christians believe the Camp Creek adherents to be lost souls. In another case, a woman has joined the Church of the Latter Day Saints but is still proud of her husband's peyote religion and helps him "put up" ceremonies. In spite of the characteristic of cooperation, there seems to be a strong tendency to keep property separate; this is particularly true of land. A woman may say, "This is _my_ allotment; my husband's is over by Fort Cobb."

Impressionistically the wife seems usually to be the dominant member of a pair, and this is especially true of older women. The situation is not extreme; most bossiness of women comes out when the couple is at home, or when women are preparing and serving food at group dinners. Most often it is the wife who decides when the couple will go to or leave town, or when they will leave a ceremony. Such behavior may be facilitated by the old cultural patterns which allowed middle-aged women to be verbally expressive of their emotions while men were supposed to be reserved and even-tempered. [53]

CHANGES IN THE WICHITA KINSHIP SYSTEM

Inferential Change

Murdock,[102] in his recent book on social structure, has set forth a technique for determining the evolution or histories of social organizations based on inferential evidence within the organizations themselves. By his own admission, he has sometimes pushed his evidence to extremes and believes that his reconstructions may contain some errors. However, he considers the method validated by the agreement of the various inferences with each other and by the available historical evidence. Among the 250 groups treated are two Caddoan tribes, the Wichita and Pawnee, who possessed a similar culture and who have been subjected to similar influences for cultural change. The present authors feel that, viewing the total evidence for the Wichita and other Caddoan tribes, a different order of past or inferential change is possible, if not probable. First, a summary of Murdock's methodology and conclusions in regard to the Wichita is pertinent.

Murdock's classification of social organizations rests on three major criteria: 1) rule of descent, 2) cousin terminology, 3) rule of residence; the first two determining the major type and the third the sub-type. These same criteria are of highest importance among those used to determine the evolution of social organizations; rules of residence are considered most susceptible to change, descent is considered next most likely to change, and cousin terminology to be the least likely, or the last, to change.[103]

Murdock, utilizing Spier's data,[104] classifies the Wichita system as belonging to the Matri-Hawaiian type because of bilateral descent, Hawaiian cousin terminology, and matrilocal residence. He also concludes that Wichita social organization has changed from a Normal-Hawaiian type to the Matri-Hawaiian type, citing as evidence the terminology for cross-cousins and the residence rule.[105] He says:

> Nomenclature for cross-cousins admits of numerous inferences. Since it usually changes later than both residence (R) and descent (D) in transitions from one stable structural equilibrium to another, it is particularly likely to have been the last of the three classificatory features to change in situations where all three are consistent with one another.[106]

In the Wichita case cross-cousins are classed with parallel cousins as siblings and since this is consistent with the bilateral rule of descent, but inconsistent with matrilocal residence, the previous type by Murdock's hypothesis must also have had Hawaiian cousin terminology. Secondly,

> Residence rules admit of numerous inferences. Since residence is normally the first of the three main classificatory factors to change in transitions from one stable structural equilibrium to another, it is particularly likely to have been the latest of the three to change

---

[102] Murdock, pp. 224-5, 330.

[103] *same*, pp. 327-29.

[104] Spier, 1924, pp. 258-61.

[105] Murdock, *Op. Cit.*, p. 345.

[106] *same*, p. 329.

when it is not consistent with the rule of descent."[107]

In the Wichita case matrilocal residence is inconsistent with bilateral descent so it is assumed to have changed in this instance from bilocal residence. Thus, on the basis of these assumptions, Murdock postulates the change of the Wichita social organizations from Normal-Hawaiian (bilateral descent, bilocal residence, Hawaiian cousin terminology) to Matri-Hawaiian.

Now we should like to suggest on the basis of consideration of a wider number of Wichita kinfolk, the kinship data of the Wichitas' close linguistic relatives — the Pawnee, Arikara, and Caddo, the distribution of kinship systems on the Low Plains and in the Southeast, and the conclusions concerning kinship change made by Eggan[108] and Spoehr[109] that the Wichita social organization nay have had a matrilineage type in its ancestry. This problem will be considered here in brief form, but it is hoped that in the future, with the aid of other Arikara, Caddo, Pawnee, and perhaps Kichai, data to give it the extended analysis that seems desirable. [54]

The consideration of a wider range of kinfolk than Murdock's male speaker's female relatives in his own and parental generations gives indication of emphasis on the maternal family. Attention can be called, for example, to separation of the mother's brother and the classing of the father's brother as a special kind of father. (Murdock's sample of female terms indirectly reflected this since calling a sister's daughter <u>niece</u> and a brother's daughter <u>child</u> is the reciprocal of designating the mother's brother uncle and the father's brother <u>father</u>.) Older ~~informants~~ cite the greater importance of the mother's brother than of the father's brother for lecturing nephews and nieces. This indicates along with the older ideal pattern of matrilocal residence and the solidarity of the lineage of women, that a definite maternal cast to Wichita social organization existed. Particularly does this seem true when viewed in the light of the known trend of change in the last hundred years: the shift from matrilocal residence and the partial equating of mother's brother and father's brother terminologically and behaviorally. The available evidence does not indicate that there has been a recent change to matrilocal residence or any maternal emphasis, but, rather, that the drift has been in the other direction.

A consideration of the affinal system of the Wichita appears to lend further support to our contention that the Wichita system was formerly of a more lineal type. Although affinal terms are applied bilaterally, they differ from the generationally applied consanguineal terms in their merging of generations. Spouses of uncles, big or little fathers, brothers, sons, and nephews are lumped under one term, and spouses of big and little mothers, sisters, daughters, and nieces are grouped under another. These terms are occasionally even used for spouses of grandparents and grandchildren. Matrilineage systems such as those of the Hopi,[110] Hano,[111] Zuni,[112] Cherokee,[113] and Mandan[114] exhibit systematic grouping, or a strong tendency toward such, of individuals marrying into ego's maternal lineage by terms which override generation. Among some, these terns can best be interpreted as <u>male-relative-in-law</u> or <u>female-relative-in-law</u>. Obviously the Wichita classification of in-laws is bilateral and not unilateral, but the terminological crossing of

---

[107] *same.*
[108] Eggan, 1937b.
[109] Spoehr, 1947.
[110] Eggan, 1950, p. 23.
[111] *same*, p. 142.
[112] *same.*, p. 183.
[113] Gilbert, 1943, p. 236.
[114] Bowers, 1950, pp. 42-3.

generations seems at great variance with the consistent generational treatment of consanguineal kin. The non-extension of the parent-in-law term to the wife's or husband's uncles and aunts, the male-relative-in-law term to a wife's brother, or the female-relative-in-law term to a husband's sister also is a non-generational feature which emphasizes their non-relationship to ego. We feel that the best inference from the affinal terminology, when taken together with the strong conviction that in-laws are not relatives but outsiders, and the somewhat greater maternal emphasis in the consanguineal system is that in the past the Wichita shifted the affinal terminology in adjustment to bilaterality, utilizing the terms formerly applied to people marrying into ego's maternal lineage. In other words, a former solidarity of maternal kin changed toward a solidarity of bilateral kin.

For another phase of our argument, we can turn to a consideration of the kinship systems of related groups. The Pawnee, Arikara, and Caddo, along with the Wichita, comprise the Caddoan language family. This means that at one time their ancestors were a single speech community, though in all fairness this may have been hundreds or thousands of years ago. As such, they must have once shared a common culture, including social organization. Present day Wichitas scoff at the idea of their language being related to Caddo, but readily concede its relationship to Pawnee. The Arikara are known only to exist somewhere up north and to speak a language like that of the Skidi Pawnee. Pawnee mythology includes dual origin myths, both of which have the Pawnee and Wichita united as a group.[115] A consideration of the Pawnee kinship data seems next in order.

Pawnee terms[116] include a number which seem to be cognates with Wichita terms. Such comparison would best be left to a trained historical linguist, however. The Republican Pawnee have a theme of alternation of generations which goes: child, grandchild, nephew, child, and so on, below that of ego's generation, corresponding to father, grandfather, mother's brother, father, above ego's generation.[117] This indicates a similarity to the Wichita system but not an identical one. In the latter the alternation is child, grandchild, [55] child below ego's generation, corresponding to parent, grandparent, parent in the generations above.

The Republican Pawnee (Figure #11) terminologically separated out the mother's brother but called the father's sister mother; children of the former were children while offspring of the latter were father and mother. This is different from the Wichita and is properly classified by Murdock as "Crow" cousin terminology. An examination of the father's matrilineage reveals a line of mothers descending from ego's father's sister. Similarly there is a line of grandmothers in the father's father's matriltneage. With the exception that the father's sister is not terminologically separated out, this approaches the matrilineal or "Crow" type system of Eggan.[118] The incomplete Skidi Pawnee terminology of Dorsey-Murie-Spoehr[119] also indicates a situation essentially the same as that of the Republican Pawnee. Spoehr has pointed out that the change from father's sister to mother, but with lineal descent preserved, is one of the first changes to occur in the shifting of the Creek and Cherokee systems from the Crow-Hopi type.[120]

---

[115] Grinnell, 1920, pp. 223-226.
[116] Morgan, 1877, Schedules 34 and 35.
[117] *same*, pp. 196-7, Schedule 34.
[118] Eggan, 1937a.
[119] Dorsey, 194.
[120] Spoehr, 1947, p. 197.

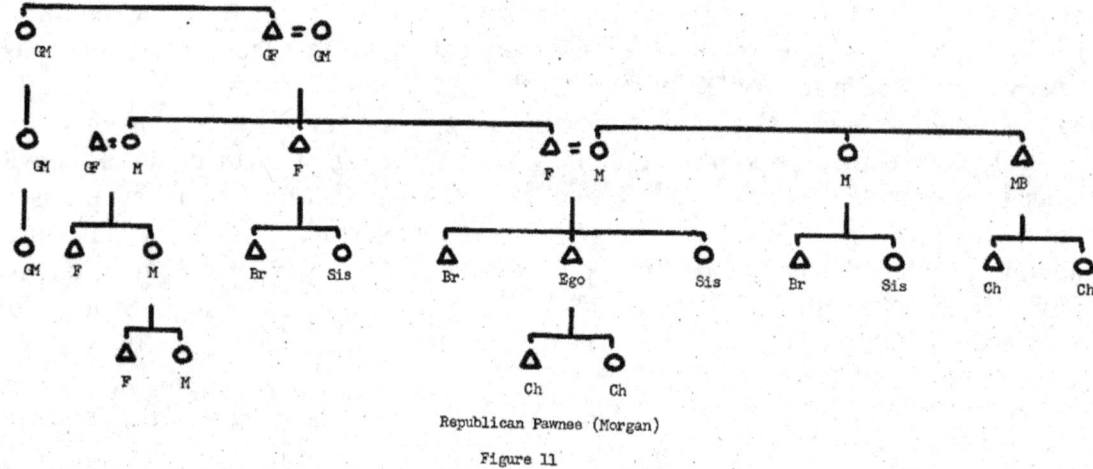

Republican Pawnee (Morgan)
Figure #11

The Grand Pawnee system of Morgan[121] (Figure #12) classes all sisters of the parents by a step-parent term. However, the offspring of the father's sister are called <u>father</u> and <u>step-parent,</u> while the offspring of the mother's brother are called <u>children</u>. Furthermore a line of fathers is indicated for the male offspring of father's sister. This feature of the Grand Pawnee schedule also suggests a variant of the Crow-Hopi or matrilineage type, almost duplicating a Choctaw situation cited by Eggan,[122] and is reported by Spoehr to be a common step in the shifting of southeastern schedules from the matrilineage type.[123]

Another characteristic of Pawnee schedules is the designation of the father's sister's husband as a <u>grandfather</u>. This feature is found in Creek, Choctaw, Cherokee, Mandan, Hidatsa, and Hopi, all of which possess, or possessed, matrilineage or Crow-Hopi type systems. Morgan's schedules also contain a number of terms which are not internally consistent or are not reciprocals of each other. These non-reciprocals, such as the application of the <u>mother's brother</u> term to the mother's mother's brother's son while the father's sister's daughter's son is called father in the Republican and Grand schedules, could have resulted from the ~~informants~~ classifying a peripheral relative by generational analogy with other closer kin — in this case with the <u>mother's brother</u>. The illogicalities of the Pawnee systems appear best explained by a shift from a lineage type system to one of a generational type: in Murdock's terminology a shift from Normal-Crow to Bi-Fox. [56]

---

[121] Morgan, 1877, schedule 35.
[122] Eggan, 1937a, p. 37.
[123] Spoehr, 1947, p. 197.

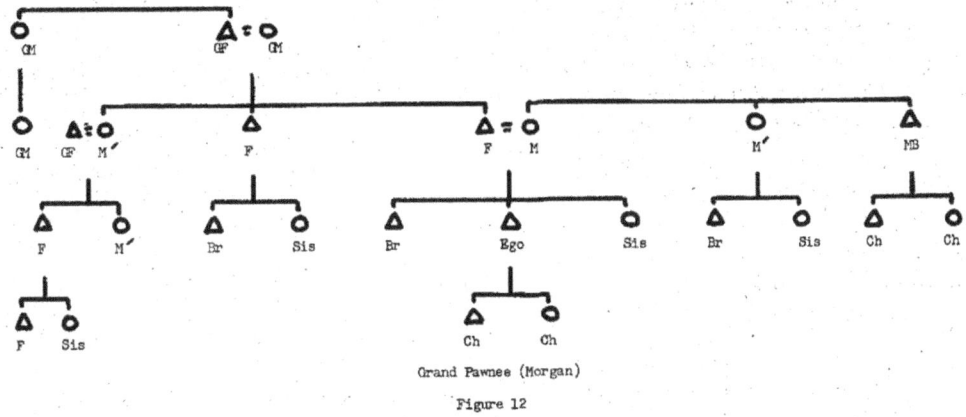

Grand Pawnee (Morgan)
Figure 12

The affinal relationship terminology of the Pawnee is not clear. However, the Skidi had a daughter-in-law term which was applied to females marrying into at least three different generations and a brother-in-law term applied to males marrying into at least two different generations in ego's family. There was also a term given as relative-in-law for the parents-in-law and a spouse's brother. A similar situation seems to have prevailed in the Grand and Republican Pawnee systems though the extension of the term relative-in-law to others besides the parents-in-law was not reported. These Pawnee systems appear to be related to that reported by older Wichitas, the Wichita male-relative-in-law and female-relative-in-law terms being used much as the Pawnee brother-in-law and daughter-in-law terms, while use of the Wichita parent-in-law term partially coincides with that of the Pawnee relative-in-law term. The major differences in the use of affinals appears to be the Pawnee use of wife for a male ego's mother's brother's wife, correlating with the temporary "fraternal polyandry" which brought ego and his uncle's wife together as spouses, and the use of grandfather for father's sister's husband: both of these decidedly were not features of Wichita terminology. All in all, however, although the Pawnee information is far from complete, there appears to be a definite relationship between Pawnee and Wichita treatment of affinal relatives.

Detailed data for the Arikara would be desirable because of their reported close relationship to the Skidi Pawnee. Unfortunately only a fragmentary schedule from Morgan[124] is available (Figure #13). This is highly suggestive. The mother's brother is terminologically separated out, while the father's sister is classed as a mother. No terms for cross-cousins are reported, but parallel cousins are brothers and sisters. For a male ego children of all brothers are called children while children of all sisters are called by nephew and niece terms. For a female ego children of all sisters are called children while children of all brothers are called by a nepotic term. This is inconsistent with classing the father's sister as a mother; apparently Morgan's ~~informant~~ was extending the mother term by analogy in the parental generation and the change was so recent that the female ego's nepotic term had not made the corresponding change to child. These Arikara data, although very meager, indicate a change toward a more generational type system and one more like that of the Wichita.

Caddo kinship data are highly conflicting though there is evidence pointing toward a

---

[124] Morgan, Schedule 36. Since the writing of this paper, the authors have collected Arikara data which definitely indicate a Skidi Pawnee type of system for the Arikara.

matrilineal emphasis. In regard to the matrilocal residence of the Caddo, Parsons said, "... the system appears quite as marked as in a culture such as the Pueblo Indian where matrilocal residence is completely developed."[125] Our own information on the Caddo tends to corroborate this statement.[126]

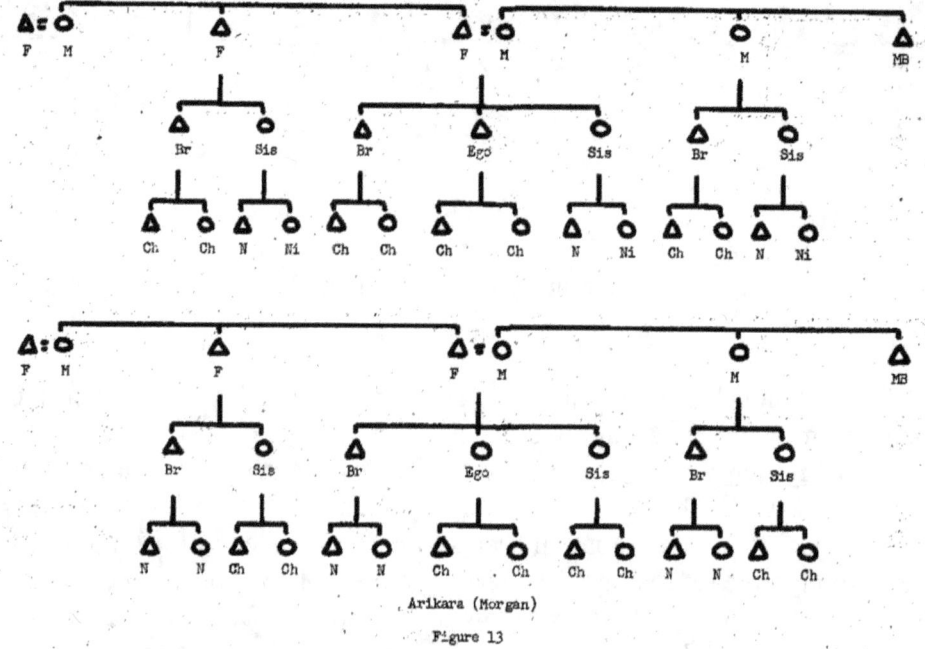

Arikara (Morgan)

Figure 13

Concerning the kinship terminology, the father's sister and the mother's brother are distinguished from other paternal siblings in all information available. It is in the treatment of cross-cousins that the data are most variable. Spier's ~~informant~~ first [57] gave a cross-cousin term, but then decided that it would apply only to second cross-cousins and that first cross-cousins mould be brothers and sisters[127] (Figure #14). Parsons' ~~informants~~ disagreed with each other; one gave the cross-cousin term, while the other said sibling terms were used for cross-cousins.[128] One of our Caddo ~~informants~~ gave the cross-cousin term for both a father's sister's and mother's brother's children and said that their children would be brother and sister. He also reported a nepotic term which is applied in line of females from a sister's daughter (Figure #15). Hunt's ~~informant~~ reported the cross-cousin term for children of a father's sister and sibling terms for children of a mother's brother. This sane individual applied the cross-cousin term to all descendants of the father's sister and said that the nepotic term was used for all descendants of a sister (Figure 16). The incomplete data indicate that the Caddo did not have a stable system in the latter part of the nineteenth century or during the first half of the twentieth century. Particularly the schedule of the last ~~informant~~ suggests a variant of a matrilineage type; the others would indicate more of a change away from such a system toward a generation type. The Caddo use of grandfather for the father's sister's husband is another similarity to other matrilineage systems.

Ethnologically and archaeologically the Low Plains area from Texas to North Dakota has been characterized by a way of life with villages of large multi-family dwellings, a heavy

---

[125] Parsons, 1941, p. 31.

[126] Recent field data acquired from the Caddo indicate a greater degree of matrilineality than shown by the data presented here.

[127] Spier, 1924, p. 262.

[128] Parsons, 1941, p. 13 footnote.

dependence on agriculture, and at least a strong secondary dependence on hunting. Essentially this way of life was characteristic also of the Southeast, where winter or fall hunting of deer seems to correspond to the hunting of buffalo, deer, and elk in the same seasons on the Low Plains. The semi-sedentary, agricultural-hunting manner of life was more widespread in the Plains area in late prehistoric and early historic times as evidenced by the Henrietta Focus[129] of Texas, the Washita River sites[130] of Oklahoma, the Antelope Greek Focus[131] of Texas and Oklahoma, the Upper Republican Culture[132] of Kansas and [59, 58 charts] Nebraska, the Nebraska Culture[133] of Nebraska, and many sites in South and North Dakota attributed to the Mandan, Hidatsa, and Arikara.[134] On an early historic level, the Caddo controlled territory into present central Texas in the 17th century; the Wichita were a populous group extending from at least the Arkansas River to present central Kansas in the 16th and 17th centuries; the Pawnee were in control of present northern Kansas and central Nebraska in the 18th century and can be traced back into the pre-historic period in the sane area via the Lower Loup Focus; and in the present Dakotas the Mandan, Hidatsa, and Arikara were well intrenched in the 18th century and apparently can be traced into the archaeological past in that area. The way of life exemplified by the above tribes was also that of the Ponca, Omaha, Kansas, Oto, and other groups to the east.

Later cultural development — that of a more nomadic, horse-buffalo culture — and the introduction of white man's diseases radically altered the distribution of the agricultural-hunting groups. By the mid-nineteenth century the Mandan, Hidatsa, and Arikara were but a small remnant of their former selves and were surrounded by nomadic buffalo hunters; the Pawnee in central Nebraska and the Wichita in southwestern Oklahoma had experienced a similar fate; the Waco, Tawakoni, Kichai, and Caddo shared a small reservation in central Texas. In addition to suffering restriction of territory and decimation of population, these tribes were also being changed by the influence of the flourishing "typical" Plains culture as exemplified by the Sioux, Blackfoot, Cheyenne, Kiowa, and Comanche. Indeed, the influence was so extensive in some cases that "typical Plains tribes," as the Crow and Cheyenne, became such by giving up the semi-sedentary villages and agriculture.

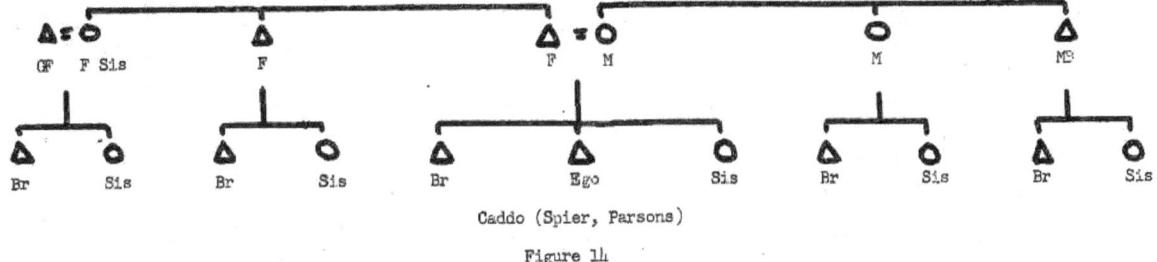

Caddo (Spier, Parsons)

Figure 14

[129] Kieger, 1946, pp. 87-150.
[130] Bell and Baerries, 1951, pp. 75-81.
[131] Krieger, Op. Cit., pp. 17-74.
[132] Wedel, 1940, pp. 310-316.
[133] Wedel, 1940, pp. 310-316.
[134] Strong, 1940, pp. 360-381.

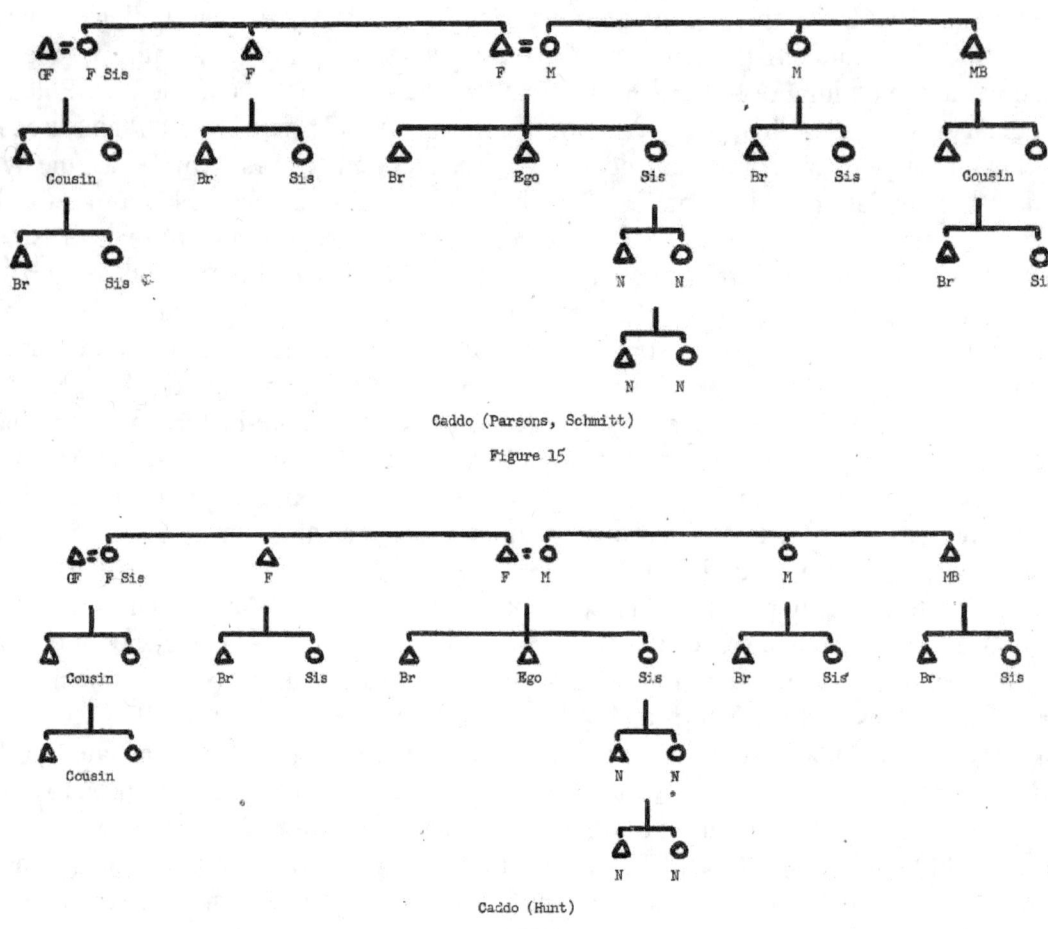

Caddo (Parsons, Schmitt)

Figure 15

Caddo (Hunt)

Figure 16

Ethnological data collected from the remnants of many of these village groups indicate there was a strong tendency to utilize the lineage principle in their social organizations. The Mandan and Hidatsa[135] and most of the well known Southeastern tribes[136] possessed Crow-Hopi or matrilineage type kinship systems and matrilineal clans. Among the Central Siouan groups — the Omaha, Ponca, Kansas, and Oto — were village tribes with Omaha or patrilineage type systems and patrilineal clans.[137]

The Omaha, although organized by patrilineal clans, had the feature of matrilocal residence when living in their villages of earth lodges and patrilocal or neolocal residence while living in tipis on tribal hunts.[138] The Osage are reported formerly to have had matrilocal residence associated with strong patrilineal clans.[139] It thus seems very possible that residence of both varieties of unilaterally organized tribes of the Missouri River area was matrilocal.

In view of the high correlation of lineal type systems with the agricultural-hunting village life in this area and the much greater extent of this way of life in late prehistoric and early historic times, it seems logical to suspect that lineage type kinship systems were once more widespread

---

[135] Eggan, 1937b, p. 93.

[136] Spoehr, 1947.

[137] Eggan, 1937b, p. 93.

[138] Fortune, 1932, p. 24.

[139] Vissier, 1827, p. 62.

also. In particular, since the Wichita and Pawnee once participated more strongly in that manner of life, they may well have had a lineage type system in their ancestry. When the Pawnee systems are found to be similar to variations reported for tribes which were in the process of changing from matrilineal type systems, and when the Wichita are found to have a system related to the Pawnee and with a maternal emphasis, it seems reasonable to conclude there is high probability that these two tribes once possessed kinship systems related to the matrilineal or Crow-Hopi type.

This tentative conclusion is counter to that which Burdock reached for the Pawnee and Wichita. In his opinion Pawnee is considered to have evolved from Normal-Hawaiian to Matri-Hawalian to Matri-Fox, or in other words to have gone from a bilateral and generational system to one which tends to emphasize lineage and maternal aspects. The next logical step in Murdock's system would have been to Normal-Crow or our matrilineage type. The Wichita social organization is considered to have evolved from Normal-Hawaiian to Matri-Hawaiian or, in other terminology, from a bilateral and generational system to a generational system with slight maternal emphasis. The crux of these deductions is the assumption that in a stable social organization the residence rule changes first and other [60] features of organization change later and toward consistency with the new rule of residence. While this may be true in many cases, other possibilities are apparent. Specifically, changes in political organization or partial adoption of new subsistence techniques, or both, presumably could influence terminology and descent patterns before alterations in residence occur. Actually, with changing cultures, it seems extremely difficult to point to one feature and say that this changed first and caused thus and so further changes. Instead one seems to have a series of mutually interrelated changes, each often reinforcing the other.[140]

Since we have criticized Murdock's conclusions concerning change of Pawnee and Wichita social organization, it seems only fair to set forth an alternative solution. We feel that Wichita and Pawnee change can best be interpreted along the lines of Spoehr's analysis of terminological change in Southeastern systems:

> The Creeks, Choctaw, and Oklahoma Cherokee terminological systems have all changed from their aboriginal forms. This change has not been entirely random, but has had a definite direction. The series of variant schedules collected from the three tribes show that two distinct processes have been operative. The first of these is a shift to a patrilineal emphasis in classifying the descendants of the father's sister, ... The second process, and apparently a more recent one, is a shift from a lineage to a generation pattern in classifying the descendants of father's sister and mother's brother.

> In the first process the overriding of generation was carried over from the old systems the second process was one of ironing out generation differences. The final result was the grouping of both parallel and cross-cousins as siblings. With the Creeks and the Cherokee the change also affected the terminology for the father's sister, who came to be classed with the mother's sister, though interestingly enough the mother's brother was not classed with the father's brother but retained his distinctive "uncle" term.[141]

The known Pawnee schedules appear most intelligible when taken as examples of Spoehr's first process; the overriding of generation is still present to a marked degree. In the Grand schedule a

---

[140] A detailed analysis of Crow and Hidatsa data, which illustrate a change from a matrilineage toward a generational type, would be most informative for this general problem.

[141] Spoehr, 1947, p. 197.

patrilineal emphasis is present in the line of <u>fathers</u> descending from the father's sister. The Skidi and Grand schedules almost duplicate Choctaw and Creek schedules of Eggan and Spoehr. The second process, that of ironing out of generation differences, is partially at work: the father's sister has become a <u>mother</u> or <u>step-parent</u>, the latter term being obviously related to the <u>mother</u> term; and in the case of the Grand band, the <u>father</u> term for the father's father's sister's son and the <u>mother's brother</u> term for the mother's mother's brother's son are not the proper reciprocals for the <u>grandchild</u> term applied to a mother's brother's son's son and for the <u>brother</u> term used for a father's sister's daughter's son and seem to be examples of reclassifying these relatives on a generational basis. However, in Morgan's Pawnee schedules the second process is not carried far since cross-cousins are not classed as siblings but still override generation, being <u>fathers</u>, <u>mothers</u>, and <u>children</u>. For the Arikara, the glaring inconsistency of a woman calling her father's sister mother while calling her brother's children by a nepotic term points up the strong possibility that the father's sister had only recently been reclassified on a generational basis.

Remembering that the Wichita were once one with the Pawnee and had close cultural similarities, we feel that the Wichita seem logically a continuation of Spoehr's two processes. In that tribe the generational differences have been ironed out by classing the cross-cousins as siblings; the father's sister has become a type of <u>mother</u>, as with the Pawnee and Arikara, while the mother's brother still retains the uncle term. The Wichita fit perfectly the end product of change in the Creek and Cherokee systems. The Grand Pawnee father's father's sister's son who is a father and the mother's mother's brother's son who is an <u>uncle</u> even point the way for change to the Wichita type: this would be correct terminology for the Wichitas and they would justify it by pointing out that those individuals are cousins (siblings) of the parents and as such have to be <u>father</u> and <u>uncle</u>.

Wichita and Pawnee kinship change, as reconstructed above, appears to have been associated with residence rules which remained relatively consistently of the matrilocal variety. Actually, for the Wichita In the 19th century, the residence rule was changing in practice, though the ideal of matrilocality existed and was practiced if possible. In view of the tremendous population decline of the Pawnee in the first half of the same century, actual residence in that tribe, too, was most certainly often at variance with the matrilocal ideal. Thus, Murdock may be right in assuming that a change in residence rule may pave the way for further changes, though the evidence Indicates the Wichita change toward bilateral or neo-local residence was concomitant with rather than prior to the kinship changes, and these latter were toward increased bilaterality. However, before this change in residence rules, partially brought about by readjustment to the population decrease, both the Wichita and Pawnee, as well as most of the tribes in or near the Plains [61] area, had other problems of readjustment. These were problems of adopting new and more efficient hunting practices associated with use of the horse and a looser political organization emphasizing more mobile bands instead of relatively sedentary villages, and oft adjusting to increased danger of warfare as other tribes became more mobile and there was conflict over control of territories. In reference to Plains life Eggan has said:

> But from the standpoint of the Plains area it is perhaps more significant that tribes coming into the Plains with <u>different</u> backgrounds and social systems ended up with <u>similar</u> kinship systems. It seems probable that conditions of Plains life favored a rather amorphous and mobile type of social organization which could vary to meet changing conditions.[142]

---

[142] Eggan, 1937b, p. 93.

All the village tribes were subjected in varying degrees to this Plains way of life, and, as Eggan has suggested, it may be possible to learn of processes of cultural change by examining a series of these groups. In the case of the Caddoan groups, there were relative differences in their exposure to the Plains culture. Both the Caddo and Wichita were in the southern Plains and seem to have had horses before 1700 and have made a partial adjustment to the new subsistence pattern. The Caddo did not get as far out on the Plains as the Wichita until the reservation period. Today, the Wichita are extremely conscious of a cultural difference between themselves and the Caddo and speak of them as "eastern Indians" and themselves as "real Plains Indians." In addition, the Caddo were in two major subdivisions, the Hainai of east Texas and the Kadohadacho of Louisiana; and the westernmost group was more exposed to Plains influences. It is perhaps significant that the Caddo informant who gave a schedule with lineage treatment of the descendants of the father's sister belonged to the Kadohadacho grouping and had close relatives who were born in Louisiana.

The Pawnee were north of the Wichita in the central Plains and further away from the source of horses and the development of buffalo and horse type Plains culture. Following Haines,[143] the diffusion of the use of the horse was not a simple south to north movement but was complicated by the fact that the Blackfeet of the northern Plains received horses via the Plateau about 1732 and about the same time or before central tribes such as the Pawnee received them from the south. Both Wichita and Pawnee informants have told us tales concerning the great walking ability of Pawnees and pointing out the scarcity of horses and the fact that the Pawnees got their first horses from the Wichita at a late date; in this case historical reconstruction and legendary material corroborate one another. It would appear, then, that the Pawnee had less chance to change to a typical Plains culture than did the Wichita and western Caddo, and thus remained more culturally conservative to the older agricultural, village life.

From the evidence which has been presented, we should assert that it is highly probable that the Pawnee kinship system changed from a matrilineal type to that represented in the schedules of Morgan and Dorsey. In this change the type of residence tended to remain the same; but descent patterns were altered to place more emphasis on bilaterality than before, kinship terms were extended somewhat on a bilateral basis and presumably some former duties which were unilaterally determined became partially bilateral. However, descent was still more matrilineal than bilateral: in cases of marriages between Individuals of different villages, the offspring belonged to the mother's town. Some younger modern individuals say they belong to "clans," such as the Pumpkin Seed clan, because their mothers belonged to such and such a clan. This appears to be a reinterpretation of the older village organization in modern terms. Similarly, offspring of marriages between individuals of different "bands" figure band affiliation through the mother.

Also, from the evidence which has been presented, we should assert that there is a good probability that the Wichita system changed to its 1850-75 form from a previous matrilineally oriented one. It is not considered that such a shift has been absolutely proven but that it is a more logical possibility of change than Murdock has presented. Again residence rules appear to have remained essentially of the matrilocal variety until a very late date while the social organization as a whole made shifts toward bilaterality.

Of course, it is possible that evolution of Wichita and Pawnee social organization did progress from Normal-Hawaiian to Matri-Hawaiian to Matri-Fox, that In the case of the Pawnee

---

[143] Haines, 1938, pp. 432-3. Haines apparently confuses Wichita groups with Pawnee groups in his discussions of the spread of the horse.

the system was in the process of change to Normal-Crow, and that intense acculturation of the later historic period upset the relatively internal change. However, in the light of the historical association of lineal terminology with the agricultural-hunting village life, and the fact that the Wichita and Pawnee were more typically "village" in their early contact days, we are of the opinion that this sequence is less likely than the one we have set forth. It should [62] be pointed out that in Murdock's terminology our hypothesis for investigation would involve a change from Normal-Crow to Matri-Fox to Matri-Hawaiian, which is the reverse of that which Murdock concludes was true.[144] Murdock does suggest that there is a possible derivation of Matri-Fox from Normal-Crow but says of this type of change:

> The derivations enclosed in parentheses are so improbable, on theoretical grounds and the evidence of our sample societies, that they can be ignored in applying the method unless specific indications of such derivation are present.[145]

It would appear that in the case of the Wichita and Pawnee, Murdock's sampling of female relatives from ego's own and parental generations was not enough to bring out the full characteristics of the systems, and that, in addition to consanguineal kin, affinal relatives should have been considered. This may well be true of other postulated derivations by Murdock.

Documented Changes

Up to this point in our discussion, we have considered only inferential changes; now we shall turn to the changes since the 1850-75 period which have been documented in the main body of the paper. During the time span, 1850-1950, Wichita life was affected by three major factors: first, the population decline which appears to have started during the eighteenth century continued on into the twentieth century; second, a part of the former subsistence economy — that of hunting buffalo, deer, and turkey — was necessarily altered by the extinction in the area of those forms; and third, the Wichita became politically subservient to the American government and were brought into continually closer contact with American cultural patterns so that now they are in many ways like any small minority group attempting to cling to a past way of life. Such radical circumstances appear to have made change in the kinship system Inevitable, though it should be expected that the change would not be random.

On a terminological level, analysis of change is a relatively simple problem. The variations from the older system which occur in the schedules of the middle group, even though they fall into no neat series, represent necessary changes in order that the older system approach the English system.[146] The uses of <u>little father</u>, or sometimes <u>uncle</u>, and <u>little mother</u> for all parental siblings and their spouses seem to represent obvious loan translations, or a reshuffling and equating of older Wichita terms with English terms: i.e., <u>little father</u> and <u>uncle</u> (mother's brother) with English <u>uncle</u> and Wichita <u>little mother</u> with English <u>aunt</u>. Similarly, the other variations involve obvious loan translations: Wichita <u>big uncle</u> for English <u>great uncle</u>, <u>big grandparent</u> for <u>great grandfather</u> and <u>great grandmother</u>, occasionally <u>big mother</u> for <u>great aunt</u>, <u>nephew</u> and <u>niece</u> for offspring of

---

[144] Murdock, pp. 324-5.

[145] *same*, p. 324.

[146] There is one exception: the confusion of terms for "big" and "little" father and mother when they are used with reference to relative age of two siblings of a parent and not with reference to that of the connecting parent.

all siblings instead of only for a man's sister's children, male-relative-in-law and female-relative-in-law for all siblings of a spouse, which makes this usage more like that of English brother-in-law and sister-in-law. These same individuals of the middle group can and do use English language kinship terms and in an essentially "right" manner. The major difference between their use of English terms and the American use of the same terms is the Wichita tendency to extend brother and sister to cousins, grandfather and grandmother to siblings of grandparents, and grandchild to grandchildren of all siblings and cousins. In the case of the monolingual, English-speaking, younger generation, a close similarity to the English terminology of the middle generation was noted. Again a much wider extension of grandparent, aunt, and uncle terms than in American usage was evident, but a consistent use of cousin for children of uncles and aunts, instead of the sibling terms used by the middle group, was obvious.

The above changes toward an English system correlate with increasing acculturation of the Wichita to "white" ways. Viewing the acculturation process through a series of generations, one finds it to be of a cumulative nature. When our informants' schedules are arranged in a typological series advancing toward the English system, we find that this series coincides well with the order of the chronological ages of the informants giving these schedules. Our informants reporting the older system are of ages of 85 plus, 74, 69, and 67 — obviously none of them really young. One of our informants of somewhat over 80 years of age did report a schedule with some loan translations) however, the Wichita speakers of the 30-60 year bracket reported schedules with many loan translations. Then, the younger English speaking generation uses English terms and overlaps with the middle, bi-lingual group in the use of such terminology. [63]

The intensive period of contact for the Wichita dates after 1850 and acculturation really was accelerated after 1870. Although Wichitas had had contact with traders, soldiers, and some administrators prior to 1870, it was not until after that date that known changes really fundamental to Wichita life occurred. After the Civil War they were sharply restricted .in territory and buffalo became extinct in their area shortly after 1878, both of these circumstances necessitating a readjustment of subsistence patterns. This was abetted largely by government aid and rations.

Soon after 1870 the first day-school was established in the Wichita village on Sugar Creek and was shortly supplanted by a boarding school near present-day Anadarko. Attendance was made compulsory by the government, though at first not with complete success. In 1874 a Creek missionary converted many leading men and villagers to the Baptist faith and many old ceremonies were no longer performed. In the words of our oldest informant: "Commence changing among Wichita when they started sending children to school. Another thing that started changing Wichita was when that missionary, Old MacIntosh, came." Although many of the first generation of school children made little progress in learning English, some of them became bilingual in Wichita and English; and what is probably more important, they spent many of their early years away from home and were not able, or desirous, of assimilating all of the old cultural ways. In addition, residence of children at school upset older patterns of home-life, since now adults had to take over what were formerly children's duties. As succeeding generations have gone to school the effects have been cumulative until the present teen-age group speaks little or no Wichita and knows little or nothing of old Wichita ways. We know of only a handful of Wichitas under 30 years of age who speak any of the Indian language.

Out of the milieu of cultural change, two factors stand forth as highly important in changing Wichita kinship toward the English pattern. These are the aforementioned attendance at schools and the American inheritance patterns and legal court actions.

Except for two known cases, all living Wichitas have attended some type of American school. All Wichitas understand some English, though a number of older individuals pretend not to and will not speak it except under pressing circumstances. Even the oldest Wichitas have long been subjected to the English kinship terminological system. In the early school period, attempts were made by the authorities to determine the kinfolk of students and give them "easy" English names accordingly. This resulted in considerable confusion, a portion of which persists to the present, because of the wide extension of the sibling relationship in Wichita. New students were often named after government personnel or famous Americans such as Robert Fulton. When another new student came in, an interpreter would be asked to whom the student was related and the reply might be, "He's Robert Fulton's brother." Actually he might be a second cousin in the American kinship system of Robert Fulton, but he would also receive the name of Fulton. Later a full-brother of Robert Fulton might come to school and be named George Clay because an interpreter chose to pick out a distant relative, Henry Clay, as his "brother." Sooner or later the white authorities realized some of the conflict between English and Wichita terminology and attempted to impress on the Wichitas that they were interested in "real" relatives.

Since 1902, problems of heirship of allotted land have increased the Wichita contacts with the English system. Hearings at the agency are often necessary since several people can claim the land of a deceased relative and the "white" authorities must decide what the division shall be. Here the conflict between the "old" Wichita system and the modern English system, which the government takes as the basis for legal decisions, is very apparent. The two following stories exemplify the resulting confusion:

> Old-lady KaiKai died and left some land. The government held a hearing to determine the heir. #H was on the stand and the government lawyer asked whether Old-lady KaiKai was a relative of his wife. H said, "She's my wife's grandmother." Then the lawyer asked if KaiKai had any grown children and #H answered, "No." Then the lawyer "jumped on H" and wanted to know how it was possible for his wife to be a granddaughter when KaiKai had had no grown children.

At another hearing a lawyer is reported to have been quizzing a Wichita man as to his relationship to several individuals. After he had gotten the reply, "He's my father," several times, the lawyer supposedly got angry and disgustedly asked, "How many fathers did you have?"

The school and court situations are illustrative of how features of American-kinship were almost forcibly taught to Wichitas. Both cane to be highly important areas of life: school was a major experience measured in years of time, and courts and land are part of the Indians' survival in the American economic pattern.

It should be pointed out that the change toward the modern American kinship system has not required drastic alterations either in terminology or behavior and that in some ways the two have become better integrated. The older patterns of respecting [64] individuals of adjacent generations and joking with these of alternate generations is not inconsistent with an English-type system since the latter also is arranged on generational lines. With respect to the affinal terms, the agreement between terminology and behavior is somewhat better than in the older system. In the latter, in-laws of the parental, first descending, and ego's own generation were lumped together by two sex-differentiating terms but were accorded highly different treatment, depending on the generation they married into. The Wichita schedules of many middle-aged individuals and those of the English-speaking younger generation have adopted uncle and aunt terms for spouses of parents' siblings, thus bringing into agreement respect behavior and respect terms. In addition the Wichita in-law terms tend now to be extended to all siblings of spouses, again bringing into harmony terminology and behavior. True, there is still the inconsistency in the middle-aged groups of calling brothers- and sisters-in-law by the same term as sons- and daughters-in-law; but the English-speaking younger generation has removed this by use of the English terms.

During this period of documented change, that of 1850-1950, other changes besides those of kinship terminology and behavior were occurring among the Wichita. Some of these have been indicated. In general, there seems, to have been a change from a more formal and rigid social organization to one that is much less formal and one that is highly factionalized. In former days tribal leaders were chosen in such a way that there was overt unanimous approval. Religion, warfare, political authority, and other areas of life were closely intertwined; and procedures were relatively ordered and blue-printed as compared to the present situation. The reservation period brought many changes in these areas, and apparently religion was one of the first aspects of Wichita culture to be affected. Some individuals became converted to orthodox Christian faiths; later others took up the Ghost Dance or Peyote. Among the factors involved here, in addition to the enforced deculturation and acculturation from without, were the population declines, often of epidemic nature, which removed many individuals who had knowledge of complex religious and social rites of the tribe.

No simple causal explanation of changes will suffice; instead, a network of interrelated factors must be recognized. A case in point is the breakup of the compact village organization. This was partially "caused" by the tribe's having two sets of "leaders," one of older religious and political authority, and a second of newer Christian affiliation who preached against the older way. At the same time, of course, the tribe was subject to decisions of the government officials and chiefly powers consequently diminished. Also, as intertribal warfare declined, scattered residence became safer and utilization of more distant desirable land became feasible. However, when the villages on Sugar Creek broke up about 1880, and the people dispersed along Sugar Creek and tributary streams, the newer residence pattern still tended to follow matrilocal patterns with extended family groupings.

It was during the period of 1875-1900 that the formal political organizations of the Wichita, Waco, Tawakoni, and Kichai disintegrated, and at the same time many of the more spectacular aspects of life vanished or decreased in importance. At present, war parties, most ceremonies, buffalo hunting, and villages of grass houses are no longer extant. Warfare went out when the United States government enforced peace on all Indian tribes, and there remain only the Indians' intense patriotism and their honoring of veterans and young men of the various armed services of the United States. The annual foot race, the Deer Dance, and even the later Ghost Dance disappeared as officials died in epidemics or were converted to fundamentalist churches, or their authority was undermined by new theories of disease. The whites slaughtered the buffalo and the last hunt was made in 1878, or shortly thereafter. During the 1930's the last of the grass houses disappeared as the cedar timber was cut, the proper native grass was replaced by ploughed fields or weeds, and modern frame houses became desirable and available. Though kinship terminology and behavior also changed, it strikes one in viewing the various aspects of Wichita life that modern kinship practices bear more resemblance, or are closer to, the older culture patterns than any other feature, with the possible exception of beliefs concerning ghosts and witchcraft. While buffalo hunting, warfare, villages, and ceremonies became obsolete, families still raised children — at least for the time: when the youngsters were not at school —, fed them, and tried to teach them the old traditions; and kinship solidarity persisted.

Spoehr in his work on the changes in Creek, Choctaw, and Cherokee kinship systems[147]

---

[147] Spoehr, 1947, pp. 199-215.

has pointed out some factors and related changes. Under stimulus to change he indicates the Importance of white settlers, the missionary, and the government agent. Among the Wichita the same stimulus was, and is, present. As we have seen, agents of the government, such as school teachers and lawyers, were particularly important in changing terminology and were responsible for more diffuse changes in behavior, such as introducing [65] new child training patterns or new inheritance patterns. White settlers, particularly after 1902, when large numbers of them came to Wichita country, had great influence on the Wichita. Wichita-white intermarriages took place, as among the Five Civilized Tribes, and often the non-Indian parent tried to raise the children by American standards. Spoehr points out that such tends to develop a social and economic cleavage between mixed and full-bloods since mixed bloods are inclined to be more aggressive in accumulation of wealth, to be more receptive to mission teaching, and to be more readily adaptive to white attitudes and usages.[148] While these things were not always true among the Wichita, we wholeheartedly agree that "As contact agent, the effect of the white settler in increasing the mixed-blood population and imparting to his descendants and Indian affinal relatives white attitudes and usages was his important contribution to change in Indian society."[149]

The role of the missionary among the Wichita as a stimulus to kinship change is difficult to evaluate. His influence in bringing about other changes is of obvious importance. Wichitas were visited by several different kinds of missionaries; Quakers, northern Baptists, Presbyterians, and Creek Baptists. The first three either operated schools, or sent children away to school, or both, while the latter were interested primarily in making converts. The influence of the first three on kinship behavior probably parallels that of the government schools in affecting primarily terminology and secondarily some aspects of behavior. With regard to relative importance of the denominations, the Baptists who belong to the Creek confederation of churches have the most members and have had the major influence. But at the present time, and apparently for some time past, there is no discernible difference in kinship behavior among the Rock Springs (Baptist) group and other Wichitas. Extended kinship ties are highly important to the church people, and indeed appear to insure success of the church, and one seems just as likely to hear obligatory joking of a rough nature on the front porch of the church as at any other Wichita gathering. Among the Wichita, the missionary as an agent of change in the social organization, except through operation of schools and creating other changes which indirectly influenced kinship, seems to have been of lesser importance than the government agent and the white settler.

Spoehr's consideration of the cultural milieu closely parallels ours, as it should, since both his groups and the Wichita are in the same general area. He considers changes in adaptation to the natural environment, violent episodes in contact relations, the peaceful expansion of white settlement with development of transportation so that physical barriers to contact are removed, and the Indians becoming largely a scattered rural population and a minority group in a white and negro society. As has been set forth, the Wichita had to adapt to a changing natural environment. Violent episodes were also a feature of Wichita life: the 1874 outbreak of Kiowas, Comanches, and Cheyennes, fights with white outlaw gangs, and the small-pox epidemic after the Civil War are examples of such. The population distribution of Wichita, and other tribes in the vicinity of Anadarko, parallels that of the Indians in the eastern portion of Oklahoma.

The known changes in Wichita kinship and related spheres seem to have occurred in the following sequence. It should be pointed out that delineation of the sequence is really only a general overall sort of portrayal, and that in actuality no great changes occurred overnight and most

---

[148] Spoehr, 1947, p. 218.
[149] *same*, p. 219.

continued over long periods of years. Some families and individuals tended to change terminology and behavior relatively rapidly, while others were more conservative — so much so, that "old style" schedules could still be collected in 1950.

The single change which seems most radical among the Wichita is the break up of village organization sometime around 1860, when extended families tended to set up separate "camps" along Sugar Creek and its tributaries. Matrilocal residence was still the ideal and was adhered to in the majority of cases for which we obtained household composition data. However, due to special circumstances, particularly the presence of orphans or near orphan girls, other forms of residence occurred; this had been true in Wichita villages as well. In these "camps" a group of women related by blood, or a form of matrilineal lineage, still was an eminent feature, and extended kinship obligations of a bilateral nature were important as they were in the village days. However, the change in population distribution seems to have been a first step in narrowing of some kinship behavior. Face to face kinship contacts diminished because of geographic distance, though actually an extensive visiting pattern and a weekly camping pattern for issue of [66] government rations worked counter to this. At the same time other changes in Wichita culture, such as cessation of intertribal warfare and much of cooperative hunting, reduced the areas of life which were characterized by highly stylized patterns of extended kinship behavior. So, the first in a sequence of documented changes appears to have been a narrowing in actual kinship contacts and a reduction in certain very formalized kinship obligations.

Then, as children started to go to government and mission schools, various loan translations from the American kinship system were made so that the terminology for parents' siblings and their spouses, nephews and nieces, and siblings-in-law changed markedly. While highly specialized kinship duties still declined, the variations of the general respect and joking behavior continued. As indicated above, since such relationships were organized on a generational basis, and since American kinship is also stratified generationally, there was no essential conflict between respect-joking behavior and the newer terminology. Actually the newer affinal terminology was more consistent with the older behavior. During this same period, practice of sororal polygyny, the levirate, and temporary "fraternal polyandry" declined but did not completely disappear. However, the terminology which was consistent with such practice has persisted strongly to the present day — but in a joking way.

After the allotment of land in 1902, families were still of the extended variety, though again at this time another dispersion of population appears to have started. Now individuals actually owned land and the tendency to neolocal residence after marriage was strengthened; however, the great majority of the Wichitas still seemed to prefer residence in extended families. Furthermore, a continuing tendency to lose control of land to white settlers worked against establishment of neolocal residences: sale of allotments or leasing of lands, including houses, forced many families to remain of the extended variety. Or, it might be said, the Wichita cultural pattern of living by extended families made the present leasing practices more feasible. At one period, that of the 1920's and early 1930's, the Wichitas became temporarily relatively affluent due to widespread oil leasing in the area, and many frame houses mere built. Some individuals bought and sold allotments and participated actively in the American economic system. It would appear that during this particular period the factors operating against extended family life and for relative independence of elementary families and a loosening of extended kinship bonds, were strongly present. But, during the late 1930's and the great depression, oil leases were cancelled and the Wichitas became poor again. Extended kinship obligations were reinforced in this time of want and have continued thus to the present date.

Terminologically the present middle group is bilingual and can use both Wichita and American kinship terms, while the younger generation of 30 years of age and under have switched almost completely to American terminology. But, the terminology is applied bilaterally to a much wider range of relatives; and behavior still tends to follow the generalized joking-respect categories, though highly formalized and special kinship duties to all intents and purposes nave disappeared. Although younger Wichitas still extend relationship more widely than in most variations of the American system, there appears some tendency toward narrowing. In the older system family exogamy was practiced and that meant anyone to whom a relationship could be traced bilaterally was forbidden as a spouse. Some of the younger Wichitas have married second or third cousins, even though elders have disapproved, and thus decreased the range of extension. However, other Wichitas in a manner still recognize the older extension and interpret the numerous extra-tribal marriages as' being necessary because the Wichita are so few and everybody is related.

Our documented material is not strictly comparable to Spoehr's data on changing Southeastern systems since his groups passed through a greater known range of change, from matrilineage systems to a variation of the American system. Actually there is a most excellent chance that Wichita kinship has gone through a similar sequence, but our earliest type of recorded system is a generational type with separation out of the mother's brother and sister's children (male speaking). As indicated above, this type is very close, if not identical, to some of Spoehr's systems where there has been a shift from lineage to generation emphasis in classifying descendants of the father's sister and mother's brother, and where the father's sister has been classed with the mother. From that point on, under influence of American culture, the change has been highly similar: in both cases attempts have been made to equate Indian terms with English terms, and in the younger generation, the Indian terms have been supplanted by English and the range of extension narrowed some. Terminologically the systems of Creek, Cherokee, Choctaw, and Wichita young people are remarkably similar. A significant point here seems to be that even though English terminology is used, and the range of relatives is reduced from former [67] days, the family organization still differs from that of white Oklahomans in that terms are bilaterally extended on a generational basis to grandparents' cousins and brothers and to parents' cousins. In other words the Wichita and other tribes are not completely assimilated to American culture as regards kinship patterns, as well as in other areas of culture, in spite of adoption of the English language. A necessary remaining step for that assimilation is a further restricting of the range and most likely an accompanying reduction of the size of the family or cooperating kinship group.

Our documented changes in the Wichita system are not particularly illuminating when Murdock's conclusions concerning changes in social organization are viewed against them. As has been pointed out Murdock's three major criteria for classification are residence and descent patterns and cousin terminology: these three aspects also are considered most likely to change in the order cited above, but he mentions that in periods of rapid cultural change, complex and overlapping sequences of change may exist. Our documented Wichita system of the middle-aged group, influenced by loan translations from English, still had Hawaiian cousin terminology and bilateral descent, but the residence pattern had perhaps shifted somewhat. Matrilocal residence was still the ideal and practiced when possible but there were a growing number of exceptions: So that step in Wichita change would be classified in Murdock's system as Matri-Hawaiian with a variation toward Normal Hawaiian (that with bilocal residence). The step to English terminology would be one that necessitates a change in type in Murdock's classification. Since cousin terminology is now of the Eskimo type and descent is still bilateral, the English-speaking Wichita system is of the Eskimo type. As to whether it would be of the Bi-Eskimo or Normal Eskimo variety we are undecided since both bilocal and neolocal residence are common among modern Wichitas. In Murdock's system no provision is made for change to Eskimo types from Matri-Hawaiian or Normal Hawaiian; the only probable change listed is from Neo-Hawaiian to Normal Eskimo with a change in cousin terminology. But it would not seem fair to test Murdock's hypothesis here because of the change from one language to another and in view of the intensive character of the acculturation process. [69, no 68]

SUMMARY AND CONCLUSIONS

The contributions of this work are of two kinds, descriptive and analytical. The kinship system of the older Wichita, in both its terminological and behavioral aspects, was described and the system of the modern Wichita was presented in comparable manner. In connection with the presentation of the older system, special consideration was given to the classificatory and theoretical aspects of joking and respect behavior. The last part of the study was devoted to an examination of change in Wichita kinship. Possible older changes were considered first and an argument advanced for a reconstruction of change different from that of Murdock. An analysis of modern kinship changes followed and suggestions were made as to factors involved. Some findings of the total study can be summarized as follows:

(1) The survey of Wichita respect and joking relationships indicates that the behavior between various pairs of relatives does not fall into a neat continuum between two poles. Understanding of such behavior and a simple, linear scaling of it is complicated by the presence of variables such as emotional intensity, intensity of interaction, amount of verbalization, and qualitative differences of behavior.

(2) Wichita data, by and large, were found to support Eggan's formulation with regard to respect and joking behavior. The application of Eggan's classification to the Wichita data was somewhat complicated by the fact that there appeared to be degrees between "possibility" and "inevitability" and between "no particular necessity" and an actual "necessity for avoiding conflict."

(3) On the basis of a preliminary comparison of Pawnee, Arikara, and Caddo data and a consideration of the general ethnological and historical perspective of the Plains, a reconstruction of past changes in Wichita social organization has been suggested. This sequence, one of change to bilaterality from a matrilineally oriented system, is different from Murdock's (Matri-Hawaiian from Normal Hawaiian) and one which he considers improbable to occur in any situation. We nave noted that the Wichita system of 1850-75 is very close to the end-type (in Indian terminology) of Creek, Choctaw, and Cherokee kinship changes. Spoehr's sequence of change in Southeastern kinship is that considered most probable to have brought about the Wichita system of 1850-75. We have suggested that Murdock's hypothesis is based on a classification which does not bring out all the pertinent characteristics of social systems and that especially a larger number of relatives, including affinals, should be considered when analyzing for evidences of change.

(4) The documented changes of the Wichita system after 1850 have been consistently toward the American or English type, and generally parallel late changes in Southeastern kinship systems reported by Spoehr. The terminological changes, with one minor exception, have been made by means of loan translations, a process of equating older Wichita terms with English kinship designations.

(5) The younger, mono-lingual Wichitas have almost completely adopted terms from the English language. However, these are still extended in a bilateral manner and indicate that the Wichitas are not completely acculturated as regards family organization.

(6) Wichita behavioral change has lagged behind terminological change, and behavior persists strongly in the present in the form of various respect and joking patterns. However, highly formalized behavior between certain sets of relatives has vanished along with other aspects of the total culture. Respect relationships which were formerly of an avoidance type have tended to become characterized by the general respect behavior accorded uncles and aunts. Joking behavior has remained relatively unchanged. The continuance of respect and joking behavior is aided by the type of kinship system of the main acculturating group: the English system has strong generational features and thus does not conflict with Wichita respect and joking patterns, which, we have seen, operate on a generational basis.

(7) Related to the terminological, and some behavioral, changes in kinship, were certain other changes in Wichita life: cessation of warfare, adoption of new religions and resulting weakening of the old native religion, disappearance of the older political organization, complete decline of hunting as a means of subsistence, and dispersal of population — first by break-up of consolidated villages and later by allotment of land. Missionaries, government agents, and white settlers were the main acculturating agents. Particularly influential, as far as kinship change is concerned, were the government and missionary schools and the inheritance court hearings since they practically forced changes in terminology and some in behavior. The fact remains, however, that kinship [70] is the least affected of the various aspects of Wichita culture and social organization. As just mentioned above, the relatively non-conflicting nature of the English system has allowed the retention of old joking and respect patterns; and, furthermore, adversities engendered by the acculturative process have tended to preserve kinship solidarity. Cutting across the political, religious, and other factions which exist today, are the kinship bonds — a cohesive force in the face of the disintegrative powers of acculturation. [71]

BIBLIOGRAPHY

Bell, Robert E. and David Baerreis
    1951. "A Survey of Oklahoma Archaeology", *Bulletin of the Texas Archaeological and Paleontological Society*, Vol. 22, pp. 7-100.

Bowers, Alfred W.
    1950. *Mandan Social and Ceremonial Organization*. Chicago.

Bolton, Herbert Eugene
    1914. *Athenase de Mezieres and the Louisiana-Texas Frontier, 1768-1780*. Two volumes. (Cleveland; Arthur H. Clark Company).

Catlin, George
    1926. *North American Indians*. Two volumes. (Edinburgh; John Grant)

Chaple, Eliott Dismore, and Carleton Stevens Coon
    1942. *Principles of Anthropology*. New York.

Dorsey, George A.
    1904. *The Mythology of the Wichita*. Carnegie Institution of Washington Publication No. 21. Washington, D.C.
    1940. *J.R. Murie; Notes on Skidi Pawnee Society*, prepared for publication by Alexander Spoehr. Anthropology Series, Field Museum of Natural History, Vol. 27, Mo. 2. Chicago.

Eggan, Fred
    1937a. "Historical Changes in the Choctaw Kinship System", *American Anthropologist*, n.s. Vol. 39, pp. 34-52.
    1937b. "The Cheyenne and Arapaho Kinship System". *In Social Anthropology of North American Tribes* (F. Eggan, ed.). Chicago.
    1950. *Social Organization of the Western Pueblos*. Chicago.

Fortune, H.F.
    1932. *Omaha Secret Societies*. Columbia University Contributions to Anthropology Vol. 14.

Freud, S.
    1919. *Totem and Taboo*. London.

Garvin, Paul L.
    1950. "Wichita I: Phonemics". *International Journal of Linguistics* Vol. 16, pp. 179-181.

Gilbert, William Harlen, Jr.
    1943. "The Eastern Cherokees". Bureau of American Ethnology, Bulletin 133, Anthropological Papers, No. 23.

Grinnell, G. B.
    1920. *Pawnee Hero Stories and Folk Tales*. New York.

Haas, Mary
    1942. "Comments on the Name 'Wichita'". *American Anthropologist*, n.s. Vol. 44, pp. 164, 165.

Haines, F.
    1938. "The Northward Spread of Horses among the Plains Indians". *American Anthropologist*, n.s. Vol. 40, pp. 429-37.

Hodge, Frederick Webb
    1907. *Handbook of American Indians North of Mexico*. Two parts, 1907 & 1910. (Washington: Government Printing Office)

Krieger, Alex

1946. *Culture Complexes and Chronology in Northern Texas.* University of Texas Publication No. 4640, Austin.

Lesser, Alexander

1930. "Levirate and Fraternal Polyandry among the Pawnees", *Man*, Vol. 30, pp. 98-101.

Lesser, Alexander and Gene Weltfish

1932. "Composition of the Caddoan Linguistic Stock". *Smithsonian Miscellaneous Collections.* Vol. 87, no. 6.

Linton, Ralph

1945. *The Cultural Background of Personality.* (New York)

Marcy, Randolph B, and Grant Foreman (ed)

1937. *Adventure on Red River.* University of Oklahoma Press.

Morgan, Lewis H.

1871. *Systems of Consanguinity and Affinity of the Human Family.* Smithsonian Contributions to Knowledge, Vol. 17.

Murdock, George Peter

1949. *Social Structure.* New York.

Nett, Betty

1951. *Osage Kinship System.* Unpublished M.A. Thesis, University of Oklahoma.

Opler, Morris E.

1936. "Kinship Systems of the Southern Athapascan Tribes". *American Anthropologist*, n.s. Vol. 38. [72]

Parsons, Elsie Clews

1941. *Notes on the Caddo.* Memoirs of the American Anthropological Association #57.

Schmitt, Karl

1950a. "The Lee Site, Gv3, of Garvin County, Oklahoma". *Bulletin of the Texas Archaeological and Paleontological Society* Vol. 21, pp. 70-89.

1950b. "Wichita-Kiowa Relations and the 1874 Outbreak". *Chronicles of Oklahoma*, Vol. 28, pp. 154-160.

Spier, Leslie

1924. "Wichita and Caddo Relationship Terms". *American Anthropologist*, n.s. Vol. 26, pp. 258-263.

1925. "The Distribution of Kinship Systems in North America", *University of Washington Publications in Anthropology* Vol. I, pp. 1-88.

Spoehr, Alexander

1947. *Changing Kinship Systems.* Anthropology Series, Field Museum of Natural History Vol. 33, No. 4. Chicago.

Strong, William Duncan

1940. "From History to Prehistory in the Northern Great Plains". *Smithsonian Miscellaneous Collections* Vol. 100, pp. 353-394.

Swanton, John R.

1942. *Source Material on the History and Ethnology of the Caddo Indians.* Bureau of American Ethnology, Bulletin 132.

Tax, Sol

1937. "Some Problems of Social Organization" in Fred Eggan (ed.), *Social Anthropology of North American Tribes.* Chicago.

Vissier, Paul
    1827. *Histoire de la Tribu des Osages*. Paris.
Wedel, Waldo R.
    1940. "Culture Sequence in the Central Great Plains." *Smithsonian Miscellaneous Collections*, Vol. 100, pp. 291-352.
    1942. "Archaeological Remains in Central Kansas and Their Possible Bearing on the Location of Quivira." *Smithsonian Miscellaneous Collections,* Vol. 101, No. 7.
Whitman, William
    1937. *The Oto*. Columbia University Contribution to Anthropology, Vol. 28.
Winship, G.P.
    1896. "*The Coronado Expedition*." 14th Annual Report Bureau of American Ethnology, pp. 339-598.

UNIVERSITY OF WASHINGTON PUBLICATIONS
IN
ANTHROPOLOGY

Vol. 1, No. 2, pp. 69-88. Maps 1-9   August, 1925

THE DISTRIBUTION OF KINSHIP SYSTEMS
IN
NORTH AMERICA.

By LESLIE SPIER.

UNIVERSITY OF WASHINGTON PRESS
SEATTLE

Tribes by # Number

Tolowa (1b) ∞ a d f g i

Hupa (1c)

Whilkut (1e)

Lassik (1h)

Wailaki (1j)

Kato (1k)

Yurok (2a) ∞

Wiyot (3)

Yuki (4a)

Huchnom (4b)

Coast Yuki (4c)

Wappo (4d)

Lutuami (5)

Shasta (6a) ∞ b c d

Achomawi (6e)

Atsugewl (6f)

Northern Yana (7a) ∞ c

Central Yana (7b)

Yahi (7d)

Karok (8)

Northern Pomo (10a) ∞ e

Central Pomo (10b)

Eastern Pomo (10c)

Southeastern Pomo (10d)

Southern Pomo (l0f)

Southwestern Pomo (10g)

Washo (11)

Northern Diegueño (15a) ∞ e

Southern Diegueño (15b)

Kamia (l5c)

Yuma (15d)

Mohave (15f)

Northern Wintun (l6a)

Central Wintun (16b)

Southeastern Wintun (16c)

Southwestern Wintun (16d)

Northeastern Maidu (17a)

Northwestern Maidu (17b)

Southern Maidu (17c)

Coast Miwok (18a)

Lake Miwok (18b)

Plains Miwok (18c)

Northern Miwok (18d)

Central Miwok (18e)

Southern Miwok (18f)

Tachi (20a)

Yauelmani (20b)

Chukchansi (20c).

Gashowu (20d)

Yaudanchi (20e)

Paleuyami (20f)

Northern Pauite (21a) ∞ d e i j l m n o r s

Eastern Mono (21b)

Western Mono (21c)

Kawaiisu (21f)

Tubatulabal (21g)

Kitanemuk (21h)

Serrano (21k)

Luiseño (21p)

Cupeño (21q)

Desert Cahuilla (21t)

Alaskan Eskimo (22)

Eskimo of Cumberland Inlet, Baffin Land, Kadiak Eskimo (23)

Tinneh (24)

Loucheux (25)

Tukuthe (26)

Hare (27)

Copper Eskimo (28)

Eskimo of Northumberland Island (29)

Cumberland Inlet (30)

Greenland Eskimo (31)

Yellow Knife (32)

Slavey (33)
Tlingit (34)
Haida (35)
Nass (36)
Tsimshian (37)
Carrier (38)
Bellabella (39b) [Nuxalk]

Bella Coola (40) [Nuxalk]
Kwakiutl (41) [Kwakwakwawakw]
Nootka (42) [Nuchalnuth]
Comox (43)
Siciatl (44)
Chehalis (45)
Squamish (46)
Cowichan (47)
Thompson (48)
Lillooet (49)

Kwantlen (50)
Songish (51)
Makah (52)
Quileute (53)
Klallam (54)
Snuqualmi (56)
Duwamish (57)
Nisqualli (58)
Shuswap (59)

Kutenai (60)
Okanagan (61)
Colville (62)
Spokan (63)
Kalispel (64)
Coeur d'Alene (65a)
Flathead (65b)
Wenatchee (66)
Yakima (67)
Klikitat (68)
Wishram (69)

Wasco (70)
Chinook (71)
Alsea (72)
Takelma (73)
Sarsi (75)

Blood (76)
Piegan (77)
Gros Ventre (78) [Atsina]
Plains Cree (79)

Assiniboin (80)
Bungi (81)
Wood Cree (82)
Swampy Cree (83)
Paviotso (84)
Uintah Ute (85)
Tabegwaches (86)
Moapa (87)
Shivwits (88)
Kaibab (89)

Havasupai (90)
Southern Ute (91)
Navaho (92)
Hopi (93)
Hano (94)
Zuni (95)
Acoma (96)
Laguna (97)
Cochiti (98)
Jemez (99)

Tewa (San Ildefonso, Santa Clara, San Juan,
   Nambe) (100)
Tesuque (101)
Santo Domingo (102)
San Felipe (103)
Sandia (104)
Isleta (105)
Cocopa (106)
Papago (107) [Tohono O'odham]
Northern Tepehuane (108)
Crow (109) [Absorika]

Wind River Shoshoni (110)
Arikara (111)
Hidatsa (112)
Mandan (113)
Uncpapa (114) [Hunkpapa]
Blackfoot Dakota (115)
Oglalla (116)

Brule (117)
Yanktonai (118)
Yankton (119)

Cheyenne (120)
Arapaho (121)
Grand Pawnee (122)
Republican Pawnee (123)
Skidi Pawnee (124)
Ponca (125)
Omaha (126)
Santee (127)
Sisseton (128)
Menomini (129)

Winnebago (130)
Sauk-Fox (131)
Iowa (132)
Oto (133)
Kansas (134)
Kiowa (135)
Wichita (136)
Osage (137)
Missouri (138)
Quapaw (139)

Caddo (140)
Ojibway of Lake Superior (141)
Lake Michigan (142)
Lake Huron (143)
Ottawa (143)
Kaskaskia (145)
Peoria (146)
Wea (147)
Kickapoo (148)
Piankashaw (149)

Timagami (150)
Wyandot (151)
Seneca (152)
Cayuga (153)
Onondaga (154)
Oneida (155)
Mohawk (156)
Two Mountain Iroquois (157)
Montagnais (158)
Abenaki (159)

Malecite (160)
Micmac (161)
Penobscot (162)
Natick (163)
Mohegan (164)
Munsi (165)
Delaware (166)
Miami (167)
Shawnee (168)
Tuscarora (169)

Cherokee (170)
Tutelo (171)
Chickasaw (172)
Choctaw (173)
Creek (174)
Yuchi (175)
Biloxi (176)
Timucua (177)
Kansas Potawatomi (178)
Ts'ets'aut (179)
Willapa (180) [Swaal]

∞ = gaps in # numbers
[ ] now preferred names

THE DISTRIBUTION OF KINSHIP SYSTEMS IN NORTH AMERICA

This paper presents a classification of kinship systems in North America and their distribution. Historical, sociological, or psychological interpretations can hardly be undertaken without such a basis.

The material has been available for some years. Lewis H. Morgan published sufficient to cover the region east of the Rockies in his Systems of Consanguinity and Affinity of the Human Family some fifty years ago. But his unfortunate manner of presentation rather prejudiced reworking the data. Many systems from elsewhere on the continent have been accumulated since, largely due, I believe to the impetus given their investigation by Robert H. Lowie. Data for part of the Pacific area were brought together by A.L. Kroeber in *California Kinship Systems* and later subjected to more intensive analysts by Edward W. Gifford in *Californian Kinship* Terminologies. With the exception of Lowie's *Sociological and Historical Interpretation of Kinship Terminologies*, no synthesis of continental scope has been attempted.

This study was begun in 1915 in an attempt to harmonize the Blackfoot data and to compare their systems with those of neighboring tribes.[150] Through the generosity of William T. Davis of New York and an anonymous friend I was then given the opportunity to classify the material from eastern North America. It has been possible to complete the task under a Fellowship in the Biological Sciences of the National Research Council in 1923-24.

The data are largely drawn from Morgan's tables. The Californian data are from Gifford's work, taken directly from his maps in most instances. I am especially indebted to R.H. Lowie for a large series of systems in manuscript, which he has placed unreservedly at my disposal, and to those who aided him in forming it. Thanks are due Alanson B. Skinner for unpublished Potawatomi and Bungi manuscripts, Pliny E. Goddard for Sarsi, Eugene A. Golomshtok for Atsugewi, and Erna Gunther for Makah, Wasco, and Salish material from Washington. Other sources are cited in the bibliography. I have made no attempt at harmonizing conflicting data. This requires linguistic specialization and further information. In most cases the several alternatives are entered on the maps, but I have been quite free in arbitrarily selecting the most harmonious data.

This is strictly an empirical classification. Beginning with the east, it was obvious that essentially the same systems were in use among tribes occupying large continuous areas. I have therefore taken a group of similar systems, determined the most frequent mode of classifying each relative, and described that as the norm. This is more difficult for the western tribes where the systems are more complex and where such features as verbal reciprocity are more frequently common to many groups which are in other respects unlike. A number of systems, such as the Navaho and Alsea, were classified with [72] difficulty. So far as the data goes — and it is as likely as not to be incorrect — they belong as much in one class as another. It seems preferable to suggest their affiliations by classifying them somewhat arbitrarily to establishing a large number of categories. No two systems are identical; a class is merely a group of systems more alike than they are individually like any other class.

To avoid misunderstanding, I wish it to be clear that I am not now asserting any historical connection between the systems of one class. The Wiyot of northern California, for example, have a system which is closer to that of the Eskimo than to that of any of their neighbors. That

---

[150]   Spier, Blackfoot Relationship Terms.

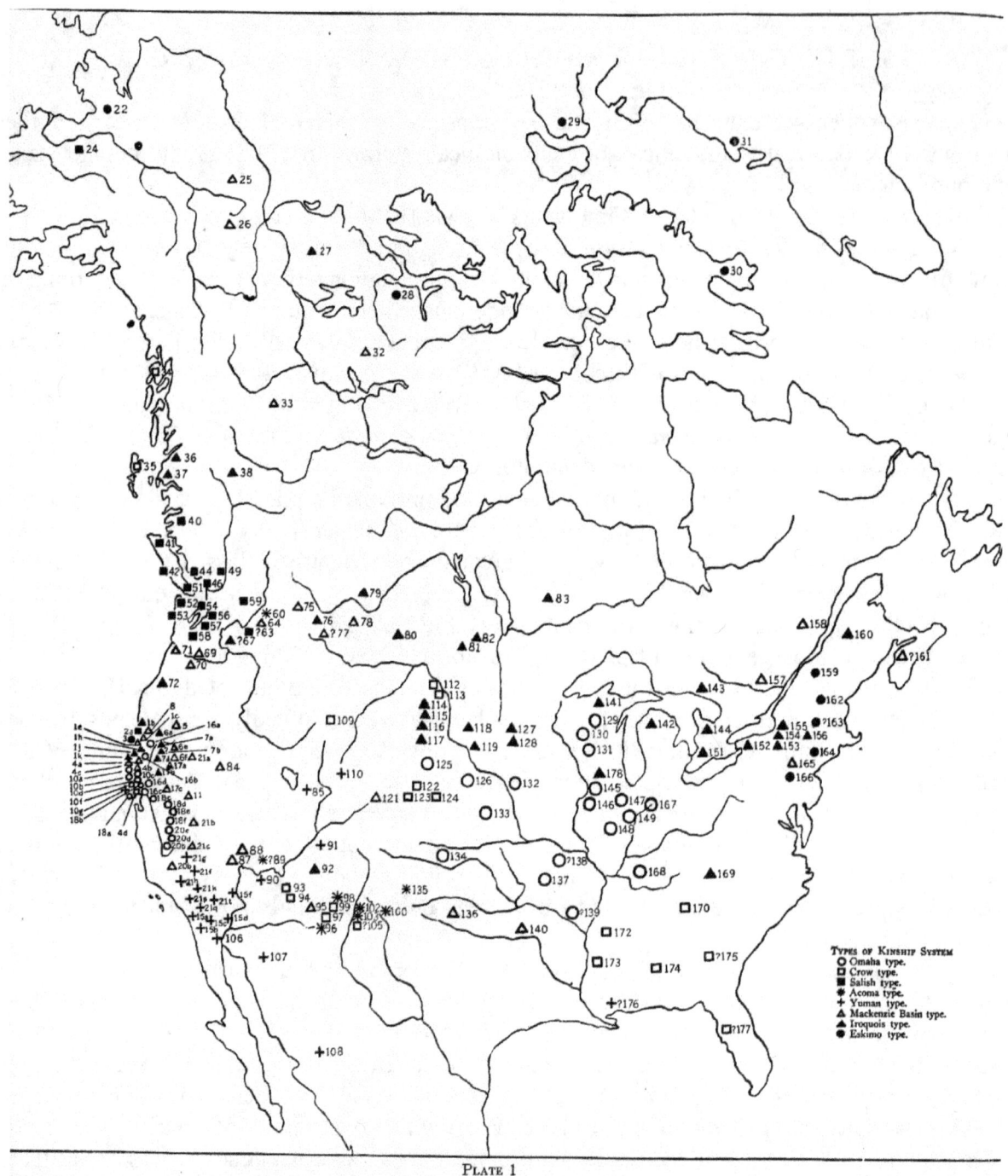

PLATE 1

is, they call all cousins of the speaker's generation by the same term, which is not sibling, as the Eskimo do. Their neighbors, Whilkut, Hupa, and Karok, share a system which classes these cousins with the siblings, although in other respects it resembles that of the Wiyot. Since I have separated Eskimo from Loucheux and Hare on this basis, I have no choice but to separate Wiyot from Hupa and to class it with Eskimo. But this does not mean that the Wiyot system is historically related to that of the Eskimo. The case is different where the several Eskimo groups are concerned. Here there is not only general similarity of systems, but as the terms are phonetically analogous, the genetic connection is unavoidable. Each of such cases will have to be argued on its merits: this study does not attempt it.

The most convenient basis for discrimination, at least in the east, is according to the method of classifying cross cousins. As a rule the systems are m other respects quite similar: the paternal and maternal siblings are separated, a corresponding distinction is drawn between sororal and fraternal nephews and nieces, and parallel cousins are classed with siblings. The Mackenzie Basin tribes, the Iroquois, and the Eskimo differ however in their terminology for cross cousins. They are also called siblings by the Mackenzie tribes: the Iroquois use special cousin terms for them, while the Eskimo class all cousins, parallel and cross, together and apart from siblings.

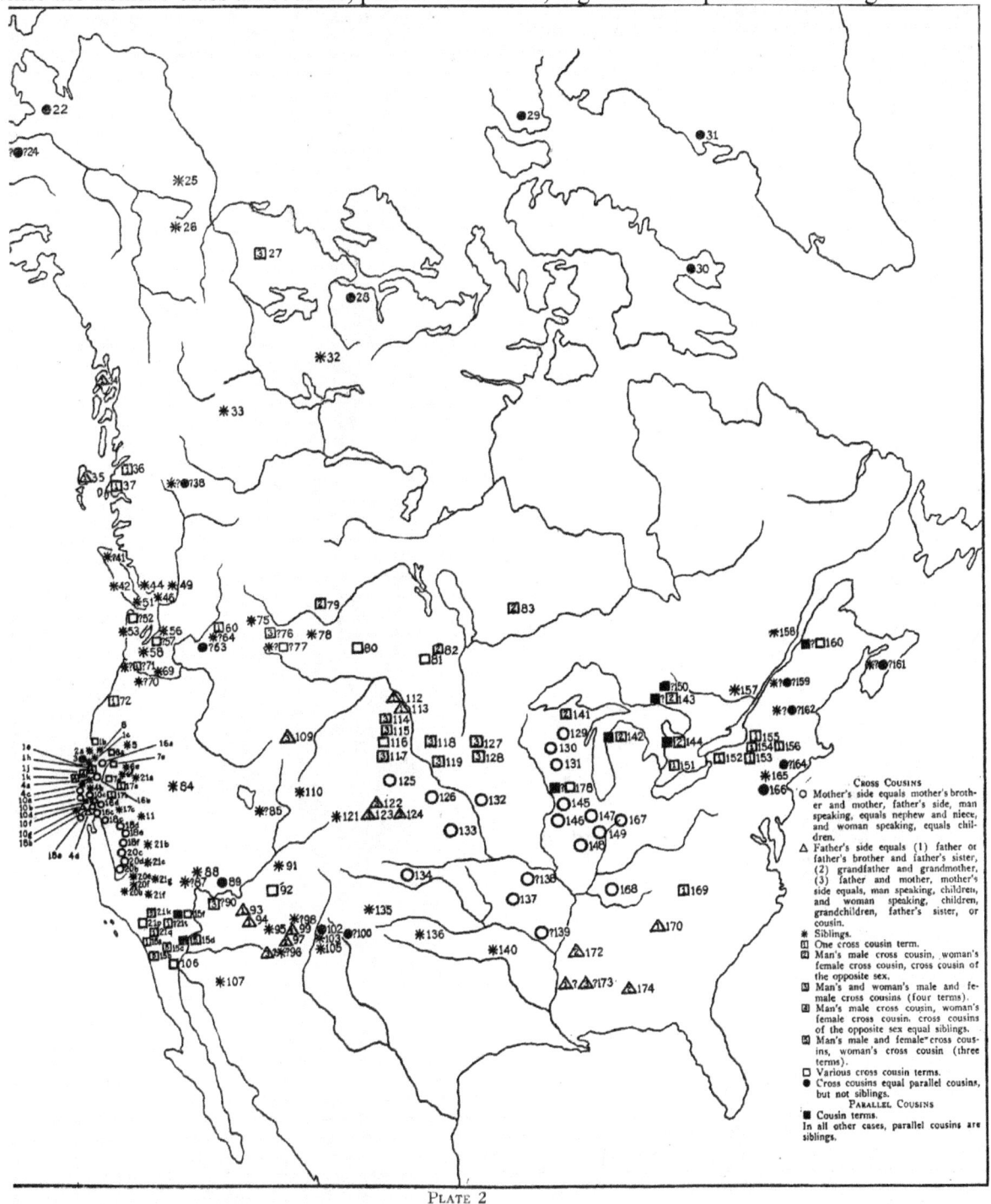

PLATE 2

The Yuman system is generically that of the Mackenzie tribes and the Iroquois, but differs in its development of age distinctions. These are consistently drawn among the parents' siblings, parallel and cross cousins, and nephews and nieces. The classification is based on the relative ages of the connecting relations.

Cross cousin terminology also offers a clue for the discrimination of the Omaha and Crow types. The first class together the mother's brother and his descendants through males: their daughters are always called mothers. The paternal cross cousins are then conceptual equivalents. Similarly systems of the Crow type class the father's sister with her female descendants through females and their sons with the father. Again, equivalent forms are used for the maternal cross cousins. That is, both systems ignore differences of generation in one or the other type of unilateral descent.

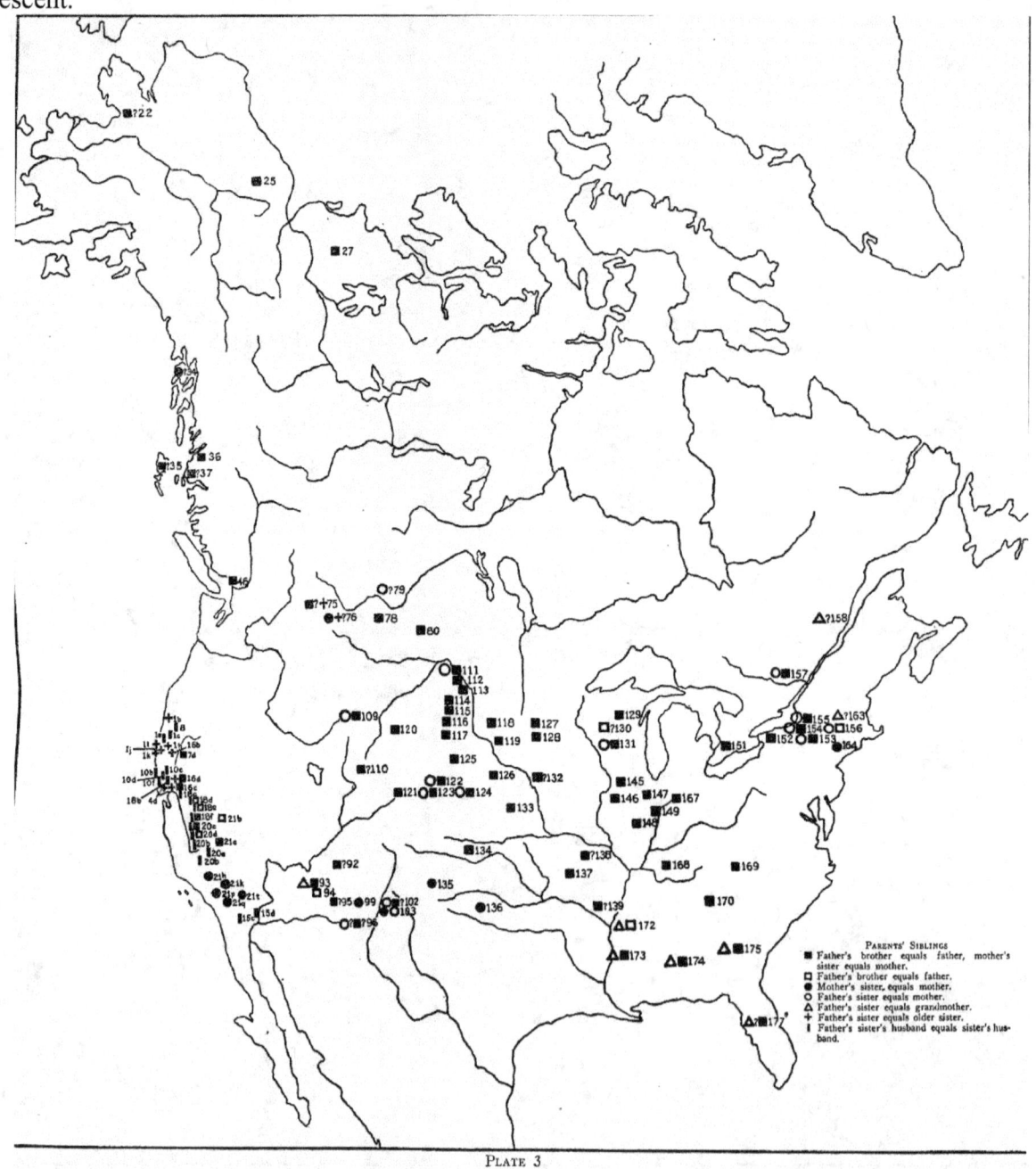

PLATE 3

In all of the preceding, paternal and maternal affiliation is taken into account, at least in the parent and child generations. But among the Salish this is not the case: relatives through males and females are merged, the basis [73] being essentially generation alone. This results in a system which operates with a minimum of terms.

I am not sure that there is justification for placing the Acoma and some of their neighbors in a separate category. Parents' sisters are merged, and this is sometimes true of their brothers. This may represent a transformation in the direction of Spanish and English terminology among these Rio Grande peoples. For the rest, they have a considerable development of verbal reciprocity and a unique way of classifying grandparents and grandchildren.

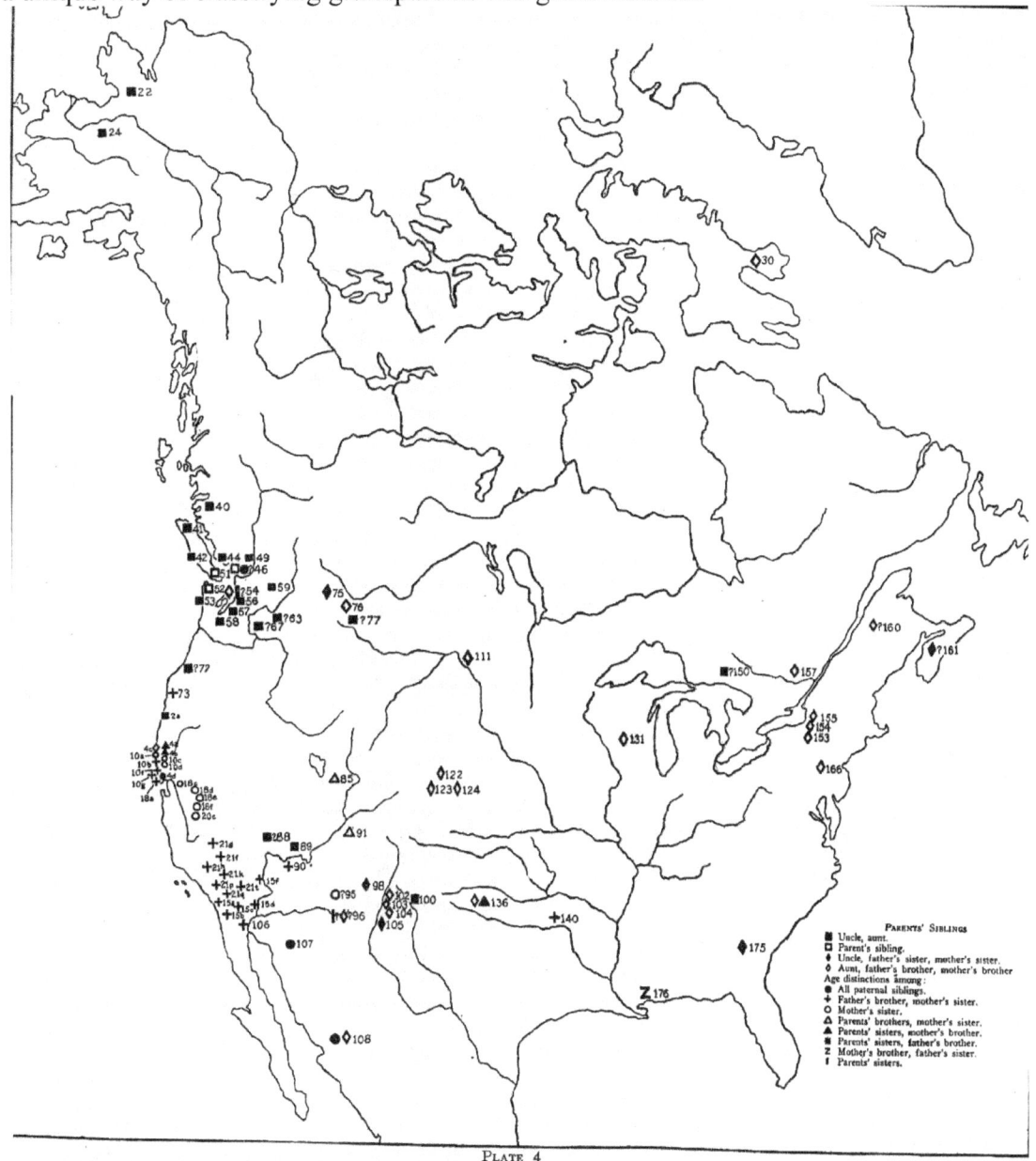

PLATE 4

The differences between these classes are not of the same order. The Mackenzie type, the Iroquois, and the Eskimo are much alike: the Yuman type only less like them with its additional age distinctions. The first two might be merged in a single class. Omaha and Crow types are alike in their unilinear groupings, but in other respects they resemble the four just named, that is in the separation of avuncular and nepotic relatives as they are on the male or female side. The Salish type is the most distinct in that it merges these relatives. As this is an empirical classification, the distinctions between the classes are not given as fundamental but descriptive.

I. OMAHA TYPE

In this system the mother's brother is an "uncle" and his male descendants through males are "uncles." The daughters of these "uncles" are "mothers," whose children are "brothers" and "sisters." The father's sister is an "aunt," her children being "sister's son and daughter" if the speaker is a male, and "son" and "daughter" if female. Their children are "grandchildren."

Ponca (125), Omaha (126), Iowa (132), Oto (133), Kansas (134), Osage (137), Quapaw? (139), Missouri? (138), Winnebago (130), Menomini (129). Sauk-Fox (131), Peoria (146), Kaskaskia (145), Piankashaw (149), Miami (167), Wea (147), Kickapoo (148), Shawnee (168).[151]

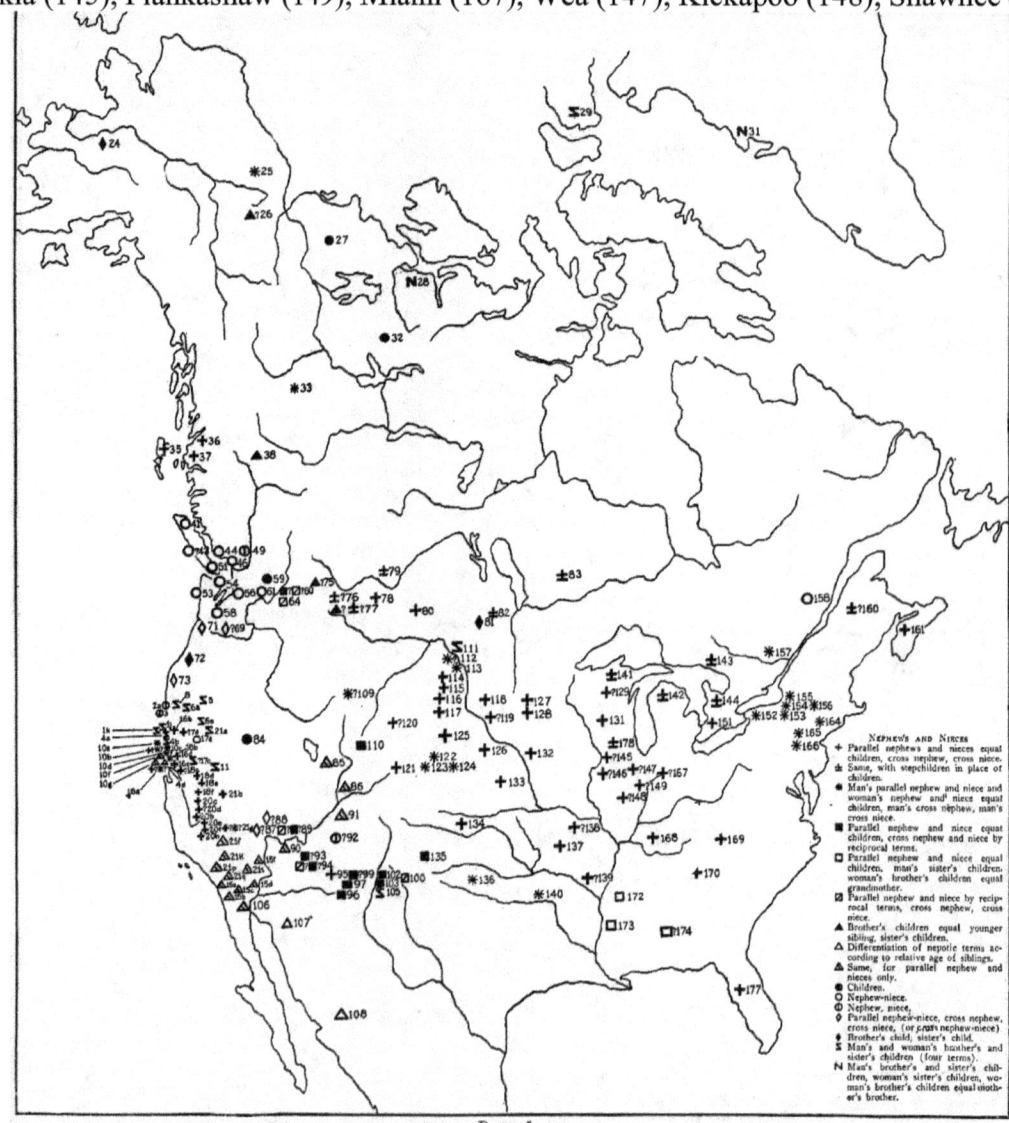

PLATE 5

In the California systems of this type the "uncle's" daughters are "mother's sisters" (as among the first seven tribes listed below), or "mother's younger sisters."

---

[151] Numbers in parentheses refer to maps at the end of the paper.

Northern Wintun (16a), Central Wintun (16b), Southeastern Wintun (16c), Southwestern Wintun (16d), Coast Miwok (18a), Tachi (20a), Gashowu (20d), Northern Pomo (10a), Central Pomo (10b), Eastern Pomo (10c), Southeastern Pomo (10d), Lake Miwok (18b), Plains Miwok (18c), Northern Miwok (18d), Central Miwok (18e), Southern Miwok (18f), Chukchansi (20c).

II. CROW TYPE

In this system the father's sister is an "aunt" and her female descendants through females are "aunts." The sons of these "aunts" are "fathers," whose children are "brothers" (or "fathers") and "sisters." The mother's brother is an "uncle," whose children are "son" and "daughter" (less commonly for a [74] female speaker) and their children "grandchildren." The children of a man's brother and a woman's sister are "son" and "daughter": the children of their other siblings are usually called by nepotic terms.

Crow (109), Hidatsa (112), Mandan (113), Grand Pawnee (122), Republican Pawnee (123), Skidi Pawnee (124), Chickasaw (172), Choctaw (173), Creek (174), Cherokee (170), Mountain Cherokee, Hopi (93), Hano (94), Jemez (99), Laguna (97), Southern Pomo (10f), Wappo (4d), Tlingit (34), Haida (35); possibly Isleta (105), Timucua (177), and less probably Yuchi (175).

III. SAL1SH TYPE

This is characterized by the merging of father's and mother's siblings: that is, there is only one term for "aunt" and one for "uncle." Conversely there is but one term for nephew or niece. There are terms for "grandparent," "child," and "grandchild." Brothers and sisters are usually distinguished as "older sibling" and "younger sibling." Sibling terms are applied to both parallel and cross cousins.

Siciatl (44), Squamish (46), Songish (51), Bella Coola (40), Lillooet (49), Shuswap (59), Snuqualmi (56), Duwamish (57), Nisqualli (58), Klallam (54), Quileute (53), Makah (52), Nootka (42), Kwakiutl (41), Tinneh (24), Yurok (2a): possibly Spokan (163). Possibly Alsea (72), Yakima (67), Kaibab (89), and Tewa (100) should be included here although I have classed them primarily elsewhere.

Two terms, "grandfather" and "grandmother," are used by the Nisqualli, Snuqualmi, Shuswap, Lillooet, Bella Coola, and Yurok.

IV. ACOMA TYPE

This differs from the preceding largely in the use of three grandparental terms, and the verbal reciprocity between grandparents and grandchildren and between avuncular and nepotic relatives. The grandparental terms are man's grandfather, woman's grandmother, and grandparent of the opposite sex. The corresponding grandchild terms are man's grandson, woman's granddaughter, and grandchild of the opposite sex. Parents' sisters are called "aunt." Mother's brother is usually a separate term: father's brother is "father" or "mother's brother," or he is called by a special term. Reciprocally a man's sister's child is "mother's brother," his brother's children are "son and daughter," "uncle," or "father's brother"; a woman's sibling's children are "aunts" Commonly three sibling terms are used, man's brother, woman's sister, and sibling of the opposite sex. Parallel and cross cousins are alike called siblings or by the same special terms:

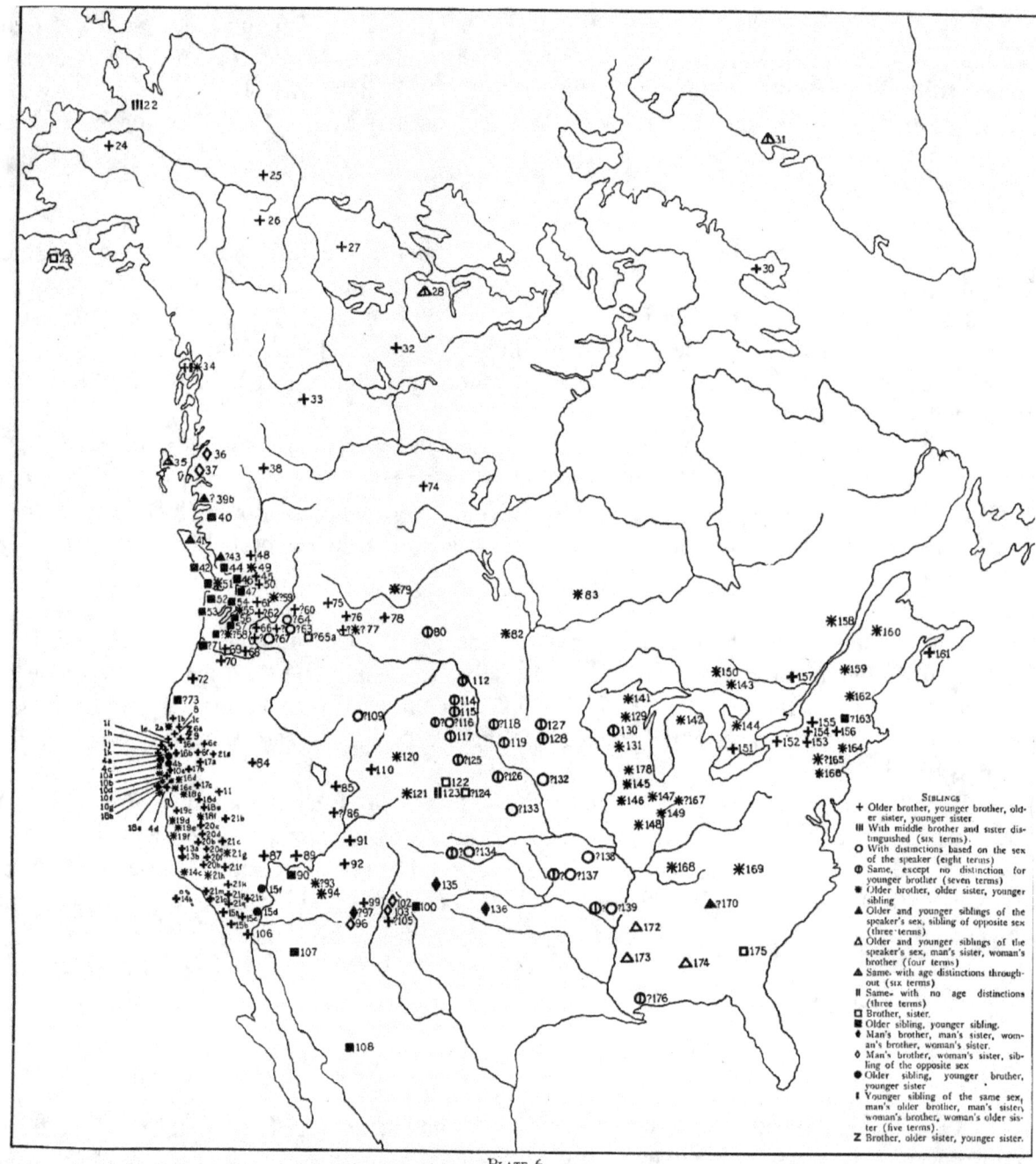

PLATE 6

Kaibab (89), Acoma (96), Cochiti (98), San Felipe (103), Santo Domingo [75] (102), Tewa (San Ildefonso, Santa Clara, San Juan, Nambe) (100), Kiowa (135), Kutenai (60).

Kaibab, Tewa, and Kiowa use terms for grandfather and grandmother: the same terms are used reciprocally for a man's grandchild and a woman's grandchild, except by the Kiowa. The Kutenai have a term for a woman's grandmother, all other grandparents coming under one caption, reciprocally these terms are used respectively for a woman's granddaughter and for all other grandchildren.

137

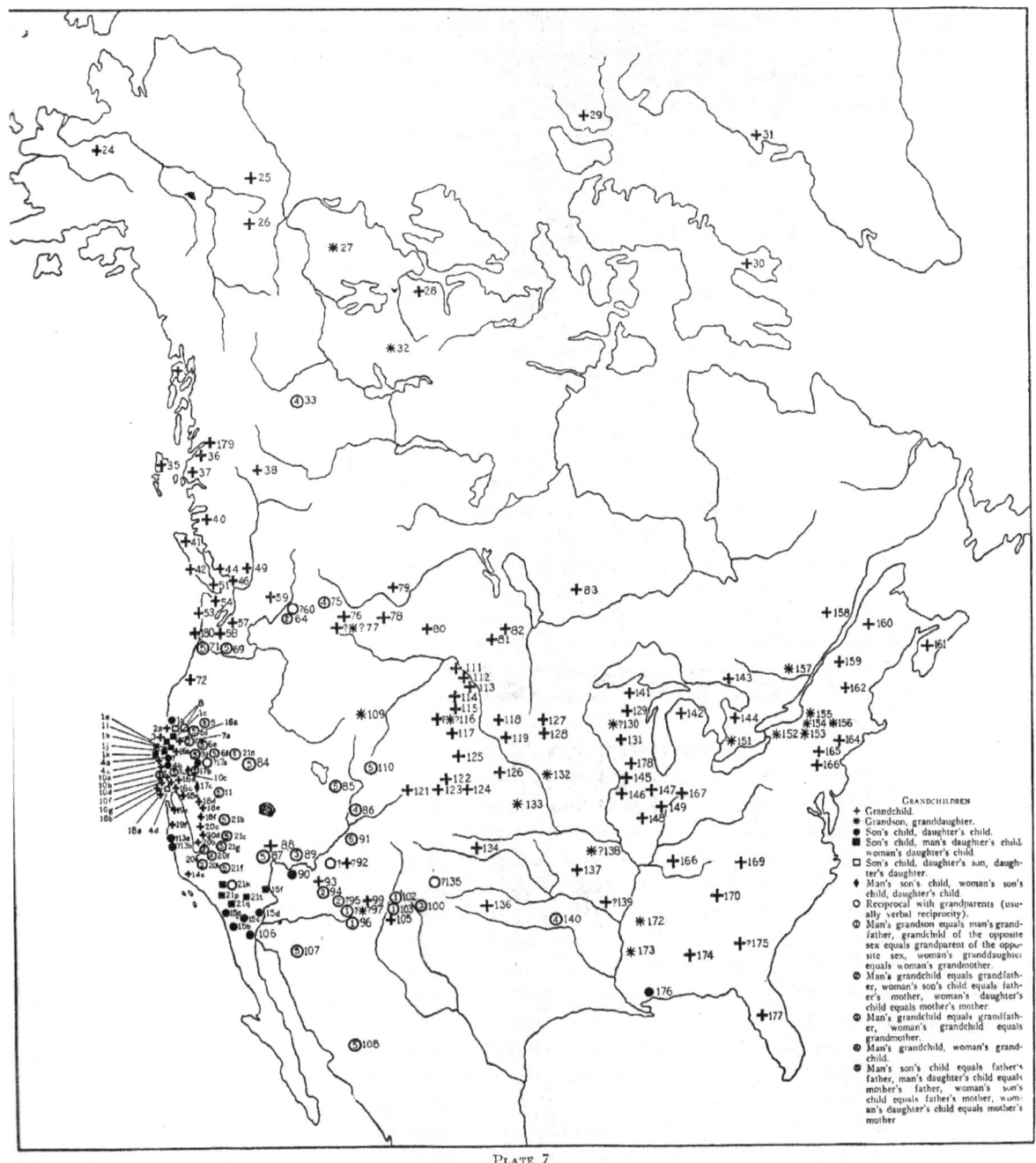

PLATE 7

Father's brother and mother's brother are included in the same term by Kaibab, Tewa and Cochiti (the last call a woman's uncle "brother"). Reciprocally a man's brother's children are "uncles," again excepting Cochiti.

An aunt is called "mother" by Acoma, San Felipe and Santo Domingo: conversely the Acoma, for whom alone there are data, call a woman's siblings' children "son and daughter."

Separate terms for man's father and woman's father are in use among Kutenai, Cochiti, Santo Domingo, and San Felipe: the last has also separate terms for mother.

Special terms are used alike for parallel and cross cousins by Kutenai, Kaibab, Tewa, and Santo Domingo. The Tewa call a female cousin "father's sister," which suggests the Crow type of system.

Among some of these groups the father's sister is "grandmother": Chickasaw, Creek,

Yuchi, and possibly Choctaw, Timucua, and Laguna. The oldest of the father's sisters is "grandmother" for the Hopi. The Pawnee groups call the father's sister "mother."

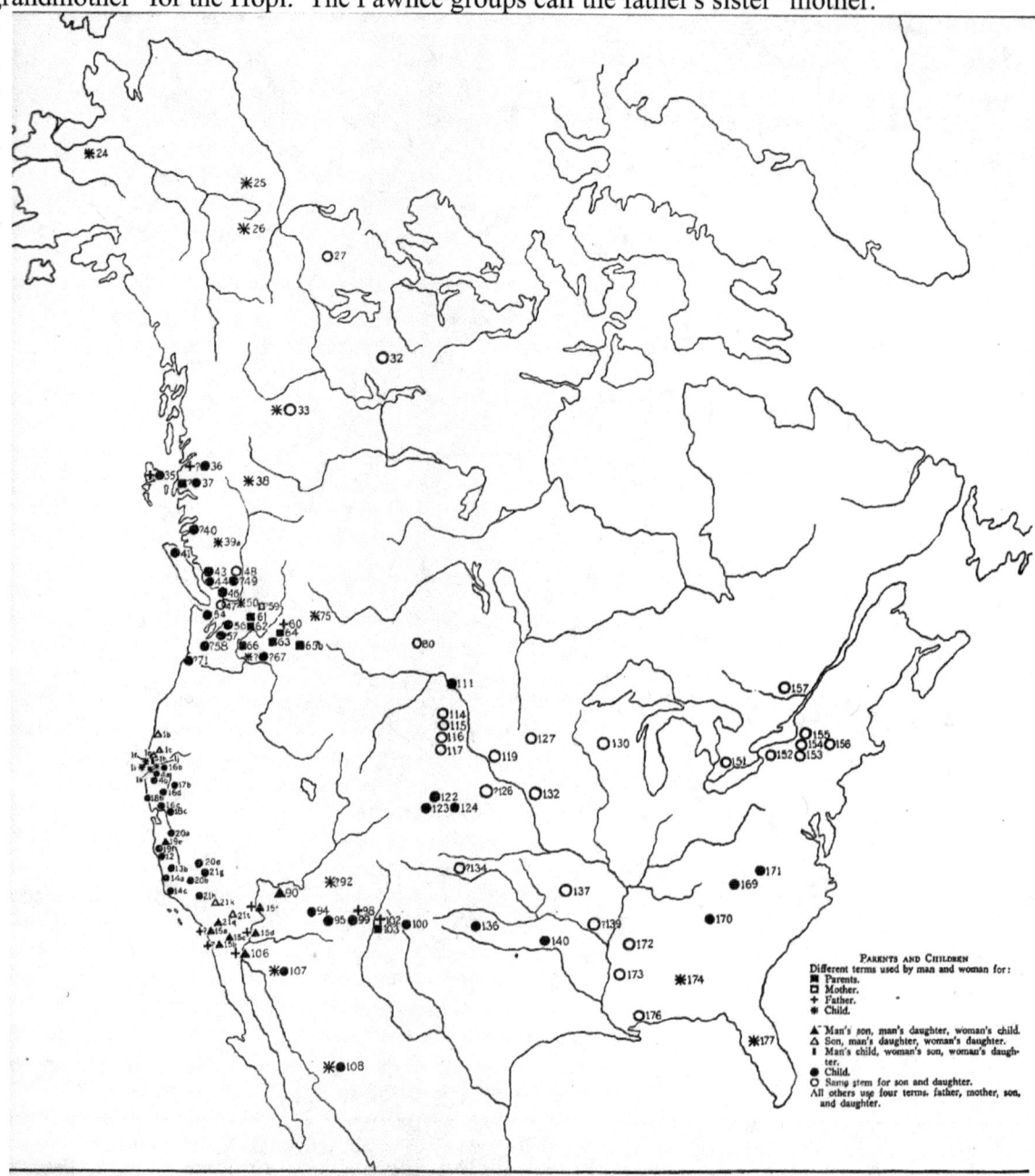

PLATE 8

V. YUMAN TYPE

The distinguishing feature here is the unusual development of age distinctions. Father's older brothers and mother's older sisters are distinguished from their younger siblings. Parallel cousins are older or younger siblings, not according to their ages relative to that of the speaker, but according to those of their parents. Similarly the children of a man's brother and a woman's sister are distinguished according to the relative ages of their parents. There are four terms for sibling; older brother, older sister, younger brother, and younger sister. Parallel cousins are siblings: cross cousins are called by special terms, or less frequently styled siblings. Children of a man are son and daughter: a woman's children are more frequently called by one term. Four grandparental terms are used; father's father, father's mother, mother's father, mother's mother, and conversely four grandchild terms, man's son's, child, man's daughter's child, woman's son's child, and woman's daughter's child.

Cocopa (106), Yuma (15d), Mohave (15f), Havasupai (90), Kamia (15c), Southern Diegueño (15b), Northern Diegueño (15a), Desert Cahuilla (21t), Cupeño (21q), Luiseño (21p), Serrano (21k), Kitanemuk (21h), Kawaiisu (21f), Tubatulabel (21g), Southwestern Pomo (10g), Wind River Shoshoni (110), Uintah Ute (85), Southern Ute (91), Papago (107), Northern Tepehuane (108): possibly Biloxi (176). Wappo (4d), Southern Pomo (10f), and even Northern Wintun (16a) might be included here, but I have preferred to class the first two with the Crow and the third with the Omaha because of their classification of the father's sister's female descendants and mother's brother's male descendants respectively. [76]

Other age distinctions are made. Older and younger mother's brother are recognized by the Uintah Ute, Southern Ute, Papago, Northern Tepehuane, and Biloxi, with comparable distinctions made among a man's sororal nephews and nieces depending on the age of his sisters. The Papago, Northern Tepehuane, and Biloxi also discriminate between father's older and younger sister, and again a woman distinguishes her older and younger brother's children. The Papago make distinctions among cross cousins as well as parallel cousins according to the age of the parents. Nepotic terms are verbally reciprocal for Uintah and Southern Ute, almost wholly so for Northern Tepehuane, and in part for Wind River, Havasupai, Papago, Serrano, and Luiseño.

Two terms, older and younger sibling, are used by Havasupai, Papago, and Northern Tepehuane. Yuma and Mohave use older sibling, younger brother, and younger sister: Tubatulabel and Kitanemuk use older brother, older sister, and younger sibling.

Cross cousins are siblings for Tubatulabal, Kawaiisu, Uintah and Southern Ute, Wind River, Papago, and in part for Mohave.

A woman's children are called son and daughter by Uintah and Southern Ute, Wind River, Kawaiisu, Luiseño, and by Serrano and Desert Cahuilla who distinguish man's and woman's daughters. Tubatulabal and Kitanemuk call a man's children child: Papago and Northern Tepehuane do the same but the term is different from that employed by a woman. Man's father and woman's father are separate terms among Mohave, Yuma and Cocopa; while Northern and Southern Diegueño have two terms which may be applied to either relative.

Grandparental terms are father's parent, mother's father, and mother's mother for Serrano, Luiseño, Cupeño, and Desert Cahuilla, and conversely grandchildren are son's child, man's daughter's child, and woman's daughter's child. These terms are all verbally reciprocal. So are those of the Kawaiisu, Tubatulabal, Wind River, Uintah and Southern Ute, and in part Papago and Northern Tepehuane, all of whom have the regular four grandparent-grandchild terms. Grandchildren are classed as son's child and daughter's child by all the Yumans, except the Mohave, and the Biloxi.

VI. MACKENZIE BASIN TYPE

The characteristic feature here is that all cousins, parallel and cross, are siblings. Four terms are ordinarily employed for these, older brother, older sister, younger brother, and younger sister. Parents are father and mother: children are son and daughter. Parents' siblings are usually father's brother, father's sister, mother's sister, and mother's brother. Nepotic relatives are commonly called by special terms. Grandparents are grandfather and, grandmother: grandchildren are called by one term, Loucheux (25), Tukuthe (26), Yellow Knife (32), Slavey (33), Sarsi (75), Wasco (70), Gros Ventre [Atsina] (78), Arapaho (121), Caddo (140), Shivwits [77] (88), Montagnais (158), Two Mountain Iroquois (157), Munsi (165), and probably Piegan (77) and Micmac (161).

The majority of the Californian and other western tribes that have this system have four terms for grandparents, father's father, father's mother, mother's mother, and mother's father. These are used reciprocally, with but few exceptions, for a man's son's child, a woman's son's child, a woman's daughter's child, and a man's daughter's child respectively.

Hupa (1c), Whilkut (1e), Yuki (4a), Huchnom (4b), Coast Yuki (4c), Lutuami (5), Achomawi (6e), Atsugewl (6f), Washo (11), Southern Maidu (17c), Northern Pauite (21a), Eastern Mono (21b), Western Mono (21c), Moapa (87), Paviotso (84), Wishram (69), Chinook (71).

Other western tribes with this system in its essentials are Paleuyami (20f), Yaudanchi (20e), Yauelmani (20b), Karok (8), Zuni (95), Kalispel (64), and Wichita (136).

There is some possibility that Moapa, Chinook, Piegan, and Micmac make use of special cousin terms.

Father's brother is called father by Zuñi, Eastern and Western Mono, Loucheux, Gros Arapaho, Two Mountain Iroquois, and older or younger father by Wichita and Caddo. Mother's sister is mother for the same groups (except the Eastern Mono) and also for the Sarsi. Again Caddo and Wichita, call this relative mother but distinguish older and younger individuals. Other age distinctions among the parents' siblings are made by the Zuñi in their alternative terms for mother's sister and by the Yuki and Huchnom for the same relative, for mother's brother, and for father's sister.

Two modes of classifying nepotic relatives stand out. A man's brother's children and a woman's sister's children are called son and daughter, child, or step-son and-daughter by Munsi, Micmac, Two Mountain Iroquois, Gros Ventre, Arapaho, Piegan (?), Caddo, Wichita, Zuni, Pauelmani, Yaudanchi, Yellow Knife, Slavey, and Loucheux. Four terms, man's brother's child, man's sister's child, woman's brother's child, and woman's sister's child, are used by most of the Californians, viz., Yuki, Huchnom, Lutuami, Achomawi, Karok, Washo, Southern Maidu, Northern Paiute, Eastern Mono, and Western Mono.

Relative age of the connecting parent enters into the classification of cousins by the Coast Yuki and possibly of nepotic relatives by the Piegan and Tukuthe. These features suggest the Yuman system.

VII. IROQUOIS TYPE

Except that there are special terms for cross cousins, this system is like the last. Parallel cousins are siblings, or in the cases where cousin terms are used these are not the same as the cross cousin terms. Four terms are most common for siblings, older brother, older sister, younger brother, and younger sister. There are separate terms for father, mother, son, and daughter. Parents' siblings are usually father's brother, father's sister, mother's brother, and mother's sister. A man's brother's children and a woman's sister's children are usually "children," with the other nepotic relatives called by two terms, nephew [78] and niece. Grandfather and grandmother are used for grandparents, with one term for grandchild.

Seneca (152), Cayuga (153), Onondaga (154), Oneida (155), Mohawk (156), Wyandot (151), Tuscarora (169), Malecite (160), Ottawa (143), Swampy Cree (83), Wood Cree (82), Plains

Cree (79), Ojibway of Lake Superior (141), Lake Michigan (142), Lake Huron (143), and Kansas, Potawatomi (178), Bungi (81), Santee (127), Sisseton (128), Yanktonai (118), Yankton (119), Oglalla (116), Brule (117), Uncpapa (114), Blackfoot Dakota (115), Assiniboin (80), Blood (76), Alsea (72), Yakima (67), Carrier (38), Tsimshian (37), Nass (36), Hare (27), Tolowa (1b), Lassik (1h), Wailaki (1j), Kato (1k), Shasta (6a), Northern Yana (7a), Yahi (7d), Northeastern Maidu (17a), Northwestern Maidu (17b), Navaho (92): possibly Natick (163) and Central Yana (7b).

Cousin terms are in use by the Carrier for the mother's sister's children, by the Navaho for the father's brother's children, and by the Ottawa and the Ojibway groups (except Lake Superior) for a man's parallel cousins and in part for a woman's parallel cousins.

The Oglalla have eight sibling terms, the sex of the speaker entering into the normal categories of older and younger brother and sister. All the other Siouan tribes have a similar usage, but with a common term for a man's and woman's younger brother, seven terms in all, except the Yanktonai who do not distinguish age among a woman's sisters. Nass and Tsimshian have three terms, man's brother, woman's sister, and sibling of the opposite sex. Shasta, Yahi, Malecite, and Bungi have individual ways of classifying these relatives.

One term for child is used by Nass, Tsimshian, Yakima (?), Northwestern Maidu, and Tuscarora.

The father's brother is called father and the mother's sister mother by a large number of these tribes: Yahi, Nass, Tsimshian (?), Navaho (?), Hare, Assiniboin, all of the Dakota groups, and all of the Iroquoian groups, except that mother's sister is recorded as father for the Mohawk, leather's sister is called mother by the Cayuga, Onondaga, Oneida, and Mohawk. The Blood likewise use a single term for aunt. Kato, Wailaki, Lassik, and Tolowa call father's sister older sister.

All of a woman's nephews and nieces are called children by Malecite (?), Seneca, Cayuga, Onondaga, Oneida, and Mohawk. The Hare call all nephews and nieces children. Special nepotic terms are used throughout by the Alsea, all the Californians (except the Yahi), but only in part by the Lassik, and possibly by the Navaho. The Carrier call a brother's children younger brother and younger sister.

Four grandparental terms, father's father, father's mother, mother's father, and mother's mother, are used by all the Californian tribes. These terms are used reciprocally for grandchildren by Shasta, Northwestern Maidu of the plains, and Yahi. Tolowa and Northeastern Maidu distinguish only son's child and daughter's child; Northwestern Maidu of the mountains a man's son's child, a woman's son's child, and daughter's child. For both Maidu groups the [79] usage is in part verbally reciprocal. Lassik, Wailaki, and Kato class them as son's child, man's daughter's child, and woman's daughter's child. The Navaho have terms for father's parent, mother's father, and mother's mother: they may use the first reciprocally for son's child. The Alsea have but a single term for grandparent. The Oglalla may have separate terms for father's mother and mother's mother. All of the Iroquois proper, Wyandot, Hare, and possibly Oglalla, distinguish grandsons from granddaughters.

VIII. ESKIMO TYPE

This system differs from the preceding in that cross cousins and parallel cousins are called by the same cousin terms. There are four terms for parents' siblings. Nepotic terms are usually man's brother's child, man's sister's child, woman's sister's child, with woman's brother's children termed variously. Two terms for grandparents are used, "grandfather" and "grandmother," with one term for grandchild.

Alaskan Eskimo (22), Copper Eskimo (28), Eskimo of Northumberland Island[152] (29) and Cumberland Inlet (30), Greenland Eskimo (31), possibly Wiyot (3), Delaware (166), and less probably Mohegan (164), Abenaki (159), Penobscot (162), and Natick (163).

Siblings are usually differentiated according to relative age. The Alaskan Eskimo resemble the Chukchi and Koryak in their tripartite division, older, younger, and youngest brother and sister.[153]

Copper and Greenland Eskimo women alike call their brother's child by the term for mother's brother. [80]

COMPARISON WITH EARLIER CLASSIFICATIONS

Resemblances between these systems have been pointed out in earlier papers, but for the most part, attention was drawn only to peculiar modes of classifying certain, relatives.

Morgan's Systems contains many references to just those resemblances between the systems east of the Rockies which form the basis of classification in the present paper. He recognizes in the cross cousin nomenclature an important means of discriminating among them. He remarks on the identity of the Iroquois, Dakota, Assiniboin, Ojibwa, Ottawa, Potawatomi, and Cree, but includes Mohegan with them.[154] The Southern Siouans, Winnebago {HoChunk}, and western Central Algonkin form a group and are distinct from the Iroquois and Dakota. The Crow and Hidatsa are coupled with the Gulf nations and the Pawnee, and a resemblance of Laguna to this group is suggested.[155] Blackfoot is more like the Great Lakes Nations than the western Central Algonkins. Yellow Knife is like Hare. Delaware is recognized as a divergent type, but Munsi is nearest Delaware. The Greenland and Northumberland Island Eskimo are alike, and markedly different from the systems to the south. Spokan and Yakima are unlike the eastern groups, and resemble the Tabegwaches in the use of verbally reciprocal terms.[156]

On the whole this is in essential agreement with my classification. Morgan believes however that these resemblances are indices of biological relationship, Seneca is the typical system: the differences which occur in other systems show in what order they have diverged from the parent stock. He is more impressed with the merging of lineal and collateral relatives in the systems throughout the whole area than with resemblances of lesser range. Accordingly he is satisfied with establishing by this evidence that all the groups, excluding the Eskimo, belong to one biologic group, the "Ganowanian."[157]

Lowie recognizes much the same groups. The Southern Siouans are grouped with some Central Algonkins: the Ojibwa, Cree, Wyandot, and Iroquois with the Dakota.[158] The similarity of cross cousin terminology among the Crow, Hidatsa, Hano, Hopi, Tlingit, Muskogeans, and Pawnee is pointed out. Another group exists in which paternal and maternal lines of descent are merged: Eskimo, Nootka, Quileute, Chinook, various Salish tribes, Kutenai, the Plateau Shoshoneans, and the tribes in a large section of California north and east of the Miwok. This is

---

[152] So I interpret Morgan's Northumberland Inlet.

[153] Lowie, *Historical and Sociological Interpretations of Kinship Terminologies*, 294.

[154] *Systems*, 166, 176, 204, 205, 222.

[155] *Loc. cit.*, 178, 179, 210-217, 188, 191, 198, 262.

[156] *Loc. cit.*, 226, 237, 221, 277, 245-252.

[157] *Loc. cit.*, 176, 192.

[158] This is not wholly independent corroboration for Lowie based his observations partly on the data assembled for the present paper.

my Salish group with the important additions.[159]

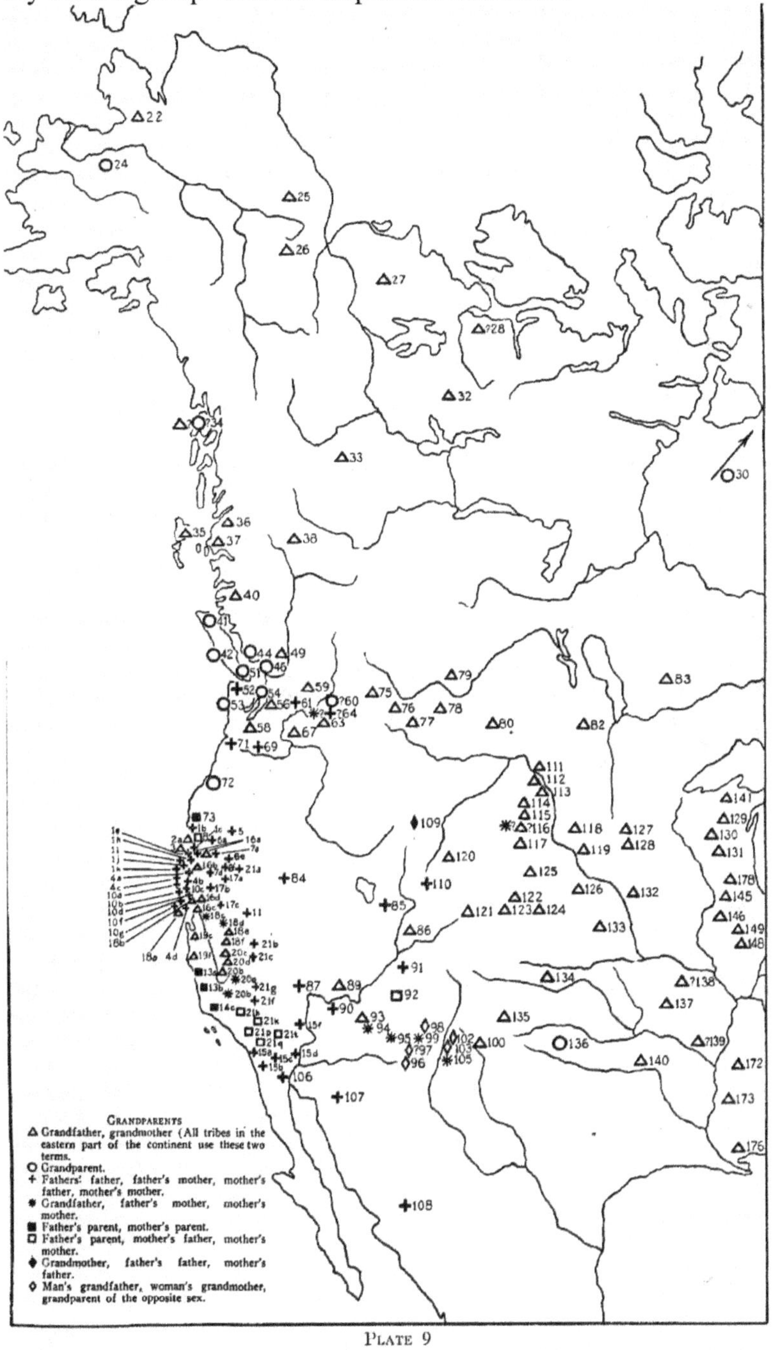
GRANDPARENTS
△ Grandfather, grandmother (All tribes in the eastern part of the continent use these two terms.
○ Grandparent.
+ Fathers: father, father's mother, mother's father, mother's mother.
✱ Grandfather, father's mother, mother's mother.
■ Father's parent, mother's parent.
□ Father's parent, mother's father, mother's mother.
◆ Grandmother, father's father, mother's father.
◇ Man's grandfather, woman's grandmother, grandparent of the opposite sex.

PLATE 9

Kroeber classifies the Californian tribes on the basis of twelve available [81] systems. These fall into three groups. Mohave and Luiseño are similar and show connections with the Southwest. Yurok is unique among Californian systems but bears resemblances to the Coast Salish and tribes of the eastern United States. This agrees with my assignment of the first two to the Yuman and the third to the Salish group. For the rest, Yaudanchi, Northern Paiute, Washo, Tubatulabal, Kawaiisu, and probably Yuki constitute a generic type distributed peripherally to Eastern Pomo, Central Miwok, and Southeastern Wintun. The latter have specialized inasmuch as their systems are simplified. This also corresponds to the present classification: these Pomo, Miwok, and Wintun systems are included in the Omaha type, the others are of the Mackenzie Basin type, except that I consider Tubatulabal and Kawaiisu similar to the Yuman systems.[160]

Gifford offers a general comparison of the Californian systems on the basis of the tripartite cultural division within the state. In such a form it is not altogether clear what relationship he sees between the northwestern systems, the southern, and those of central California. In the northwestern area Wiyot is noted as different from the Athabaskans, Yurok, and Karok. According to my scheme it is possibly to be classed with the Eskimo, the others being of Mackenzie and Iroquois type. Yurok is not recognized as exceptional. In southern California there is some difference between the Shoshonean and Yuman systems, the divergence increasing' with remoteness from the Yuma. This does not

---

[159] *Historical and Sociological Interpretations*, 296; *Kinship Systems of the Crow and Hidatsa*, 341; *Culture and Ethnology*, 124, 153, 167.

[160] *California Kinship Systems*, 378-382.

contradict my inclusion of all southern Californian Shoshoneans with the Yuman tribes, but it does not directly confirm it.[161]

Two groups are recognized in central California; a Sacramento-San Joaquin valley core with a peripheral mountain group. This corresponds fairly well with the present classification, at least so far as the valley group is concerned. All the tribes in the valley group shown in Gifford's Map 24, with two exceptions, have systems of the Omaha type. These two, Southern Pomo and Wappo, might be classed with the Crow or Yuma.[162] Elsewhere Gifford has suggested the resemblance of the Central Miwok to the Omaha.[163]

The mountain tribes are seen as a less homogeneous group. Yet the similarity of Shasta, Northeastern, Northwestern, and Southern Maidu, Lutuami, and Achomawi is noted. In this I concur, but I have separated the first three from the others on the basis of their cross cousin nomenclature, classifying them as of Iroquoian and Mackenzie type respectively. Gifford has also calculated the degree of inter-relation within the whole central Californian area. If we take those systems having least resemblance, i.e. with less than fifty per cent of their categories in common, we have a series of systems which differ on the whole from the others. These are Achomawi, Lutuami, Coast Yuki, Kawaiisu, Tubatulabal, Southern Pomo, Wappo, Southern Miwok, and Central Pomo. [82]

The first three belong to my Mackenzie Basin type; the others to the Crow, Yuma, and Omaha types.[164]

On the whole the present classification agrees with Gifford's in separating the southern Californians, the Wiyot, and the Interior valley systems from those of the mountain tribes. I have gone further in classifying this remainder with the Salish, Iroquois, and Mackenzie Basin groups.

---

[161] *Californian Kinship Terminologies*, 199, 200.
[162] *Loc. Cit.*, 203.
[163] *Miwok Moieties*, 188.
[164] *Californian Kinship Terminologies*, 202, 210.

BIBLIOGRAPHY

Barnum, Francis *Grammatical Fundamentals of the Innuit Language* (Boston, 1901, 264-5).
[Alaskan Eskimo; Nushagak to St. Michael's Is.]

Boas, Franz *Second General Report on the Indians of British Columbia* (Report, British Association For the Advancement of Science, 1890, 688-692).
[Bella Coola, Kalispel, Lillooet, Okanagan (61), Shuswap, Squamish.]

The Vocabulary of the Chinook Language (American Anthropologist, N.S., 6, 1904, 134-5).

Tsimshian Mythology (Thirty-First Annual Report, Bureau of American Ethnology, 1916, 489-495.)   [Kwakiutl, Tlingit, Tsimshian.]

Kinship Terms of the Kutenai Indians (American Anthropologist, N.S. 21, 1919, 98-101.)

Boas, Franz and Goddard, Pliny Earle. *Ts'ets'aut, An Athapascan Language From Portland Canal, British Columbia* (International Journal of American Linguistics, III, 1924, 15-16).
[Ts'ets'aut (179).]

Vocabulary of An Athapascan Dialect of the State of Washington (*same*, 41).
[Willapa ? (180).]

Chapman, John W. *Manuscript of Tinneh Terms, Anvik, Alaska*, 1905.

Dall, W.H. *Tribes of the Extreme Northwest* (Contributions To North American Ethnology, I, 1877, 117-119, 122, 137, 145).
[Bellabella (39b), Eskimo of Cumberland Inlet, Baffin Land, Haida, Kadiak Eskimo (23), Kwakiutl, Nass, Tlingit, Tsimshian.]

Dorsey, J. Owen *Omaha Sociology* (Third Annual Report, Bureau of Ethnology, 1884, 252-255). See Riggs, Stephen R., xvii-xxiii.
[Biloxi, Dhegiha, Hidatsa, Kansas, Mandan, Osage, Quapaw, Santee, Tciwere, Tutelo (171), Winnebago.]

Farrand, Livingston *Notes on the Alsea Indians of Oregon* (American Anthropologist, N.S. 3, 1901, 244).

Frachtenberg, Leo *Manuscript of Quileute Terms.*

Franciscan Fathers *An Ethnologic Dictionary of the Navaho Language* (St. Michaels, Arizona, 1910, 435-6).

Freire-Marreco, Barbara *Tewa Kinship Terms From the Pueblo of Hano, Arizona* (American Anthropologist, N.S., 16, 1914, 269-287). [84]

A Note on Kinship Terms Compounded With the Postfix 'E In the Hano Dialect of Tewa (*same*, 17, 1915, 198-202).
[Hano, Nambe, Santa Clara.]

Gibbs, George *Tribes of Western Washington and Northwestern Oregon* (Contributions To North American Ethnology, I, 1877, 252-3, 270-1, 345).
[Bella Coola, Colville ? (62), Coeur d'Alene (65a), Comox (43), Cowichan (47), Flathead (65b), Kalispel, Kuwalitsk, Lillooet, Nisqualli, Okanogan, Shuswap, Spokan, Thompson (48), Wakynakaine, Wenatchee (66).]

Gifford, Edward Winslow *Miwok Moieties* (University of California Publications in American Archaeology and Ethnology, 12, 1916, 139-194).

Tubatulabal and Kawaiisu Kinship Terms (*same*, 12, 1917, 244-7).
[Uintah Ute, Kaibab Paiute.]

Californian Kinship Terminologies (*same*, 18, 1922, 1-285).

Goddard, Pliny Earle *Manuscript of Sarsi Terms.*

Goldenweiser, A.A. *On Iroquois Work, 1912* (Summary Report For 1912, Anthropological Division, Geological Survey of Canada, 1913, 471).

Golomshtok, Eugene *Manuscript of Atsugewi Terms.*

Grinnell, George Bird *Blackfoot Lodge Tales* (New York, 1917, 210).

Gunther, Erna *Manuscript of Duwamish, Klallam, Makah, and Wasco Terms.*

Haeberlein, Hermann K. <Haeberlin, Herman> and Gunther, Erna *Ethnographische Notizen Uber Die Indianerstamme Des Puget-Sundes* (Zeitschrift Fur Ethnologic, 1924, 1-74).
[Nisqualli, Snuqualmi.]

Harrington, John P. *Tewa Relationship Terms* (American Anthropologist, N.S., 14, 1912, 472-498).
[Tewa of San Ildefonso, Santa Clara, San Juan, and Nambe, Isleta, Taos, Jemez.]

Hawkes, E.W. *Manuscript of Alaskan Eskimo Terms, 1916.*

Hill Tout, Charles *Report on the Ethnology of the Siciatl of British Columbia, A Coast Division of the Salish Stock* (Journal of the Anthropological Institute of Great Britain and Ireland, 34, 1904, 80-1).

Report on the Ethnology of the Statlumh of British Columbia (*same*, 35, 1905, 206-7).
[Cowichan, Lillooet]

Report on the Ethnology of the South-Eastern Tribes of Vancouver Island, British Columbia (*same*, 37, 1907, 352-4).
[Songish.] [85]

Jenness, Diamond *Manuscript of Sarsi Terms.*

The Life of the Copper Eskimos (Report, Canadian Arctic Expedition, 1913-18, 12, 1922, 83-4).

Jones, William *Kickapoo Ethnological Notes* (American Anthropologist, N.S., 15, 1913, 333-5).

Kroeber, A.L. *The Arapaho* (Bulletin, American Museum of Natural History, 18, 1902, 9-10, 150).
[Arapaho, Gros Ventre]

Arapaho Dialects (University of California Publications in American Archaeology and Ethnology, 12, 1916, 75).

California Kinship Systems (*same*, 12, 1917, 358-361).

Zuni Kin and Clan (Anthropological Papers, American Museum of Natural History, 18, 1917, 51-88).
[Acoma, Laguna, Zuni.]

Lowie, Robert H. *Manuscripts of Yankton and Hopi Terms.*

The Northern Shoshone (Anthropological Papers. American Museum of Natural History, 2, 1909, 209).

The Assiniboine (*same* 4, 1909, 36-38).

Social Life of the Crow Indians (*same*, 9, 1912, 207-212, 248).

Exogamy and the Classificatory Systems of Relationship (American Anthropologist, N.S., 17, 1915, 223-239).

Historical and Sociological Interpretations of Kinship Terminologies (Holmes Anniversary Volume, 1916, 293-300).

The Kinship Systems of the Crow and Hidatsa (Proceedings, Nineteenth International Congress of Americanists, 1917, 340-343).

Notes on the Social Organization and Customs of the Mandan, Hidatsa, and Crow Indians (Anthropological Papers, American Museum of Natural History, 21, 1917, 11-15, 26-42, 56-

74).

A Note on Kiowa Kinship Terms and Usages (American Anthropologist, N.S., 25, 1923, 279-281).

Notes on Shoshonean Ethnography (Anthropological Papers, American Museum of Natural History 20, 1924, 287-291).

[Moapa and Shivwits Paiute, Paviotso, Southern Ute, Wind River Shoshoni.]

Mason, J. Alden *Manuscript of Papago [Tohono O'otam] Terms.*

Matthews, Washington *Ethnology and Philology of the Hidatsa Indians* (U.S. Geological and Geographical Survey of the Territories, Miscellaneous Publications, 7, 1877, 55-57).

Michelson, Truman Notes *On the Piegan System of Consanguinity* (Holmes Anniversary Volume, 1916, 320-334).

Morgan, Lewis H. *Conjectural Solution of the Origin of the Classificatory* [86] *System of Relationship* (Proceedings, American Academy of Arts and Sciences, 7, 1868).

Systems of Consanguinity and Affinity of the Human Family (Smithsonian Contributions To Knowledge, 17, 1871).

[Arikara (111), Cheyenne (120), Spokan (63), Tabegwaches (86), Tesuque (101), and Others.]

Morice, A.G. *The Western Denes — Their Manners and Customs* (Proceeding's, Canadian Institute, Third Series, 7, 1889, 120-1).

[Carrier.]

Parsons, Elsie Clews *Manuscript of Acoma, Jemez, Laguna, and Navaho Terms.*

Further Notes on Isleta (American Anthropologist, N. S., 23, 1921, 149-153).

[Isleta, Sandia (104).]

Laguna Genealogies (Anthropological Papers, American Museum of Natural History 19, 1923, 147-203).

[Acoma, Laguna, San Felipe, Santo Domingo.]

Petter, Rodolphe *Sketch of the Cheyenne Grammar* (Memoirs, American Anthropological Association ,1905-7, 443-478).

Radin, Paul *Manuscript of Cochiti Terms.*

The Winnebago Tribe (Thirty-Seventh Annual Report, Bureau of American Ethnology, 1923. 128-133).

Riggs, Stephen Return *Dakota Grammar, Texts, and Ethnography* (Contributions To North American Ethnology, 9, 1893, 45, 203, 204, 207).

[Santee.]

Rinaldini, Benito *Gramatica, Diccionario Y Catecismo* (Mexico, 1743).

[Tepehuane (108).]

Ross, Alexander *Adventures of the First Settlers on the Oregon or Columbia River* (London, 1849, 326).

[Okanagan of Washington (61).]

Sapir, Edward *Manuscript of Nootka Terms.*

Notes on the Takelma Indians of Southwestern Oregon (American Anthropologist, N.S., 9, 1907, 268-9).

Takelma Texts (Anthropological Publications, University of Pennsylvania Museum, 2, 1909).

[Takelma (73).]

A Note on Reciprocal Terms of Relationship In America (American Anthropologist, N.S., 15, 1913, 132-8).

[Kaibab Paiute, Uintah Ute.]

Terms of Relationship and the Levirate (*same*, 18, 1916, 327-337). [87]

Kinship Terms of the Kootenay Indians (*same*, 20, 1918, 414-8).

Corrigenda to "Kinship Terms of the Kootenay Indians." (*same*, 21, 1919, 98).

Nass River Terms of Relationship (*same*, 22, 1920, 261-271).

A Haida Kinship Term among the Tsimshian (*same*, 23, 1921, 233-4).

The Algonkin Affinities of Yurok and Wiyot Kinship Terms (Journal De La Societe Des Americanistes De Paris, N.S., 15, 1923, 36-74).

Skinner, Alanson *Manuscript of Bungi and Potawatomi Terms.*

Social Life and Ceremonial Bundles of the Menomini Indians (Anthropological Papers, American Museum of Natural History, 13, 1913, 32-4).

Notes on the Plains Cree (American Anthropologist, N.S., 16, 1914, 73-4).

Societies of the Iowa, Kansa, and Ponca Indians. (Anthropological Papers, American Museum of Natural History, 11, 1915, 735-8, 766-9).

Speck, Frank G. *Ethnology of the Yuchi Indians* (Anthropological Publications, University of Pennsylvania Museum, I, 1909, 68-70).

Notes on the Mohegan and Niantic Indians (Anthropological Papers, American Museum of Natural History, 3, 1909, 193-4).

Family Hunting Territories and Social Life of Various Algonkian Bands of the Ottawa Valley. (Memoir, Geological Survey of Canada, 70, 1915, 24-5).

[Timagami (150).]

Kinship Terms and the Family Band among the Northeastern Algonkian (American Anthropologist, N.S., 20, 1918, 143-161).

[Abenaki, Malecite, Micmac, Montagnais, Passamaquoddy, Penobscot.]

Correction to Kinship Terms among the Northeastern Algonkian (*same*, 22, 1920, 85).

Spier, Leslie *Manuscripts of Havasupai, Kalispel, Nisqualli, and Wishram Terms.*

Blackfoot Relationship Terms (American Anthropologist, N.S., 17, 1915, 603-7).

Wichita and Caddo Relationship Terms (*same*, 26, 1924, 258-263).

Swanton, John R. *Social Condition, Beliefs, and Linguistic Relationship of the Tlingit Indians.* (Twenty-Sixth Annual Report, Bureau of American Ethnology, 1908, 424-5).

[Haida, Tlingit.]

Contributions to the Ethnology of the Haida (Memoirs, American Museum of Natural History, 8, 1909, 62-6).

Letters To R.H. Lowie *Concerning Chickasaw, Choctaw, and Creek Terms*, May 9, 1914, Dec. 13, 1915.

Terms of Relationship in Timucua (Holmes Anniversary Volume, 1916, 451-463). [88]

Early History of the Creek Indians and Their Neighbors (Bulletin, Bureau of American Ethnology, 73, 1922, 366-8).

[Timucua.]

Swanton, John R. and Murie, James *Manuscript of Skidi Pawnee Terms.*

Tolmie, W. Fraser and Dawson, George M. *Comparative Vocabularies of the Indian Tribes of British Columbia* (Geological and Natural History Survey of Canada, Montreal, 1884, 14-109).

[Bella Coola, Carrier, Chehalis (45), Chilcotin, Chinook, Haida, Kalispel, Klikitat (68), Kutenai, Kwakiutl, Kwantlen (50), Kyuquot, Lillooet, Nakuntlen, Nanaimo, Snohomish, Songish, Tiakluit, Tlingit, Tsimshian.]

Trumbull, James Hammond *Natick Dictionary* (Bulletin, Bureau of American Ethnology, 25, 1903).

Uhlenbeck, C.C. *Flexion of Substantives in Blackfoot, A Preliminary Sketch* (Verhandelingen Der Koninklijke Akademie Van Wetenschappen te Amsterdam, Afdeeling Letterkunde, n.r., 14, 1913).

    [Piegan.]

  Some General Aspects of Blackfoot Morphology, A Contribution To Algonquian Linguistics. (*same*, 14, 1914).

Walker, James R. *Oglala Kinship Terms* (American Anthropologist, N.S., 16, 1914, 96-109).

Wells, Roger, and Kelly, John *English-Eskimo and Eskimo-English Vocabularies* (Circular, Bureau of Education, Washington, 2, 1890).

    [Alaska Eskimo.]

Wissler, Clark *The Social Life of the Blackfoot Indians* (Anthropological Papers, American Museum of Natural History, 7, 1911, 14-6).

KARL SCHMITT, 1915-1952

By FRED EGGAN

COLLISION with a train while driving near Magdalena, New Mexico, on August 6, 1952, resulted in the death of Karl Schmitt and serious injuries to his wife, Iva. He was on the threshold of a brilliant career in anthropology and all who knew his warm personality will feel a deep sense of personal loss.

Karl was born December 20, 1915, in Albany, New York, the son of Karl and Beatrice Schmitt, but the family soon moved to Washington, D.C., where Karl attended William McKinley High School and George Washington University, obtaining his B.S. degree in geology. During his youth he had become interested in local Indian artifacts and had spent much of his time in making archeological collections in the Tidewater area. As a result his interests shifted from geology to archeology. He entered the University of Chicago to study under Dr. Fay-Cooper Cole in the autumn of 1938, after a summer with the U.S. National Museum archeological excavations in western Missouri.

At Chicago his range of activities broadened but archeology remained his central interest. He took part in the Kincaid excavations, but also maintained his relations with the U. S. National Museum, participating in its excavations in Kansas and Virginia. From March 1941-March 1942 he served as archeologist at Ocmulgee National Monument, Macon, Georgia. During this period he married a fellow student, Iva Osanai; their twin children, Sigrid and Kirk, were born February 18, 1944.

Soon after receiving his M.A. in the spring of 1942, he was inducted into the army. His background in natural sciences led to his assignment to the meteorological school at the University of Chicago from which he received a certificate of professional competence in meteorology and a commission in the Air Force. He served at various stations in the United States and then was sent to Morotai in the Southwest Pacific. After separation in March, 1946, 1953 as a major in the Air Force, he returned to the University of Chicago to continue his studies.

Karl served as a teaching assistant in the department of anthropology while completing his doctoral dissertation on "Archaeological Chronology of the Middle Atlantic States" which was summarized in J.B. Griffin (ed.), *Archeology of the Eastern United States*, University of Chicago Press, 1952. He received his Ph.D. in 1947 and accepted a position as assistant professor of anthropology at the University of Oklahoma.

When he went to Oklahoma his area of specialization again shifted, this time from archeology to ethnology. The large Indian population, with its opportunities for ethnological and social anthropological research, offered a new challenge. With his wife and children, he spent weekends and summers in the field, primarily among the Wichita and Caddo, but also with other groups. He retained his archeological and historical interests but the problems of contemporary change and development began to take precedence. The new "pan-Indian" culture in Oklahoma, the development of factionalism, and the study of changes in social organization and kinship became the major foci around which he organized his researches.

His published papers reflect the variety of his interests. Some, such as his "Notes on Morotai Island Canoes," were by-products of war-time assignments. Of his more recent studies, only his and Iva Schmitt's Wichita Kinship: Past and Present had gone to press. This is a notable addition to our knowledge of Plains social organization and an important contribution to the study of problems of social and cultural change. It combines historical and comparative studies in admirable fashion, and develops hypotheses which are both important in themselves and as stimuli to further research. Several manuscripts on various archeological sites, Caddo kinship, Factionalism, and Pan-Indian culture in Oklahoma are largely completed and it is hoped that they can soon be published. His M.A. thesis is to appear in revised form in T. Dale Stewart's *The Historic Indian Village of Patawomeke, Stafford County, Virginia.*

Karl loved his work and he and Iva made many friends among the Indians whom they studied. At the Memorial Service held in Norman, October 5, 1952, a great many Indians came long distances to attend, and the Caddo family which had adopted them spoke of their love and esteem for him. A few days later the Caddoes presented a radio program dedicated to his memory. The University had also recognized his worth and promise. He had recently been promoted to associate professor of anthropology and was to have taken over the chairmanship in September. Karl was a member of the American Anthropological Association, the Society for American Archaeology, the Texas Archaeological and Paleontological Society, and the Oklahoma Archaeological Society, and has been elected to Sigma Xi.

Karl's many friends, both white and Indian, will feel his loss deeply. Their [239] sympathy goes to his wife and children, with a hope that Iva Schmitt can carry forward the research which she and Karl had been pursuing so fruitfully.

UNIVERSITY OF CHICAGO
CHICAGO, ILLINOIS

BIBLIOGRAPHY
Compiled by Robert Bell

"Patawomeke, An Historic Algonkian Site," M.A. thesis, Univ. of Chicago. 1942

"A Dated Silt Deposit in the Ocmulgee River Valley, Georgia," *American Antiquity*, Vol. VIII, pp. 296-297. 1943

"Notes on Morotai Island Canoes," *Man*, Vol. 47, Article 127, pp. 119-122. 1947

"Notes on Some Recent Archaeological Sites in the Netherlands East Indies," *American Anthropologist*, Vol. 49, pp. 331-334. 1947

J. S. Slotkin And Karl Schmitt, "Studies of Wampum," *American Anthropologist*, Vol. 51, No. 2, April-June, pp. 223-236. 1949

"Two Creek Pottery Vessels from Oklahoma," *The Florida Anthropologist*, Vol. 111, Nos. 1-2, May, pp. 3-8. 1950

"The Lee Site, Gv-3, of Garvin County, Oklahoma," *Texas Archaeological and Paleontological Society*, Vol. 21, Sept., pp. 69-89. 1950

"Wichita-Kiowa Relations and the 1874 Outbreak," *The Chronicles of Oklahoma*, Vol. XXVIII, No. 2, pp. 154-160. 1950

"Archaeological Chronology of the Middle Atlantic States," in *Archaeology of the Eastern United States*, edited by J.B. Griffin, pp. 59-70. 1952

"Wichita Death Customs," *The Chronicles of Oklahoma*, Vol. XXX, No. 2, pp. 200-206. 1952

Karl And Iva Schmitt, *Wichita Kinship: Past and Present*, Univ. of Oklahoma Book Exchange, Norman. 1952

Karl Schmitt pp237-239 *American Anthropologist* 55, 1953
https://anthrosource.onlinelibrary.wiley.com/doi/pdf/10.1525/aa.1953.55.2.02a00070

WICHITA-KIOWA RELATIONS AND THE 1874 OUTBREAK

By Karl Schimitt*

A feature of Indian life in and around Anadarko, Oklahoma which is soon obvious to the interested observer is the tribal ethno-centrism which still exists. One aspect of this is pride in one's own tribe and its ways; a second aspect is that of applying stereotypes, frequently uncomplimentary, to other tribes. Particularly striking are the prejudices which the Kiowas and the Wichitas, as groups, hold against each other.[165] A full understanding of the present status of Kiowa-Wichita relations would require an analysis of the complex situation from cultural, psychological, and historical viewpoints. This paper is limited to a consideration of an important historic factor: the series of events now referred to by older Indians as the "74 Outbreak" consisting of an uprising by some bands of the Kiowa and Comanche and their subsequent subjugation by the United States military forces. Wichita, Caddo, and Delaware scouts aided in rounding up the dissident bands. The outbreak has been described by Indian agents[166] and by Army personnel.[167]

Included in this paper is an account of the "74 Outbreak" as remembered by an elderly Wichita woman. Her story not only agrees well with the published materials but also furnishes further details and background information. In addition it has an advantage in that the viewpoint is that of an Indian and includes data pertinent for understanding the actions of the Indians involved.

Setting of the 1874 Outbreak

The Southern Plains area was the scene of many movements of tribes and populations in historic times. These movements were particularly complex during the period of the Civil War. The [155] conclusion of the war found the Kiowa scattered in small groups extending westward from the vicinity of present-day Anadarko into the area of the Wichita Mountains. Following the war, the Wichita, including the Waco, Tawakoni, and Kichai, returned from the vicinity of what

---

[165] *The Chronicles of Oklahoma* 1950: 154-160 Summer.

* Karl Schmitt, Assistant Professor of Anthropology, Department of Anthropology, The University of Oklahoma, Norman, is a graduate of George Washington University (B.A., Geology, 1938), and of the University of Chicago (Ph.D., Anthropology, 1947). For the past three years, he has been concerned with the ethnology of the Plains Indians with special reference to that of the Wichita, conduced under the sponsorship of the Department of Anthropology and the Institute of Human Studies of The University of Oklahoma. His published articles relate to the subject of archeology in Georgia, Oklahoma, and the Netherlands East Indies, — Ed.

/ 1 As is frequently the case in the application of stereotypes, individual exceptions are made. Kiowa and Wichita individuals do fraternize and attend each others ceremonials. At a recent Wichita gathering at which the writer was present, Kiowas were among the guests of honor. There are also now a number of intertribal marriages.

[166] / 2 Annual Report of the Commissioner of Indian Affairs to the secretary of the Interior for the year 1874, pp. 72, 221, 238. Washington: GPO, 1874.

[167] / 3 Record of Engagements with Hostile Indians within the Military Division of the Missouri from 1868 to 1882. Washington: GPO, 1882, p. 41.

is now Wichita, Kansas, and settled on their reservation, the southern boundary of which was the Washita River, in what is now Caddo County.[168]

The Wichita bands inhabited separate, though adjacent, villages. The Wichita proper under two chiefs named *Tsodiako* and *Kawhaydis* lived on the east side of Sugar Creek near the present homes of Mr. Clarence Standing and Mr. Hugh Miller; one band of the Tawakoni under the leadership of Tawakoni Dave lived on the hill just north of the Standing home; the Waco led by Buffalo Good inhabited a village on the west side of Sugar Creek across from the Wichita; a second band of the Tawakoni, "Tawakoni Jim's bunch", were also on the west side of Sugar Creek and a little north of the Waco; the Kichai lived several miles to the west in the flats of the Washita, just under the "Old Shirley Place," and were led by Chief "Just Another Day."

The period of the early 1870's was one of great stress for the Plains tribes, since they had been forced to alter radically their former type of life: the buffalo were practically extinct and this meant that the main subsistence of tribes like the Kiowa, Comanche, and Cheyenne was gone; the older form of obtaining' prestige and wealth by warfare and raiding was discouraged by the United States government; American expansion had greatly reduced Indian lands and forced many different tribes to live in close proximity; and tribal autonomy no longer existed since they were not free to move about as they pleased and were subject to the authority of Indian agents and Army personnel in many matters. Some tribes, such as the Wichita and Caddo, threw their lot with the government whereas others, including the Kiowa, Comanche, and Cheyenne, tended to resist authority. This environment of unrest, insecurity, and conflicting attitudes toward the government was a natural setting for intertribal friction.

An important feature of Indian life at this period was the weekly distribution of rations by the agencies. Rations included beef cattle, flour, coffee, sugar, lard, bacon,[169] and other items to which they were entitled as a result of treaties with the United States. The Wichita Agency had been established just north of [156] the present town of Anadarko to handle the administration of the Wichita, Caddo, and Delaware. Another agency was at the site of the present Fort Sill to administer the Kiowas and Comanches. However, one band of Comanches and a number of Kiowas found it more to their convenience to procure their rations at the Wichita Agency. Rations were issued on Saturdays and for those occasions large numbers of Indians camped about the agencies and spent their time visiting and gambling. It was at the Wichita Agency on one of these issue Saturdays that the main fracas of the 1874 outbreak occurred. There follows below an elderly Wichita woman's version of the event.

A Wichita Account of the 1874 Outbreak[170]

The Kiowa were fussing about the government cutting down their rations. They also didn't

---

[168] / 4 For a summary of movements of the Wichita during and shortly after the Civil War consult Gladys Esther Gates, The Wichita Indians from 1859 to 1868, Unpublished Master's thesis, History Department, University of Oklahoma, 1926.

[169] / 5 The Wichita and Kiowa threw away five gallon tins of lard and sides of bacon because to them it smelled bad and was considered inedible. Older individuals even refused to eat beef because of its bad smell and taste.

[170] / 6 ~~Informant~~ #A is a woman who is acknowledged to be the oldest member of the Wichita tribe. She was officially born in 1868 but other data indicate her birth dale to have been 1863 or 1864. The account has been edited by the author. Changes were largely confined to grammatical construction; most words and idioms are those of the informant.

want to send their children to school. In addition Kiowa warriors had been raiding in Texas and the agent had been getting letters from Washington telling him to control those Indians. The government and the agent were expecting some trouble so they had two companies of soldiers camped at the agency and they threw up a little fort in the hills just north of the agency.[171] The agent had cautioned the Wichita chiefs to keep their people away from crowds and out of possible trouble. However, when the fighting broke out some young Wichita men joined in. There were lots of Wichitas in the '74 outbreak; they weren't supposed to be, but they were. It happened right after school started, it must have been September.[172]

The trouble started on Saturday, on an issue day. The agent called in the Kiowa chiefs and they got to fussing. Trouble started in the office when Kiowas started abusing government employees and the soldiers arrested one or two chiefs.[173] Talk got around to other Indians and they just started shooting everybody that was [157] white. The soldiers took refuge in their fortification on the hill and withstood all attacks. The rebels fanned out over the country. They burned John Osborne's father's store. He was married to Black Beaver's daughter. Osborne had five wagon loads of goods coming in. He said, "I'd better get out and warn those people." He went out to meet the wagons. The Indians killed him, the five drivers, and a Negro cook, just east of what is now Anadarko. They killed the teams, too. I was way down on Sugar Creek when the fighting started. Only the old people and children were left at home. We could hear the shooting. The women came home and most of the men, too. The women, children, and old people deserted the villages and went over to Cottonwood Grove.[174] Most of the men stayed behind at the villages.

There were three of us on our horse. The people used to kid me afterwards and tell me how I kicked the side of my horse and said, Lets go!" They used to tell me that I "sure must like to ride." One old man kept stirring up the women. Everytime they would quiet down, he would get excited and say he heard those rebels coming, and off everybody would run again. Finally, a Wichita man came over and told us not to go so far because the rebels weren't after us. It was way after dark when we got back to our village. *The Kiowa had even made a raid on our village*! The sacks of corn were cut and the grains were lying about. They claim the Kiowas did it!

After the excitement passed, it was found that the Kiowas had left to get away. They had gone down to Texas. At this time a group of Wichita, Caddo, and Delaware were recruited as Indian scouts under the leadership of Captain Pratt. The United States Army with the aid of the Indian Scouts rounded up the rebel Kiowas and brought them back. *This was the only time the*

---

[171] /7 According to the Kiowa agent's report, there were four companies. The Wichita agent states that the companies were there to arrest two Comanche chiefs who were not enrolled at any agency and who were at the Wichita Agency against orders. Annual Report of the Commissioner of Indian Affairs to the Secretary of the Interior for the year 1874, Washington; GPO, 1874, pp. 221 and 238.

[172] /8 Both the Kiowa and Wichita agents state that the incident occurred in August and, according to the Kiowa agent, specifically on the twenty-second of the month. *Ibid.*

[173] /9 According to the agents' reports, the trouble started near the commissary and involved the two Comanche chiefs as well as the Kiowas. The Wichita agent relates that, when the general in command of the forces tried to arrest the Comanche chiefs, the Kiowas fired upon him. The Kiowa agent's version is a little different: Red Food, one of the Comanche chiefs, started to run away and was fired upon by a guard, whereupon the Kiowas, led by Lone Wolf, commenced shooting at the troops.

[174] /10 This was the site of a former Wichita village of that name and now the site of Verden, Oklahoma.

Wichitas went against the Kiowas. Kiowa sure did hate the Wichita after that! The leading Kiowa chiefs were imprisoned and later sent to Florida for a period of years. There they learned Christian hymns. I remember when the Kiowa chiefs were brought home. They were brought in wagons to the old Wichita School which was located just north of present day Anadarko. The Wichita, Caddo, and Delaware school children were taken out to meet the returning chiefs. The authorities made the Kiowa chiefs sing old gospel songs for the children. Then the Kiowa families came in and claimed their men.

Another detail concerning the outbreak was furnished by ~~Informant~~ #B.[175] One of the Wichita scouts was *Ichitowax* who was a "war chief." *This man whipped a Kiowa Chief named Big Tree and* [168] *tied his hands and 'brought him in*. It should be remembered that striking a live enemy was one of the highest coups or war honors that a Plains Indian could perform.

Discussion and Further Statements

There undoubtedly was some mutual suspicion between Kiowas and Wichitas before 1874. It would be foolish to say that the 1874 outbreak was the main cause of Kiowa-Wichita ill-feeling. There must have been previous historic facts which could be used to explain why most Wichitas sided with the United States Government against the rebellious Kiowas instead of joining them. However, in the minds of present-day individuals that date marks the break in what was previously an overtly friendly relationship between tribes. After the rebels had been rounded up there was great antagonism between the two tribes. The general feeling of the Kiowas is understandable; in their opinion former friends and allies had deserted them and sided with the enemy whites. In addition Wichitas had actually participated in the campaign against them and one of their chiefs had been humiliated by a Wichita chief. An added insult came with the enforced concert for the children of the Wichita, Caddo, and Delaware when the Kiowa chiefs returned from Florida.

The general feeling of the Wichitas included a reaction against the ill-feeling of the Kiowas plus certain resentments of their own. The Wichitas had lost a considerable amount of property[176] in the Wichita agency incident and no doubt held this against the Kiowas. Also present seems to have been indignation over what they considered to be general preferential treatment of the Kiowas and unfair treatment of the Wichitas by the United States Government. The Wichitas had long made efforts to co-operate with the whites and had received a relatively small reservation which was in effect reduced in size by the settlement of other tribes. The Kiowas, who were relatively new-comers to the area and who had been notoriously antagonistic to whites, were given a large reservation and one which included much of the Wichita's traditional territory.

By the time the Kiowas had been brought back to the reservation following the uprising and order had been established, the mutual antagonism between the Kiowas and the Wichitas had become crystalized around the events of the outbreak. This antagonism continued as an important factor in Kiowa-Wichita relations for the next three quarters of a century. There follow some, statements from Wichita ~~informants~~ which illustrate the continuance of the antagonism over a period of years.

~~Informant~~ #C, a Wichita man who attended school during the 1880's and 1890's, said that when he was a boy there were two [159] schools. One was on the north side of the Wichita and was for Wichita, Caddo, and Delaware children, while the other was on the south side of the river and

---

[175] / 11 A Wichita man who was officially born in 1876, though other data indicate that 1868 is more probably correct.

[176] / 12 See account of ~~Informant~~ A and also Wichita agent's report, *op. cit.*

was for Kiowas. Whenever they caught a Kiowa on the north side of the river, "they tried every way to kill him, they would kick him in the stomach, in the head, they "would kick him anywhere." On the south side of the river there were four stores or trading posts. "When the Wichita children would go over to the stores, and the Kiowa boys saw them, they would be given similar treatment by the Kiowas. My ~~informant~~ says "you had to run as fast as you could to get across the river and get away." The wife of this man said that the above "sounded awful but that the kids learned to dislike the Kiowas from their parents."

~~Informant~~ #B, who was a school boy during the 1870's and 1880's, tells of a more formalized type of mayhem which was practiced. The Wichitas had a game in which two sides of boys just kicked each other until one side ran the other off. When Wichitas played this among themselves they did it "just for fun — they kick each other around and when they want to quit they quit — nobody hurt." However, this same game was played with Wichitas and Caddoes on one side and Kiowas on the other, and "when play with Kiowas — not for fun!" In these intertribal kicking games, which were planned ahead of time, the contestants tried to inflect actual bodily, harm on each other.

~~Informant~~ #D, a Wichita man who was born about 1901 and later went to school at Chilocco, related how he got the Kiowas "stirred tip" when a student at that school. There was a pageant in which a Kiowa boy played the part of a chief and a Wichita boy kneeled in front of him. He said, "I think there is something wrong with that, it ought to be a Kiowa kneeling before a Wichita chief." This was a direct reference to events in the 1874 outbreak.

Present-day hostilities seem to be largely verbal and are reflected in derogatory statements made by members of both sides about purported general characteristics of the other groups. Wichitas tend to stereotype the Kiowa in terms of what they consider undesirable personality traits, while the Kiowa seem to stereotype the Wichita largely on the basis of unattractive physical traits.[177]

Summary and Conclusions

The account of the 1874 outbreak illustrates that descriptions by living ~~informants~~ of events long past are not to be regarded lightly. In this particular case the related account checks rather well with accounts published soon after the occurrence,[178] and in [160] addition adds pertinent details omitted, or not known, by the early reporters. Obviously much of the informant's story was not the result of actual observation of events but was gained by listening to elders discuss the affair. In a situation of this sort it would not be surprising if distortion or ethnocentric slanting of information occurred. This is not obviously the case.

Even if distortion does occur, such information should not be ignored. What individuals consider to be true is equally important in explaining present attitudes and behavior as the actual truth. In this case information gained by Wichitas from parents and grandparents concerning what the Kiowas have done or are like, and vice versa, constitutes the facts and basis of actions for many individuals of both tribes.

It should be pointed out, lest it be thought that the Wichitas and Kiowas are at each other's throats, that the situation is not nearly that extreme. There are factors operating against the continuance of antagonistic feelings. A number of these factors are the same as those more general

---

[177] / 13 Specific details of present stereotypes would add little to the present paper and could conceivably perturb individuals.

[178] / 14 Published accounts themselves do not agree on details.

factors -which tend to tear down all tribal barriers. Attendance of Kiowas and Wichitas at the same schools teaches individuals that persons of the other tribe can he worthwhile human beings. There are now several inter-tribal marriages among members of the younger generation, a very rare occurrence in the past. Membership in organizations which cut across tribal boundaries, as the United States Army, the Native American Church, and the Baptist Church, also tends to create a common set of interests and erase old tribal animosities. Time has a soothing effect, and the loss of tribal customs by members of the younger generations leads older members of rival tribes to meet and talk amicably of by-gone days, and often to sing and participate in each others "pow-wows."

    In conclusion, one can say that individuals of the Kiowa and Wichita tribes still hold adverse stereotypes of each other and in the minds of the people, at least, much of their mutual prejudice can be traced back to the "74 outbreak." However, animosities are not as intense as those which existed fifty years ago and a continuing diminution of ill-feeling is to be expected.

WICHITA DEATH CUSTOMS[179]
By Karl Schmitt

Introduction

A purpose of archaeology is to reconstruct in so far as possible the culture or way of life of extinct groups of people. Ethnology has an aim of understanding the life of living groups of people, or of groups in the ethnological present. Ethnologists can arrive at their goal through actual observation of people in action, through conversing with and questioning ~~informants~~, through reading descriptions of past observers, or through combinations of these techniques. Archaeologists, of necessity, base much of their reconstruction on the analysis of material remains. But, since both archaeologists and ethnologists are concerned with culture, there is an overlapping of interests. Particularly in the realm of death and burial practices is this so. Archaeologists place great emphasis on burial practices in determining relationships, and ethnologists, often find the rites and behavior at this time of crisis most illuminating in understanding the total patterning of a given culture. A presentation of the data concerning Wichita death customs may be of help in identification of archaeological sites of possible "Wichita provenience and aid in the interpretation of material from known Wichita sites.

Present Wichitas are the consolidated and intermarried remnants of several groups which formerly were politically independent and of much greater population. The Wichita proper, the Waco, and the Tawakoni were culturally and linguistically similar, while the Kichai, although similar in general culture, were divergent linguistically. The Wichita proper were visited in central Kansas in 1541 by Coronado. The Waco and Tawakoni, if they were separate groups at this time, presumably ranged south in what is now present Oklahoma. The Kichai at the same period appear to have been much further to the south and associated with Caddo-speaking groups. After this time there was a southward movement of the Wichita-speaking groups and by 1760 they were established in villages along [201] or south of the Red River. With later declines in population there was a general northward movement which finally culminated with the consolidation of the Wichita-speaking groups and the Kichai in the Indian Territory in 1859. The descendants of these groups form the present Wichita tribe. Although Caddo groups and one band of the Delaware were also placed on the Wichita Reservation at the same time, they preserved their cultural identity and in particular still have different burial customs.

Thus, the "Wichita and other related groups have lived within the boundaries of the present states of Kansas, Oklahoma, and Texas during the last three centuries, and presumably have left a

---

[179] *The Chronicles of Oklahoma* 1952: 200-206 Summer.

/ 1 This paper was presented at the 1951 meetings of the Texas Archaeological and Paleontological Society at San Angelo. Data were gathered from modern Wichitas in the vicinity of Anadarko, Oklahoma during the years of 1947-51 when the author was conducting ethnological investigations under the auspices of the Facility Research Committee, the Institute of Indian Studies, and the Department of Anthropology, all of the University of Oklahoma. Although a number of ~~informants~~ were used, one individual, Mrs. Cora West, was the principal source of information and gave the most complete data. This is partially because she is one of two Wichitas who lived in the last concentrated Wichita village and thus actually participated in the old culture. She was born near present Wichita, Kansas during the Civil War, when the Wichita and related groups sought refuge there, and is the oldest member of her tribe.

number of archaeological sites which have not been historically identified. The data presented herein refer specifically to the period of the 19th century but may furnish links to help in the identification of older sites.

Descriptive Data

People who were seriously ill were moved to a tipi set up in the family's housing area, and treated there by medicine men or "doctors." My oldest ~~informant~~ became very emotional when the possibility of a death occurring in a grass house was posed, and said, "Nobody die in grass house!" Close association with menstruating women, women near parturition, and sick people could be detrimental to the health of others, particularly men; such people were often separated from the rest of the household. When death appeared imminent word was sent for all the relatives to assemble and even distant cousins (who were "brothers" and "sisters" in Wichita terminology) were expected to come. After death occurred there was no set period of time before burial took place; instead it was considered desirable to have the interment as soon as possible. However, all the relatives had to gather first. At this time a hair cutting ceremony took place:

> CW was present at such a ceremony when she was a little girl. Her aunt and step-mother took her to a tipi where a relative had died. On her arrival, she noticed a deceased girl covered up on the ground south of the central fire and a pile of hair and a butcher knife between the corpse and the tire. There were a lot of people present — "just family and friends." Everybody had to cut off part of their hair "to show respect." CW's aunt cut her own hair with the knife and then CW's. All hair was placed on the pile near the tire. A grandmother or an aunt sat at the feet of the deceased and "had charge of hair cutting business." Women cut their hair straight around while men cut theirs on one side only.[180] Afterwards some of the women took the hair and scattered it into the water of a nearby creek.

Soon after the relatives had shown their respect, the actual interment occurred. Non-relatives dug the grave and were rewarded [202] with presents of blankets or robes. The family would ask some old person, usually a woman, to dig the grave and she in turn would ask someone else to help her. Graves were in a cemetery area adjacent to the village and preferably on a hillside, although occasionally there were burials in bottom land. The cemetery of the last consolidated village[181] of the Wichitas occupied during the 1870's was on a hillside to the north and slightly east of the village. In shape the grave was an approximate rectangle and oriented east and west.

The body was washed in warm water and dressed in the deceased's best clothes, and the face was painted. If a man had been a warrior, his "warrior's outfit" consisting of bow and arrows, rawhide shield, warbonnet, and medicine bundle might be placed in the grave also. However, the deceased might have expressed a desire that a nephew[182] or a son have his paraphernalia and then

---

[180] / 2 Men wore their hair loose and shoulder length. A few early photographs of prominent Wichita individuals have been examined. Several had hair longer on one side than the other. CW said this was due to their having been in mourning.

[181] / 3 Karl Schmitt, Wichita-Kiowa Relations and the 1874 Outbreak, *The Chronicles of Oklahoma*, Vol. 28, No. 2, p. 155 (Summer, 1950).

[182] / 4 Only a man's sister's son was a nephew in the older Wichita kinship system. In later times a brother's son also was considered a nephew and could share in the inheritance.

it would not be included in the grave. CW said it seemed that men gave such material to a nephew rather than to a son. Even if the uncle had not specifically made a verbal will, the nephew could take such paraphernalia for his own. Similarly a man's friend, who was also a special war partner, could claim the man's possessions. Deceased persons who had been doctors might be accompanied by their medicine objects, and CW mentioned in particular a type of whistle made from a "deer-shank" or metapodial bone which was part of the paraphernalia of "deer doctors." Women might have implements placed in the grave.

The body was wrapped in blankets and rawhides. After 1880-90, canvas and cotton sheets were used. First rawhides were placed in the grave, and the encased body was laid on them. Then more rawhides were placed over the body. The rawhide wrappings were often perforated and laced. The body was extended on the back with the head to the east.[183] This position seems to symbolize a separation of the living and dead; present-day Wichitas remember how disturbed grandparents and other relatives got when they as children started to sleep with their heads to the east instead of in the approved position of having the head to the west. Dirt would be thrown into the grave by the non-relatives who had done the digging.

During the burial the women present would wail, particularly if the deceased had been a young person or in the prime of life. A young warrior's death occasioned the greatest display. Death of a very old person did not need to be mourned much, if at all, since [203] the individual had had a long life and death was to be expected, and he would really be better off in the after-world. I have the impression, though cannot prove it, that old people sometimes were suspected of having long lives through the practice of witchcraft and as such were not deserving of mourning. Persons actually executed as witches were not mourned, even by close relatives, since grieving would be a tantamount to admitting that the mourner was himself a witch. The name of the deceased ideally was never mentioned again unless he was thought to be a witch and not worthy of such respect.

At the site of the grave an aged man might be asked by the family to talk and offer prayers, particularly if the deceased had been prominent or a young warrior. The mother or some close female relative often cut up tipi poles and erected a structure over the grave. This consisted of two crossed pieces at each end of the grave, a bar connecting the two, and pieces leaned against the bar from both sides — in final result, a tent-shaped structure. No dinner honoring the dead person was held and food was not offered at the grave.

Following the burial, the tipi was smoked with cedar and aired out and could be used again by the family. If the death had occurred on a war expedition, and the body not brought back, there was no symbolic burial, but the grass house in which the deceased had lived was smoked with cedar and the family continued to inhabit it.

Following the funeral, members of the family were still in mourning. If they were one of the leading families in the village, or a family of means, then non-relatives came to mourn with them. CW described this as follows:

> When son or daughter of a first-class, well-to-do, principal family die, the whole village go to the home of the deceased and wail, cry, and mourn with the family. People just keep coming in. Each group stay about ten minutes. The mother or sister (of the deceased) go around to every visitor and take hand and wipe tears off their faces and say, "Let's quit crying — we've cried long enough." Take dishpan and wash visitors faces —

---

[183] / 5 At the present time "white" undertakers have charge of burials and their custom of placing the head to the west causes middle-aged and older Wichitas some concern. Tombstones erected by Wichitas are on the east end of the grave plot.

give visitors shawls, blankets, and other presents. Then other people come in. By time mourning (is) over, family hardly got anything left — give away everything they have. They stay in mourning for a month or more. Kinfolks bring things they really need, 'til they establish their own home again.

The close relatives of the deceased were in possible danger of death since the spirit could return and try to entice them to joining it in the afterworld. To counter this, one or two ceremonies were held. CW described them as follows:

Family has lost close relative, a brother, a mother. After burial, in next four days, they get medicine man to bathe them in medicated water, then smoke them in cedar leaves. After that they are clear of association with dead ones. If they didn't give the bath and smoke, every night she see him (dead relative). Then she sort of pine, gets sickly. [204] Then people say she ought to get her bath. After that is done they seem to straighten out.

When anybody dies in family, after burying is over — a few days after, they call some old man, a doctor, to come to that family to make smoke for them. He has a long pipe. He goes in house. All family is together. Whenever doctoring anybody, do it on south side of tipi. Doctor gets coal for pipe from south side of tire, takes four puffs. (He) blow up in air. Just puff straight up and not to the directions. Throws head up. He makes tall;, just like praying to God — God is up. He says, "this family. this death would turn them loose from any more death." Then the doctor starts pipe — first father, then mother, then goes clean around as many as are in) family and back to doctor (clockwise). Then he makes smooth place south of fire and empties bowl on ground. He mixes ashes up with dirt and rubs in hands. Doctor goes clean around whole family, rubs hands down them starting at head — that frees them. (The "power" from above, the smoke, and the earth is in his hands.) Folks give doctor blanket of own free will.

Most ~~informants~~ agree that the medicated bath formerly was given m a nearby creek and not in the house, but in the present-day situation such baths are given in the houses. Curtis mentions that baths were taken in the creek on each of four days after death of a relative.[184]

The death of any person was observed with a four day mourning period by the entire village. During this time no dancing, games, or gambling were indulged in. At the end of the four days a representative of the family would have it announced by the town crier that the people had mourned long enough and that it was now all right for them to go ahead and beat the drum and enjoy themselves. Then the village returned to its normal activities. As late as 1949, a group of Wichitas conservative to the older religion delayed a scheduled dance for four days after the death of a young man.

A surviving spouse and the close relatives of the deceased observer a much longer mourning period, which was ended in a ritual described by CW as follows:

When a man dies his people take over looking after his wife. She's supposed to give away everything she had — wasn't allowed to put on any gay clothes or paint, or look good. His people would set a time that they would turn her loose. Husband's family, the women folk, gather up everything a woman wears and pick a certain day. They go to her house and present her with new things — things to eat, pans, dishes. They take her, put on new clothes, comb and braid hair, paint her face, put on beads and bracelets — full dress.

---

[184] /8 Edward S. Curtis, *The North American Indian*, Vol. 19, 1930, p. 42.

Always have some old woman in bunch — the dead man's grandmother. She talk to her (the wife) and advise her how to live — how good it was to live right, think of her people, never leave them. Then have a feast. Dead boy's mother goes wailing and crying — gives daughter-in-law a talk, too. She say, "Now you are loose, go ahead and live as you want to." They (the man's family) didn't have no more to [205] do looking after her. She can marry anytime she wants to. They warn her to take her time, pick out a good man.[185]

When a man loses his woman they aren't so strict. He's supposed to guard himself — not go to doings. They don't hold a man as long as they did a woman. When they turn him loose they take presents to him — man's clothes. The girl's people take the presents. (The presents are taken to the man since at the death of his wife he goes home to his mother's or sister's place.)

After death the spirit left the body and was thought to go to one of a number of villages up in the sky. There it and other spirits lived a life like that lived on earth. It was said that the dead in the villages above knew what was happening in the villages of living people below. Sometimes people would say after a death, "His people must be glad to see him." Not all spirits went to the after-world; those of murderers, suicides; and inveterate gamblers could not be with the rest. It was not reported specifically what happened to those of murderers and suicides: however, since Wichitas did and do believe strongly in ghosts that remain around burial areas and even old haunts of the living, it would appear that they remained on earth. Spirits of individuals who had gambled to excess lined the road or pathway which went to the afterworld. Young people who were inclined to gamble were told, "When you die, you don't want to be a castaway!" The spirits of gamblers are lined "on the pathway — they just sit there gambling."

Interpretation and Conclusions

1. It should be emphasized that, with few exceptions, the data herein reported are in ideal patterns. Furthermore, these patterns would be ones to which "leading families," or ones prominent in village affairs, would try to adhere. Only important families would go through with complete and ornate hair-cutting, burial, give-away, bathing-smoking, and spouse-freeing ceremonies. In Wichita thinking, lower-class families, poor families, and small families (in the extended sense) seem synonymous. Thus, one hears sayings such as, "He is poor, he doesn't have any relatives." Less fortunate families would make "the best approach possible to the ideal, but ceremonies — particularly the give-away and spouse-freeing — would suffer because of the small number of relatives involved, because of the lack of property, and because of no need for "putting up a front."

2. Obviously a great majority of the traits associated with. Wichita death customs would not be preserved in archaeological sites. However, Wichita burials of the 19th century, and perhaps the latter half of the 18th, would be expected to occur in cemetery areas and to exhibit rectangular or long oval burial pits, east-west [306] orientation, and an extended position of body with the head placed in an easterly direction. Artifacts accompanying burials should vary widely, with few or none being found in many interments. Graves of poorer individuals would not be expected to have very many artifacts. But also, due to extensive "give-aways" and the rights of

---

[185] / 7 Often, particularly if there were children, a young woman would marry a brother of her husband; or a man would marry a sister of his wife. This practice of levirate and sororate does not seem to have been absolutely obligatory, but to have had strong positive sanctions.

nephews and friends, graves of well-to-do people could be relatively barren of materials. Grave goods to be expected occasionally would be: stone and metal arrowheads, knives, whetstones, flint strike-a-lights, and guns with male burials; very occasionally pottery or metal containers and various bone or metal gardening and skin-working tools with female burials; bone or glass beads and metal trade ornaments remaining from costumes with burials of both sexes; and deer- or eagle-bone whistles, bone or horn sucking tubes, and a wide range of miscellaneous objects remaining from medicine bundles accompanying both male and female "doctors." Generally speaking grave goods would be expected to be scarce.[186]

Since the Wichita occupation of Kansas-Oklahoma-Texas was late in time and since portions of these states have relatively small amounts of annual precipitation, ordinarily perishable materials should occasionally be found with burials. This would be particularly so if the body was well laced in rawhides with other hides above and below.

3. A comparison of the data presented here and those reported by Dorsey is of interest.[187] Although I had read Dorsey previous to doing field work, his data did not influence the gathering of mine. In collecting' data, I had my ~~informants~~ "volunteer" statements on general topics, such as death and burial. Also, although some of my ~~informants~~ were aware that a man named Dorsey bad once written something about the Wichita, they appeared to have been uninfluenced '-9 by that source. Dorsey's and my material are in agreement in major outline and in moat details. This is of interest because it is indicative of the fact that 'two ethnological observers can duplicate or verify each other's work, and perhaps of greater interest since Dorsey did his field work in 1901-3 and I almost fifty years later.

---

[186] / 8 After the delivery of the paper, Mr. Ed Jelks of the Smithsonian Institution River Basin Surveys commented on the two burials excavated at the Stansbury site on the Brazos River above Waco, Texas. This site is thought to be that of one of the two Tawakoni villages visited by de Mezieres in 1772. The two burials were near each other in long, oval pits, extended on the back and with heads to the east. One had no accompanying artifacts, while the other had only a few glass beads.

[187] / 9 George A. Dorsey, *Wichita Mythology* 1904.

KARL SCHMITT, 1915-1952

By FRED EGGAN

COLLISION with a train while driving near Magdalena, New Mexico, on August 6, 1952, resulted in the death of Karl Schmitt and serious injuries to his wife, Iva. He was on the threshold of a brilliant career in anthropology and all who knew his warm personality will feel a deep sense of personal loss.

Karl was born December 20, 1915, in Albany, New York, the son of Karl and Beatrice Schmitt, but the family soon moved to Washington, D.C., where Karl attended William McKinley High School and George Washington University, obtaining his B.S. degree in geology. During his youth he had become interested in local Indian artifacts and had spent much of his time in making archeological collections in the Tidewater area. As a result his interests shifted from geology to archeology. He entered the University of Chicago to study under Dr. Fay-Cooper Cole in the autumn of 1938, after a summer with the U.S. National Museum archeological excavations in western Missouri.

At Chicago his range of activities broadened but archeology remained his central interest. He took part in the Kincaid excavations, but also maintained his relations with the U. S. National Museum, participating in its excavations in Kansas and Virginia. From March 1941-March 1942 he served as archeologist at Ocmulgee National Monument, Macon, Georgia. During this period he married a fellow student, Iva Osanai; their twin children, Sigrid and Kirk, were born February 18, 1944.

Soon after receiving his M.A. in the spring of 1942, he was inducted into the army. His background in natural sciences led to his assignment to the meteorological school at the University of Chicago from which he received a certificate of professional competence in meteorology and a commission in the Air Force. He served at various stations in the United States and then was sent to Morotai in the Southwest Pacific. After separation in March, 1946, 1953 as a major in the Air Force, he returned to the University of Chicago to continue his studies.

Karl served as a teaching assistant in the department of anthropology while completing his doctoral dissertation on "Archaeological Chronology of the Middle Atlantic States" which was summarized in J.B. Griffin (ed.), *Archeology of the Eastern United States*, University of Chicago Press, 1952. He received his Ph.D. in 1947 and accepted a position as assistant professor of anthropology at the University of Oklahoma.

When he went to Oklahoma his area of specialization again shifted, this time from archeology to ethnology. The large Indian population, with its opportunities for ethnological and social anthropological research, offered a new challenge. With his wife and children, he spent weekends and summers in the field, primarily among the Wichita and Caddo, but also with other groups. He retained his archeological and historical interests but the problems of contemporary change and development began to take precedence. The new "pan-Indian" culture in Oklahoma, the development of factionalism, and the study of changes in social organization and kinship became the major foci around which he organized his researches.

His published papers reflect the variety of his interests. Some, such as his "Notes on Morotai Island Canoes," were by-products of war-time assignments. Of his more recent studies, only his and Iva Schmitt's Wichita Kinship: Past and Present had gone to press. This is a notable addition to our knowledge of Plains social organization and an important contribution to the study of problems of social and cultural change. It combines historical and comparative studies in admirable fashion, and develops hypotheses which are both important in themselves and as stimuli to further research. Several manuscripts on various archeological sites, Caddo kinship, Factionalism, and Pan-Indian culture in Oklahoma are largely completed and it is hoped that they can soon be published. His M.A. thesis is to appear in revised form in T. Dale Stewart's *The Historic Indian Village of Patawomeke, Stafford County, Virginia*.

Karl loved his work and he and Iva made many friends among the Indians whom they studied. At the Memorial Service held in Norman, October 5, 1952, a great many Indians came long distances to attend, and the Caddo family which had adopted them spoke of their love and esteem for him. A few days later the Caddoes presented a radio program dedicated to his memory. The University had also recognized his worth and promise. He had recently been promoted to associate professor of anthropology and was to have taken over the chairmanship in September. Karl was a member of the American Anthropological Association, the Society for American Archaeology, the Texas Archaeological and Paleontological Society, and the Oklahoma Archaeological Society, and has been elected to Sigma Xi.

Karl's many friends, both white and Indian, will feel his loss deeply. Their [239] sympathy goes to his wife and children, with a hope that Iva Schmitt can carry forward the research which she and Karl had been pursuing so fruitfully.

UNIVERSITY OF CHICAGO
CHICAGO, ILLINOIS

BIBLIOGRAPHY
Compiled by Robert Bell

"Patawomeke, An Historic Algonkian Site," M.A. thesis, Univ. of Chicago. 1942

"A Dated Silt Deposit in the Ocmulgee River Valley, Georgia," *American Antiquity*, Vol. VIII, pp. 296-297. 1943

"Notes on Morotai Island Canoes," *Man*, Vol. 47, Article 127, pp. 119-122. 1947

"Notes on Some Recent Archaeological Sites in the Netherlands East Indies," *American Anthropologist*, Vol. 49, pp. 331-334. 1947

J. S. Slotkin And Karl Schmitt, "Studies of Wampum," *American Anthropologist*, Vol. 51, No. 2, April-June, pp. 223-236. 1949

"Two Creek Pottery Vessels from Oklahoma," *The Florida Anthropologist*, Vol. 111, Nos. 1-2, May, pp. 3-8. 1950

"The Lee Site, Gv-3, of Garvin County, Oklahoma," *Texas Archaeological and Paleontological Society*, Vol. 21, Sept., pp. 69-89. 1950

"Wichita-Kiowa Relations and the 1874 Outbreak," *The Chronicles of Oklahoma*, Vol. XXVIII, No. 2, pp. 154-160. 1950

"Archaeological Chronology of the Middle Atlantic States," in *Archaeology of the Eastern United States*, edited by J.B. Griffin, pp. 59-70. 1952

"Wichita Death Customs," *The Chronicles of Oklahoma*, Vol. XXX, No. 2, pp. 200-206. 1952

Karl And Iva Schmitt, *Wichita Kinship: Past and Present*, Univ. of Oklahoma Book Exchange, Norman. 1952

He is buried with Osanai at

Resthaven Funeral Home & Memory Gardens
500 SW 104th St, Oklahoma City, Oklahoma, *United States*, 73139
405-691-1661 ·   *resthavenokc*.com.

Karl Schmitt pp237-239 *American Anthropologist* 55, 1953
https://anthrosource.onlinelibrary.wiley.com/doi/pdf/10.1525/aa.1953.55.2.02a00070

Iva Osanai **Teruko Schmitt Springstead**
1917 – 1969

Iva was born in 1917 in Nebraska to Japanese immigrants. The family moved to Chicago in the 1920s, and Iva attended the University of Chicago field school at the Kincaid Mounds site in Illinois in the summer of 1937. While at Chicago she met Karl Schmitt, a fellow anthropology student, and they married in 1941. In 1947 they moved to Oklahoma with their two children, Karl E. and **Sigrid S.**, and he became an assistant professor in Anthropology, then was appointed as curator of Ethnology at the Stovall Museum in July of 1952. In August of 1952 he was killed in a car-train accident in Magdelina <Magdalena>, New Mexico.[188] Sometime after this in 1952, Iva was appointed to the curator position, which she held until 1958. Her many roles in museum programs and events included leading tours, giving lectures, analyzing new collections, and even filming museum tours for public television and radio programs. She also sponsored the University of Oklahoma (OU)'s Japan Club, which would later become the Asian Student Association. In 1958, she and her second husband, Clarence Springstead, left Oklahoma, and eventually moved to Hachinohe, Japan, where she passed in 1969.

She is a co-author on two notable anthropological publications – *Navajo Eschatology* with Leland Clifton Wyman and Willard Williams Hill in 1942 and *Wichita Kinship: Past and Present* with Karl Schmitt in 1952. Her and Karl's field notes from their work in Anadarko, OK with Caddo, Pawnee, and Wichita peoples, as well as Creeks and others, are in the collection of the Western History Center at OU.

https://www.findagrave.com/memorial/229120557/iva_teruko_springstead

Census records in Nebraska associate her with Thomas Curtis Elliott and Mary Mae Keister, born in Virginia. In 1940, Mary May (53) is married to Thomas Osanai (61) and living at 6100 East 61st Street, Chicago, Cook County, Illinois, where Tom is a cook, Iva (22) is a laboratory assistant, and Elliot Myron (31), surely Myron Elliot, is a stepson born in Virginia, high school graduate, working as a clerk.

Thomas was born 21 Aug 1879 in Japan, died in Oklahoma on 30 April 1961, and is buried at Resthaven Gardens Cemetery.

Iva's second husband Clarence 2nd remarried in 1970 to Hisae (Miyake) at Nagoya, then moved to Iowa.

---

[188] Magdalena, named for an image evoking Mary Magdalene on Magdalena Peak, is on Highway 60 west of I-25 at Socorro and east of Datil, Pie Town, and Quemado, as well as the National Radio Astronomy Observatory Very Large Array (NRAO VLA) of 28 radio telescopes, each 25-meters across, aimed at the universe. It is south of Cibola National Forest and Alamo Navajo Reservation. It is indeed on a railroad spur.

Magdalena grew in 1866 when lead, zinc, and silver mining began in the surrounding mountains, particularly at the Kelly mines. Magdalena became an incorporated municipality in 1884; a railroad spur was built between Magdalena and the smelting industry in Socorro.

Clarence Springstead
1929 – 1996

BETTENDORF – Services for Clarence S. Springstead, 67, of Bettendorf, will be 10:30 a.m. Saturday at Davenport Memorial Park. There is no visitation.

Mr. Springstead died Tuesday, Sept. 10, 1996, at Genesis Medical Center-East Campus, Davenport.

McGinnis, Chambers & Sass Funeral Home, Bettendorf, is in charge of arrangements.

He retired in 1986 as quality assurance instructor after 11 years at U.S. Army Management Training Agency, and had earlier worked at Blue Grass Army Depot in Kentucky.

During the Korean War, he served in the Air Force.

He was born Dec. 14, 1928, in Patterson, N.J. He married Hisae Miyake in 1970 in Nagoya, Japan. Memorials may be made to Disabled American Veterans.

Survivors include his wife; sons, Timothy and Gordon Springstead, both of Lexington, Ky.; his mother, Beatrice Springstead, Falls Church, Va.; and brothers, Lester, Falls Church, and Bert, Carlisle, Pa.

Hisae (Miyake) Springstead
1935 — 2018

DAVENPORT — Hisae (Miyake) Springstead of Davenport, passed away on Tuesday, June 26, 2018, at Clarissa Cook Hospice House. Private graveside services are pending at Davenport Memorial Park.

Hisae was born on March 12, 1935, in Japan and came to the U.S. with her husband, Clarence "Clancy" Springstead, following his U.S. military service in Japan. She embraced life in this country and together they established many lifelong friends as they traveled extensively with his career. They settled in Bettendorf, Iowa, where they enjoyed their life and retirement years together.

Hisae had a talent for creating pottery, cooking and gardening. She had a passion for art and music and was vibrantly independent. Her home was always warm and inviting. Hisae was very devoted to her many friends and family. She will be deeply missed by all those who loved her, including her friends at Ridgecrest Village and the many others far beyond. She leaves behind her remaining family members in Japan, including a brother and a nephew.

From the September 12, 1996, edition of *The Quad-City Times* (Davenport, IA) form F8-192

11-19-51

okd 9/9 ws

e-ssa

AMERICAN FOREIGN SERVICE

REPORT OF THE DEATH OF AN AMERICAN CITIZEN

American Consulate, Negoya, Japan, Sept. 25, 1969

Name in full   Iva Osanai Springstead   Occupation   Housewife

Native xxxxxxxxx   Born on May 30, 1917 in Nebraska, U.S.A.   Last known address in the United States 815, South 5th St., Chambersburg, Penn., U.S.A.

Date of death Sept. 22 11:55 AM 1969   Age   52

        (Month) (Day) (Hour) (Minute) (Year)   (As nearly as can be ascertained)

Place of Death   Aichi Cancer Center, Tashiro-cho, Chikusa-ky, Nagoya, Japan

        (Number and street) or (Hospital or hotel) (City) (County)

Cause of Death   Certified by Dr. Makoto Ogawa, attending physician at Aichi Cancer Center,

        (Include authority for statement)

Nagoya, Japan to be mammary cancer.

Disposition of the remains   Cremated at Yagoto Crematory in Nagoya, Japan, and ashes will be buried at Daijiji Temple in Hachinoi City, Aomori Pref., Japan

Local law as to disinterring remains   Application to city authorities is required.

Disposition of the effects   in the custody of husband, Mr. Clarence S Springstead.

Person or official responsible for custody of effects and accounting therefor

    Mr. Clarence S Springstead.

Informed by telegram:

NAME	ADDRESS	RELATIONSHIP	DATE SENT
xxx			

Copy of this report ~~send~~ given to:

Mr. Clarence S Springstead	9-3, 1-chome, Sannomaru Naka-ku, Nagoya, Japan	Husband	9/25/69
Mr. Timothy O. Springstead	" <ditto>	Son	
Mr. Gordon B. Springstead	" <ditto>	Son	

Other known relatives (not given above)

Cpt. Karl E. Schmitt	USASSG, ACSA, DA Camp Zama, Japan	Son
Mrs. Sigrid S. Illes	c/o Cpt James M. Illes USAMEDC, APO S.F. 96331	Daughter

    This information and data concerning an inventory of the effects, accounts, etc., have been placed under File 234 in the correspondence of this office.

Remarks: U.S. Official Passport No. Y644220 issued on Dec. 14, 1967 cancelled and returned to husband, Mr. C. Springstead. Mrs. Springstead's Social Security number is 440-36-3821.

(Continued on the reverse if necessary)

Peter P. Pease

(Signature on *all* copies)

<u>Vice Consul</u> of the United States of America.

[seal]

No fee prescribed

54-597 Army AG Admin Cen-Japan 1M

Entries are by titles or first names, grouped family names, subjects,
page numbers ending in #0 refer to a scattered ten page span
#f refers to a five page span
* marks a main entry

Cover image is *Wee-ta-ra-sha-ro* ~ Wichita Chief by George Catlin 1834

Please Help Fight Off Typo Gnomes!

Sold @ Amazon.com

www.ingramcontent.com/pod-product-compliance
Lightning Source LLC
Chambersburg PA
CBHW080412290526
45791CB00008BA/2245